MUSICAL PERFORMANCE

Music is a performing art yet our experience of it is usually through recorded media. The musical sounds we most often hear have often been electronically edited and sculpted by sound engineers, and many such sounds derive entirely from computers. Music has become increasingly remote from performance.

Stan Godlovitch in his unique book, *Musical Performance*, addresses this relatively recent phenomenon. He examines the musical enterprise not from the usual vantage point of the composer or the audience, but from that of the performer. Playing traditions go back many centuries, largely because what players use, particularly in classical music, has not changed significantly in that time. Many musicians still strike strings, blow through pipes, or pound stretched membranes, all of which involve immediate physical contact with the sound source. This physical immediacy belongs with any traditional craft in demanding refined physical skill. Much of musical tradition has been conservatively devoted to the development and achievement of physical mastery to serve expressive ends. And much of the value in music has derived from the very depth of technical and expressive skill certain players have reached – especially their ability to display it then and there to attentive listeners.

These traditions have been challenged by electronic technology which has made live human performance seem a mere transfer medium. After developing a full model of traditional performance, the book asks how well performance proper has stood up, and where (if anywhere) its unique value lies.

Stan Godlovitch is Senior Lecturer in Philosophy at Lincoln University, New Zealand.

MUSICAL PERFORMANCE

A philosophical study

Stan Godlovitch

London and New York

First published 1998
by Routledge
11 New Fetter Lane, London EC4P 4EE

Simultaneously published in the USA and Canada
by Routledge
29 West 35th Street, New York, NY 10001

Typeset in Galliard by Routledge
Printed and bound in Great Britain by TJ International Ltd,
Padstow, Cornwall

British Library Cataloguing in Publication Data
A catalogue record for this book is available from the British Library

Library of Congress Cataloging in Publication Data
Godlovitch, Stanley, 1947–
Musical performance: a philosophical study / Stan Godlovitch.
p. cm.
Includes bibliographical references and index.
1. Music–Philosophy and aesthetics. 2. Music–Performance.
ML3845.G6 1998   98–11832
781.4`3`01–21   CIP
MN

ISBN (hbk) 0–415–19128–9
ISBN (pbk) 0–415–19129–7

CONTENTS

ACKNOWLEDGEMENTS

Portions of the following papers have found their way into this essay: 'Music Performance and the Tools of the Trade', *Iyyun* (1990) 39: 321–38; 'Artists, Computer Programs, and Performance', *Australasian Journal of Philosophy* (1990) 68: 301–12; 'Music – What to Do About It', *Journal of Aesthetic Education* (1992) 26: 1–15; 'The Integrity of Musical Performance', *Journal of Aesthetics and Art Criticism* (1993) 54: 573–87; and 'Innovation and Conservatism in Performance Practice', *Journal of Aesthetics and Art Criticism*, (1997) 55: 151–68. For kind permission to make use of this material, I thank the editors and the journals.

Among friends and colleagues, special thanks are owed to Steven DeHaven, Shmuel Keshen, Tom Leddy, David Novitz, and Eddy Zemach for comments and discussion. For helpful suggestions on the manuscript, I am grateful to Alex Neill and Aaron Ridley. Far and away the most substantial philosophical debt of gratitude I owe to John H. Brown, Stephen Davies, and Jerry Levinson for their patience, encouragement, indulgence, and ever-thoughtful reflections.

And, as for Glen and Daniel – well, it goes without saying.

INTRODUCTION

Central themes

Music is a performing art. Music is made. So much our long-standing musical traditions take for granted. What these conceptions of music imply and how our traditions fare in the face of modern challenges are main themes in this essay. As a focus, I offer an idealized model of the complete performance which comprises a complex network of relations linking together musicians, musical activities, works, listeners, and performance communities. Through this model, I aim to make explicit the interactive features of the total performance environment. The richness of the performance environment gives prominence to a number of issues. Very generally:

• performance merits as much philosophical attention as has been shown toward musical ontology (the metaphysical aspect), the expressive content and meaning of musical sound (the affective and semantic aspect), and the listener's experience (the phenomenological aspect);

• by taking seriously the integrated workings of the performance environment, one's sympathy increases for the view that art and art-making travel together;

•musical performance provides an interesting framework for broader philosophical concerns about action; notably about intention, purposiveness, skill, communication, and creativity.

More specifically, I aim to show that:

• performance in a primary idealized sense is represented most aptly as a highly intricate event comprising players, sounds, works and listeners in a ritual setting;

• performance, as it has historically evolved, belongs squarely within the craft tradition as a professional practice governed by inherently conservative standards of manual skill and expertise. These standards are staunchly sustained and applied by a performance practice community which emulates many of the regulatory powers and obligations of the Guild tradition;

• tradition has exemplified music as that which is presented in and through performance;

1

• the ritual aspects of performance and the hierarchical structure of performance communities explain the tendency of performance practitioners and their audiences to resist otherwise serious challenges to performance traditions brought on by new technology and experimentalism in music.

The traditional view of music as a performing art guided by the performer's craft, however consistent, may no longer faithfully represent the general musical enterprise. Though some experimental options have arisen through the influence of changes in other artforms, the most significant alternatives to tradition have come from technology, especially the development of electronic and computer-based sound-processing machines. Such technology, which can neither be ignored by nor absorbed within the traditional structure, signals major changes to come in our conception of music and performance. Certainly, developments in electronic sound-making technology already give the impression that the tradition of performance as a skilled manual craft occupies, at best, one amongst a plurality of musical options for the production and display of sound.

Performance and the aesthetics of music

For some time now, two primary factors have marked much of Western art music; namely, (1) composing, or the creation of musical works, and (2) performing, or the presentation of such works in sound. For a millennium, composing has involved registering created works in replicable notated scores which represent certain elemental features of the work. Besides being media for the storage of works, scores are also instruction sets for their presentation in sound. Performing makes works accessible to the ear through the physical activity of musicians who typically work initially from score. A third factor, (3) listening or audition, is the active apprehension of sounds in performance. Composition, performance, and audition are functionally and physically separable, and often attach to three distinct sets of participants – composers, musicians, and audiences. In music studies, the division into theory and analysis, performance practice, and ear-training and appreciation reflect these functional compartments.

Each of these three factors is indispensable. Music is an art of structuring sound for display in sound. The designers of musical structures, the presenters of musical sound, and the recipients of those displayed structures all play interdependent roles in our musical culture. One person busy in all three enterprises conceivably constitutes a self-sufficient (albeit minimal) musical community, but no musical community lacks any one of these factors. Any comprehensive musical aesthetic must attend equally to the creation and nature of musical works, the making and displaying of musical sound, and the experience of music made.

Though these three components defy complete separation, independent treatment of one or another is often a practical necessity and a theoretical convenience. The tripartite division of musical labour reinforces the attractiveness of such separate treatment. Each approach emphasizes specialized problems and interests. For instance, concern about musical works, the composer's sphere, prompts discussion about their ontology, their essence and formal structure, how they are represented, and how they relate to performance.[1] Those partial to performance, the practising musician's domain, attend primarily to such issues as virtuosity, improvisation, the nature and role of the act of playing, what the performer owes to the composer, the work, and the work's historical context, and what the performance does with the work.[2] Concern about sound, the listener's sphere, raises questions about the content and meaning of music, expression, affect, representation in music, musical appreciation and understanding, and the listener's response.[3]

Performance can become inadvertently minimized in focused approaches by assigning to it a merely subservient role or neglecting its influence altogether. Work-centred accounts may treat performance purely functionally as merely one means to reveal the work in sound, thus reducing it to a kind of messenger mediating between composer and listener. More formal accounts of works may portray performances as simply token instances of the work type while underestimating the significant fact that works massively underdetermine their performances. Listener-based accounts may leave the impression that the immediate cause of the experienced sound is incidental both to its expressive qualities and to a full musical appreciation of it. Such accounts often treat musical sound as a purely disembodied phenomenon, a private sensuous array for the auditor – however informed the listener about the context of creation of the work. We may open up such tightly framed perspectives by reminding ourselves of the near platitude that music is a performing art, an attribution which is surely central to musical tradition. Of course, that music, unlike dance and drama, is not *necessarily* a performing art turns out to be an intriguing if unsettling discovery of our own time.

The contents surveyed

Though this essay falls into two parts, its structure is not strictly linear. Part I is a relatively self-contained core around which selected satellite themes and problems orbit in Part II.

In Part I, 'Central aspects of performance', an idealized model of traditional performance is elaborated. At the risk of stressing a metaphor, Part I explores the ecology of performance. Although grounded on various common intuitions about performance, the model emphasizes the richness of the performance environment and the complex interconnectedness of its constituents. The conception which emerges constitutes a model of a model performance, so to speak, one in which all the overt and tacit conventions are fully realized.

Part II, 'Challenges to the model', considers various ways in which the primacy of traditional performance in music may seem to be ignored, defied or threatened. I look at various recent innovations in the visual arts as well as experimental and computer-based music. Although these challenges fail to damage the model's internal coherence or show it to be inconsistent, they do expose the traditions behind it as ever more local. Such traditions are perhaps best viewed as sturdy historical monuments increasingly forced to share space with newer, taller, leaner structures.

Part I, 'Central aspects of performance', represents performance as a value-driven, value-laden, communicative exercise of specialized manual skill. It is characterized as governed by powerful historical conventions of training and expertise. These conventions are established and internally regulated by performance communities, the structure and organization of which are determined by long-standing inherited norms. The idealized model in Chapter 1, 'A model of musical performance', draws upon the Socratic theme of *technē* and presents performance as an agent-centred intentional enterprise which invokes special skills to create musical experiences for attentive listeners. At the hub of musical enterprise, performance is portrayed as a complex network of relations connecting musical agents, works, sound, and listeners. These relations range from purely structural ones to normative ones, in which the obligations of performers and listeners figure. The model is meant to make explicit the many interwoven factors in the performance environment and bonds these together under a single conception as components of performance itself. Among its less intuitive aspects, the model requires that performances have third-party attentive listeners. In this and other ways, the model attempts to lay out optimal success conditions for performance.

Chapter 1 concentrates on the immediate environment of performance in progress; that is, the setting and circumstance of performance events especially as they define the relationship between player, sound, work, and listener. Chapter 2, 'Skills and Guilds', casts a wider net and explores the mechanisms and institutions of performance practice by placing the player within the context of standing performance communities. Performance is a highly structured practice essentially built upon and employing task-related primary manual skills. The value in and of performance thus depends not only on the music as made, but on the way in which it is made. The requirement and refinement of musical skill is the glue binding musicians to performance communities. A strong kinship is established between performance practice and the craft tradition in their common emphasis upon skill acquisition and training. This concept of performance as craftwork leads to an examination of the professional communities and institutions which promote and regulate the music-making enterprise. Performance communities share much in common with trade and professional guilds which regulate their membership through traditionally established common standards and highly structured hierarchies of accomplishment. Central to the preservation of performance ideals is the perfectionism characteristic of the craft tradition generally. Because the performance community is highly protective of its norms and goals, it tends to react conservatively to any suggestions for change.

4

Part II, 'Challenges to the model', looks at problems for the model from the vantage point of alternative musical possibilities. Five central features of performance developed in Part I involve the place of the musical work, primary agency, the craft tradition, intentional agency, and the performing context. In Part II, these features are confronted with alternative conceptions of what principally counts in music, and more interestingly, with newly and potentially available non-traditional options for performance. The core features challenged are these:

• the musical work – performance, far from being simply a faithful delivery of goods from composers to their listeners, is an active collaborative constituent of the full work itself. The notation typically available to musicians is a mere musical framework;

• direct causation (primary agency) – performance involves the direct, immediate, physical causation of sound by an agent;

• the craft tradition – primary skill and traditions of expertise are essential to performance, and integral to our regard for music-making;

• intentional agency – performance is essentially an intentional activity; more pointedly, an activity characteristic of beings with typically human cognitive and affective constitutions;

• the performing context – the musical sounds created by a performer do not exhaust the full content of the performance which also comprises the presence, activity, and manner of the performer.

Chapter 3, 'Performances and musical works', considers the view that, because performers are principally musical brokers fulfilling a contract between composers and listeners, performance is properly subordinate to the musical work it delivers. Although part of the sentiment behind this derives from a romanticized form of composer (or 'authenticity') worship, a more formal element plays a part; namely, that the work is to its performances as a type is to a token of that type, or a universal is to one of its particular instances. This formal view creates an asymmetry of independence and autonomy between works and performances. In countering this conception, Chapter 3 takes seriously the significance of the fact that works underdetermine their performances. In considering different forms of instantiation, the view emerges that, far from being subordinate to works, performances operate at least in collaboration with the notated frameworks, and, like elaborations of stories, help create the works themselves in that collaboration.

Chapter 4, 'Computers, readymades, and artistic agency', examines very generally the effect of computers and of readymades on primary causation and on the skill and crafting traditions. The decline of primary agency has largely been due to the use of indirect, non-manual, abstract causal processes epitomized in electronic and computer-based graphics and music. When primary causation – physically immediate art-making – is thus displaced, conceptions of art and, with it, performance undergo major change. Computer-based artforms are generically distinct and unify sound and colour as merely different manifestations of information, their common substrate. Both primary causation and traditionally valued manual techniques were upset by the readymades introduced by Marcel Duchamp. The implications created by the readymade for the traditional link between art-making and technique are explored. There it is argued that when skill is acceptably absent, many value-regulating mechanisms must be abandoned. To survive, the artform may make such adjustments and detach artistic value from technical accomplishment. Though this has occurred in the plastic arts, nothing quite like it has taken place in music.

Chapter 5, 'Experiments with musical agency', looks more closely at intentional agency and the performing context. Emulating selected readymade themes, certain musical experiments have aimed to rid music-making of the centrality of primary agency and the expertise of the crafts. These experiments affect both the presentation of music and the hegemony of performance communities. The varieties of experimental music discussed include event pieces, found sound, and chance music. I consider whether such experimental music constitutes another musical form in its own right, forces performance communities to re-cast their traditional foundations, or must answer to, and possibly fail, traditional norms. I conclude that, despite their undoubted impact upon conceptions of composition and music generally, these modern experiments have little effect on the standard notion of performance and leave it much where it has been. Far from upsetting the prominence of established performance traditions, much experimental music has not quite freed itself from them; and, where it has, it ceases to be performance music altogether. That said, such experiments leave much in doubt the centrality of traditional performance to the music enterprise generally.

The final chapter, 'Artists, programs, and performance', uses a thought experiment to question the necessity of human intentional agency in performance. Computer programs currently exist which compose music, and which produce reasonably convincing pieces in the styles of the past. One can imagine a computer-driven performance machine which takes notation as input and generates unique, imaginative, and musically convincing renditions of standard repertoire – so convincing that they cannot be distinguished from those of accomplished human performers. Such machines would first analyse the interpretive techniques of great human players, and eventually would develop their own individual performance styles – functionally, much as humans do in learning new skills. At some stage, these machine performances will impress listeners as much as any fine performance. Consider a competition amongst such performance machines. Could a completely program-driven music competition eventually supplant human contests without aesthetic loss much along the lines of machine chess competitions? Whatever the technological success, I argue that the traditional object of apprehension and judgement involves much more than the mere sound experienced by the listener, and indeed, more than the nexus of constituents making up the model developed in Part I. The chapter ends with a sketch of an enriched complex of conventions and expectations which underwrite our experience and appreciation of performing artists as persons. These conventions and expectations draw not only upon primary skills and practice traditions but also upon the messy, diffuse context of human ability, fallibility, personality, choice, and growth. From our appreciation of these very general aspects of the kinds of creatures we are comes the value we currently identify in rigour, skill, and creativity. Thus embedded culturally and psychologically, performance turns out to be seamlessly continuous with human pursuits generally. Peculiarly, though, the more the player is like the rest of us, the more we can value the music made; and yet the more extraordinary the performance, the more we value the player.

Unfinished business

The essay raises issues wanting further treatment. Five areas wanting discussion are: (1) the implications for ontology, (2) the primacy of performance, (3) creativity and invention in improvisation and score-playing, (4) the nature of interpretation, and (5) the implications of recording studio techniques. Regarding (1), I could profit from a distinction between compositions or frame-works and works proper. The former are given to us by composers and are usually in score, while the latter are what performers collaboratively create in performance in using compositions. In this sense, performers contribute in making the musical work which is, necessarily, underdetermined by its composition. This distinction requires much development. I flirt with it in Chapter 3. As to (2), I think performance not merely central to our tradition, but essential to any tradition which sustains anything like the framework/work distinction just mentioned. In some electronic music, the distinction all but collapses. In that music, performance fails to figure. Because electronic music will eventually carry most of our musical business, greater heed will have to be paid to the hegemony of music as a sound art. With (3) is raised the whole question of the dispensability of compositions and notated works as we know them. Improvisational traditions boost performance stock by giving the performer greater discretion and creative opportunity than the score-guided player has. Properly speaking, any paradigm of primary performance should be founded upon improvisational traditions. Whether our score-dominated musical culture is a performance compromise, an equal but distinct alternative, or an equal member of the same paradigm deserves further treatment. Regarding (4), interpretation merits expansive treatment in itself. For convenience, I conceive interpretations as procedural operations which represent technical and expressive options for presenting passages, often in keeping with practice conventions. Interpretive moves are standardly concerned with expressive potential and how best to realize it. Interpretation seems primarily linked with a musician's concern about achieving certain determinate acoustic effects and the best means to do so. That said, what it is about compositions which qualifies them as bearers of musical interpretations at all, and as bearers of certain proper interpretations in particular needs clarification, especially if one cannot appeal to anything semantic or quasi-linguistic. Finally, (5) the recording studio has transformed performance and audiences along with it, much as film and television have spirited away theatre and given us oddly captivating ghosts. Why have we been so willing, so eager to swap real people in real time and space for engineered traces? Whatever we have lost, ever so much more seems to have been gained, given our preferences. Someone must soon do an aesthetic audit.

Part I

CENTRAL ASPECTS OF PERFORMANCE

1
A MODEL OF MUSICAL PERFORMANCE

Introduction

What is the nature of musical performance? Intuitively, performances are occasions of musical sound – musical events – intentionally brought about by musicians for listeners. More abstractly, they are conceived formally as instances or tokens of certain universals or kinds; namely, musical works. In this chapter, I outline a model of performance which reflects and yet complements various intuitive considerations. I also aim to build sympathy for a performance-centred conception of music, the overall plan being to epitomize a tradition of music-making.

Why focus thus on performance? Music, after all, has many facets. The activities of composers, musicians, and listeners, and, by association, the works, performances, and experienced sounds of music, offer different perspectives from which to view music. Still, music is characteristically classified as a performing art. Since music typically lives in and for its public sounds which derive from performance, there is reason enough to regard the musical enterprise generally from the performance standpoint. More strongly, if music is essentially a performing art, the performance perspective is clearly privileged.

Four primary constituents of the musical sphere are typically drawn together in performance: sound, agents, works,[1] and listeners. Plausibly, any standard performance consists of sounds made by some musician instancing some musical work for some listener. These four factors will clearly figure in any model of performance.

Ordinary language embodies a concept of performance more relaxed than the model to be proposed. While respectful of the intuitive view, the emerging picture brings to the foreground certain otherwise understated intentional and contextual factors affecting performers and listeners. The resulting model is thus more determinate than some intuitions about performance; for example, in requiring the presence of attentive audiences and properly informed musicians. Further, the model outlines a cluster of success conditions for performance, the realization of which constitutes an idealized paradigm of music-making. Rather than assembling a stereotype which faithfully mirrors what would ordinarily count as an acceptable performance, the model depicts the fully successful or exemplary performance. That successful performance serves as an analytical benchmark derives in part from the sense of achievement internal to descriptions like: 'Williams performed the Giuliani *Concerto Opus 30* in Jasper, Alberta on January 2nd'. Such expressions imply not merely something undertaken, but something fully completed or accomplished. Note, the notion 'fully successful' does not here connote the highest levels of individual accomplishment captured in expressions like 'exceptional' or 'definitive' performance which mark a given occasion as superior to most others. The success conditions outlined in my account are meant to heighten conceptual undercurrents which are often implicit in standing conventions and discourse. From this idealization emerges a model of the model performance, cleaner at the edges than real life, against which one can assess one's typical expectations.

I focus on solo performance not only for its relative simplicity but because of its ultimacy. Analyses of ensemble performance derive directly from or contrast with it. Solo performance, broadly conceived, covers cases where one performer's musical decisions and actions predominate. With fully collaborative ensembles like string quartets, one may conceivably postulate a supra-individual performer, the quartet, to facilitate attributions of global sound quality as well as global praise since each quartet player is equally responsible for the joint venture.

Again, for simplicity, I emphasize instrumental music-making throughout. Instrumental music counts for much of music-making, and the separateness of musical agents and their instruments brings into high relief aspects of physical challenge and control which will figure strongly in the account. Further, the presence of language and meaning in song would needlessly complicate the picture presented of what music-makers must accomplish at a very primary level of agency. Even if song were historically prior to instrumental music, the latter is constitutionally prior, so to speak, by being semantically leaner. Even if instrumental music were not analytically more primitive than song, song verges, at least in comparison, towards the mixed media, blending melody and poetry or melody and narrative. That said, the voice can be and is used purely to make musical sound. When so used, my account applies fully to voice.

Preliminary groundclearing

Performance falls within a family of music-making activities. While general terms like 'work', 'piece', and 'number', standardly attach to whole items of music, another group of terms typically describes general music-making activity; for example, 'play', 'perform', and 'execute' (and, relatedly, 'performance', and 'execution'). These last verbs differ in various ways. We can draw a distinction in level between playing and performing.

'Playing' refers to more general and generic activity than the more specialized and formal 'performing'. Though every case of performing involves playing, one may succeed in playing without having succeeded in performing. 'Performing' invokes occasion and ritual; 'playing' leaves such contextual imputations open. Sight-reading for amusement, say, is also playing but not performing in most cases. 'Playing' neutrally captures occasions of creating musical sound. 'Performing' applies more restrictedly as a species of playing.

Performing is not the sole species under the genus 'playing'. Besides sight-reading, one may rehearse, practise, jam, noodle, and so on. These too are more determinate than playing, and distinct from performing. Terms like 'concert', 'recital', and 'show' typically relate to relatively prominent performance occasions. 'Rehearsal', 'practice session' and 'jam session' denote less formal episodes. Performances tend to be special ritualized occasions, considerably more constrained than rehearsals, practice, or recreational playing. For present purposes, I will take the familiar recital as a standard performance setting.

'Perform' and 'performance' have both singular and general uses. Singular uses include 'Paganini performed the *Tarantella* just once', and 'The performance tonight of *Brandenburg III* starts at 8pm sharp'. The general use occurs in 'Performance of *Finlandia* strengthened the people's resolve to resist the enemy', and 'Among other instruments, O'Dette performs on cittern'. 'Performance' occasionally means 'recital', 'show', or 'concert'; for example, 'The matinee performance has been cancelled': while 'perform' relates analogously to a general manner of playing; for example, 'He performed with bravura last night'. In what follows, 'performance' is not used synonymously with 'recital' or 'concert'. Instead, individual performances in the sense intended attach to individual works rather than designated venues.

Constituents of performance

As mentioned, performances draw together sounds, agents, works, and listeners. Each of these occupies a role within performance, and collectively they comprise the large, complex, integrated events which performances are. I shall examine these critical constituents and indicate how they are woven together in successful performance.

Sound sequences

Every performance necessarily has sound as a constituent, but no sequence of sounds, considered purely as sound, constitutes a performance. Still, claims like: 'I heard a performance of Britten's *Nocturnal* last night', suggest that performance can be viewed exhaustively as an object of hearing. Suppose 'performance' in the claim refers just to a temporally-bounded ordered set of sounds which fall under a physical-acoustical description involving a transmission medium, sound waves, and wave qualities like frequency and amplitude. Although the sequence presumably was deliberately caused by some human, this forms no explicit part of the reference. But, can the description of a performance fail to coincide with any description of any musical activity?

13

Surely acoustic properties alone are insufficient to enable one to identify, let alone adequately constitute, any performance, even if such ingredients are elementally required. If there were a 'music of the spheres' – perfect oscillations of cosmic crystals – the very detachment of the sound from any obvious agent would disqualify it as a performance. It would be space noise, however melodious. More dully, one cannot differentiate through sound alone the music players create and the non-musical tappings of their shoes while playing it, both of which co-exist and result from the movements of their body. To identify performances one must supplement sound sequences by reference to works and performers at least.

Attributing self-sufficiency to sound sequences rests on the odd notion that performances can be identified and characterized independently of players and works. What inspires such a belief?

Recordings might influence such views because of the temptation to say that they capture performances proper rather than mere performance sound. This, however, involves an uncritical assimilation of dissimilar paradigms. Many creative activities – for instance, painting, cooking, sculpting, writing, lute-making – yield independent and independently identifiable results. These activities result in moveable, saleable, collectable things which live independent lives and often outlive their creators. Recordings share these features and may influence conceptions of performance on analogy with the detachability and autonomy of paintings.

Recordings of performances, however, are not performances. Recordings are just traces or records of performances, and no more performances in their own right than photos are the objects photographed. The temptation to neglect this likely stems from the stunning excellence of the resemblance, and its often capturing everything that certain parties are concerned with in the original, while dispensing with the seeming side-effects of live music-making. Common idioms are misleading. Having heard a recording or taped broadcast of the *C# Minor Prelude*, one typically remarks: 'I heard a performance of the *C# Minor Prelude* last night'. But if the performer is dead, to say: 'I heard Rachmaninoff perform his *C# Minor Prelude* last night' is awkward, surely, because literally false.

Performances are essentially events. That alone should make clear their difference from discrete, independent physical objects. Performance sound ceases with the cessation of its generative source, the activity of music-making, and hence is causally dependent upon that source. Even if some sound outlasts the activity (through echo, say), the entire performance cannot outlive all the activity. Most performance sounds overlap with the sound-making. Cause and effect here travel together. Such is not true of detachable, transportable things like paintings.

One may be tempted to reify musical sound if one supposes that auditory experience captures all that is musically significant. One may close one's eyes at a concert the better to absorb the music. So some listeners believe. But this says less about sound exhausting the musical significance in a performance than it does about the psychological means through which sound may be appreciated and savoured by certain music consumers.

If musical sound alone is not sufficient for performance, perhaps sound is not necessary either. John Cage wrote *4′33″* to make this very point. Lasting four minutes and thirty-three seconds, *4′33″* involves pure silence and yet calls for everything else normally featured in performance – performers, instruments, audiences, venues. Each of the three sections of *4′33″* is marked 'TACET'. *4′33″* is meant for any instrument, and was premiered by David Tudor in Woodstock, New York, 29 August 1952. Tudor, at the piano, indicated the duration of each section by opening and closing the keyboard cover.

Does Cage merit serious regard? Cage purportedly used *4′33″* to stress the equal importance of sound and silence in music. Most pieces contain elements of both; but some, like perpetual motion pieces, contain just sound. Why deny musical status to a work consisting of pure silence? If this is the main point of *4′33″* it seems a silly analogue to a sight gag. Imagine a culinary cousin, a gourmet's delight called *Holes* which consists of an empty folded napkin served with fresh coffee. The message: to stress the equal importance of air and solids in doughnuts. Some doughnuts, the ones with holes, contain elements of both, while others, jelly doughnuts, contain just solids. Why deny culinary status to doughnuts emphasizing pure air? Ignoring general worries about the nature of art, it is questionable whether *4′33″* is even a musical work.[2] If it is not, then performing it cannot be a musical performance. That should caution us against taking it centrally into account.

Most pertinently, *4′33″* only works in contrast against a prior paradigm involving sound. Pieces like *4′33″* could never be musically typical.

Musical agency

Four aspects of agency are pertinent to performance: causation, intention, skill, and intended audiences. Below, I elaborate upon the claim that musical performances are activities brought about by human agents with certain abilities and with certain intentions about their activities and beneficiaries.

Causation: making music happen

As events, performances have causes, but performances, clearly, are not mere occurrences, but actions undertaken by agents. As such, performance points both to its origin and purpose. The cause of musical performance is standardly some human being.

That said, we talk comfortably about the performance of machines. Taken generically, human and machine performances share certain features. Consideration of machine performance involves attention to specifications, statistics, and ratings. The specifications and statistics describe what the machine can do under given conditions relative to an assigned task, while the ratings tell us how well it operates relative to other machines. 'Isaac performed the *Chaconne*', describes at least what Isaac did. He caused the *Chaconne* to be sounded. Isaac's performance rating: 'He did it well, given the pressure'.

Similarities fade once individuality enters. 'Isaac gave a startlingly original performance of the *Chaconne*', departs from shop talk. Machines are often of value only if they are reliably replicable, and instances of a particular line are designed to be uniformly reliable and interchangeable in their job. Though I may admire the performance of my particular vacuum cleaner, I do not expect more than uniform reliability and, discounting sentimental attachments, am happy to replace it with another which performs as well. From human performance we customarily expect distinctiveness which, as a norm, is not built into machine performance. Much musical performance thrives on the virtues of unique variety and the unexpected by design which are characteristics of creative, that is, anthropoid, agency.

Musical performance is typically a humanly caused sound sequence. Since humans usually make such sound with certain instruments (including voice), one may expand this with 'using some specified musical instrument'.

Do player pianos give performances? To eliminate such prospects, one may appeal to the lack of intention in such devices.[3] Although intention figures in any paradigm of performance, one may rule out the player piano on other grounds. Player pianos are merely playback devices and so more like record, CD, and tape players than they are like paradigm performers. The roll or magnetic insert functions like a tape or CD. The only difference is the output mechanism. Whether or not the roll played back was punched out by an actual human performance is incidental. The pianola does not interpret its roll. The changes in any sequences of playings can be explained by appeal to determinable environmental changes; for example, the roll is worn in parts, there was a slight power surge, a hammer stuck, etc. What counts is who or what created the roll in the first place. Sound-making devices which actually perform must meet certain elemental causal conditions which player pianos lack; that is, they must programme their own renditions.

Intention: the performer's plan

Performances are deliberate, intentionally caused sound sequences. They are never involuntary like sneezes, nor accidental or inadvertent. A person, unaware of a certain piece, who plays something sounding just like it by casually running a bow across a cello could only generously be said to have performed that piece. Such a person could not claim the credit that is normally due to one who has given a performance. The intention to perform and beliefs about the immediate context are integral to performance.

What do performers intend in causing sound? Roughly, one intends to cause a certain sound sequence with certain qualities at a certain time. (Works and

16

means also figure, though reference to them here needlessly complicates matters.) Generally, one intends to play well, to meet and even exceed certain standards of proficiency. Time and circumstance may frustrate one's desires. Delays in opening occur as do mistakes in execution. Sometimes fortune smiles when things go as, or even better than, one had wished. Players surprise themselves occasionally with spontaneous expressiveness.

Questions about certain performance details reflect upon intention and prior planning; for example, 'Did you really want such a big *diminuendo* in measure 15', 'to slow down that much in bar 22?', 'to employ such a brittle sound in the repeat?'. Highly deliberate, self-monitoring players may answer these confidently. Others may not. Some may hold false beliefs about their performance until tapes or reviews set the record straight. One's performing intentions may be more or less rich depending upon one's preparatory deliberations. Performance may be pre-planned down to microscopic details, or run more thinly on rough-hewn notions of overall effect. Whatever the degree of pre-planning, performers must have some notion about the desired outcome, some relatively determinate conception of their intended sound.

One cannot have a plan so thin it regulates virtually nothing; for example, the intention to play some sounds or other. This is to renounce all plans, rather like answering 'Breathe, eat, and sleep' in response to 'What do you plan to do with your life?'. In such cases, it cannot matter what sound one causes. In performing it always matters. What of very thin plans; for example, just to cause this sound sequence? Though possibly appropriate in practice as one gears up to conquer technical obstacles, such thinness is at best preparatory only. In itself, it promises nothing of musical interest. Should musical interest arise, it does so arbitrarily and incidentally. Of course, we must exclude cases of apparent thinness, where the player's past experience and knowledge operate tacitly in the background. There is a minimal thinness of plan below which performance proper either fails completely or fails to get going at the outset.

To perform is to intentionally generate and to regulate the generation of some sound sequence. Such regulatory intentions shape the sound by making certain effects happen. They also comprise a normative template which informs the player how well the performance is going and how it went. Without such templates, no performance ranking is possible. Individuals commonly rank their own performances, not necessarily by audience response, but by conformity to their own ideals. Though one may achieve this conformity by luck, one cannot consistently so achieve it.

That performers must adopt a plan of action against which the relative success of a certain caused sound sequence is assessed suggests that performance has both intrinsic as well as instrumental value. By this I mean that value attaches not only to the results one achieves, but also to how they are achieved. The value of many purposive activities resides almost exclusively in the external results achieved. So, the value of gold mining derives from the gold recovered, and not from the exercise of mining itself.

17

On this simplified analysis, performance intentions are, in many ways, personal since they involve performers creating and satisfying their own standards of achievement. External regulations exist, however, which flow from the performer's regard for the listener, the work being performed and its performance traditions, the performer's immediate performance community, and the formal rituals and institutions of performance like the recital, concert tour, conservatory juries and so on. These public matters are taken up later.

Skill: agency refined

The causal path from intended sound to the sound itself cannot be haphazard. Causing the sound one intends to cause requires control over one's actions and the instruments of action. The mark of full control is being able to cause the sound one intends when one will, and to do with the sound as one will. Naturally, while being in full control does not presuppose being infallibly in control, such control does presuppose a high degree of reliability.

One major indicator of control is the power to cause repeatedly at will certain intended sound sequences reliably and consistently. Duplicating a result at will minimizes the influence of luck. Duplicating also minimizes the uncertainty that one's success rides on hidden facilitating factors which are randomized out by repetition. The greater the variety of circumstances under which one can replicate one's planned actions, the greater one's control over them. The power to duplicate results increases our confidence about future success just as do any reliably confirmed regularities. (On analogy with experiment design and hypothesis testing, the greater the number of varying conditions under which a given prediction is confirmed, the greater the degree of confidence we have in the hypothesis from which the prediction flows. Skill and verisimilitude are kindred.) This consistently reliable ability to cause sound to match one's intentions is one mark of dependable control, commonly known as skill.

Is skill required in performance? Having skill and knowing that one has skill allow one to predict with some accuracy the likelihood of succeeding at causing certain intended sounds. If players chronically lacked confidence in their power to realize on call a musical plan in sound few would perform. Otherwise, what point could there be in formulating musical plans, announcing them in public, while wondering all the while whether any of this would or could be realized? The only way to satisfy desires to make music is by acquiring the skill to do so.

Being a performer involves the ability to produce and re-produce certain results on call. Skill is not required for each performance but is surely constitutionally and professionally necessary for musicians. Musicians lacking skill will enjoy short musical careers as do those who lose skill through inactivity. A person lacking enough skill for a certain repertoire may, at best, luckily perform it passably, once, possibly twice. Though one can have skill without exercising it, no skilled player would deliberately forsake that skill. One may perform as if one had never played the work previously, but this itself requires the skilled contrivance of a Victor Borge. Performers count on their skill, evidence for which they accumulate in practice and rehearsal. Performance can thus be described as the human causing of certain intended sound sequences with skill.

The links between skill and physical causation, and where skill fits in performance communities and traditions are explored later. Here I will canvass a few matters of immediate concern.

An initial point: if skill hangs on willed repetition, can skill be manifest in a single unrepeated episode? Listeners do not withhold attributions of skill just because they have heard a performer only once. Listeners, however, may not care whether skill is truly present so long as their experience has been satisfying. The so-called skill they admire may just be their appreciation of that performer's effect upon them. Still, would-be listeners count on skill as outlined. They assume the performer has preparation enough to fulfil the promise of a performance.

Suppose a performer successfully tries something new, thus creating the excitement of an improvisation.[4] Is this not an exercise of skill? Yes, but the novelty here may mislead somewhat. Much that happens usually depends upon exercising already entrenched skills in a new context. So, a player's established skills at linking intricate chord sequences and interweaving musical quotations may be applied in certain melodic contexts, the outcome of which is unexpected. The skills remain as ever. Sometimes where great risk is taken (for example, pressing the tempo or wandering into distant harmonic regions), talk of skill may be inappropriate. Some musicians may think themselves lucky at having survived intact. The next time, however, counts differently.

Perhaps we should distinguish between having a skill and acting skilfully. Using the latter to mean 'acting as one with skill would act', we reserve judgement about the full attribution of skill. Acting skilfully is evidence – not necessarily conclusive – of skill. Performers tend to be conservative. They often need more convincing as to their skills than one skilful (possibly just lucky) break.

A second concern is that skill is usually associated with the ability to perform relatively difficult tasks. The account above ignores this and seems consistent with saying that blowing my nose is a skill just because I can do it repeatedly at will.

Skills are essentially bound up with challenges. Any analysis of skill must capture the sense of overcoming some challenge and the value assigned to overcoming it as a result of the exercise of skill. Challenges, ever relative to circumstance, are contextualized difficulties. For those with shattered spinal cords, walking is a challenge, and walking gracefully a masterful skill. Any human activity may become a challenge. Mastering any activity can become a skill for some group for whom the activity is a challenge and overcoming it reliably is a victory.

Skills arise relative to acknowledged limitations in means relative to ends which, for convenience, I call 'handicaps'. Chapter 2 examines conventional music as relying in part on certain deliberate handicaps. I may withhold regarding something as a skill until I am aware of the handicaps. Certain handicaps are institutionalized; for example, having to cut a clean dovetail joint with a chisel in cabinet-making class even though using a power router and jig is much easier. One can make a competition for any skill (arising from a challenge due to handicap), and thus establish ranks of accomplishment.

Others may attribute to one a skill even if one fails to appreciate it as a skill one has. The activity may seem to one altogether effortless. One feels no challenge present and hence, has no sense of accomplishment. If one has always found mathematics easy, one may not think oneself endowed with mathematical skills. Certain expressions almost underrate the mastery implied in skill by somehow withholding full credit for certain abilities; for example, I may regard myself as having an aptitude or flair for mathematics, or consider myself a 'natural'. Perhaps it is best to say I have facility, skill without toil.[5]

Skills can be acknowledged without being admired. Some skills may impress us more because we admire the overcoming of certain handicaps more than others. We may admire a skill because we value the results it achieves, results we would like to achieve but cannot. We may derive pleasure just watching someone overcome odds, however contrived they are. Even if such appreciation is wanting, one can acknowledge the skill in what one otherwise regards to be a pointless, violent, tasteless, immoral, or juvenile pursuit.

Music-making is skilful because human handicaps in manual (or glottal) dexterity and facility are plain, especially if one tries to imitate a virtuoso. Our respect for musicians stems largely from a regard for their musical skills. Of course we admire talent, but talent without skill is like power without authority – unsteady, capricious, unreliable. Talent is the promise of high merit, given skill; facility, the blessing of skill without sweat. Though musicians and listeners alike may be disillusioned by recklessly undeveloped talent, facility never disappoints.

The skills musicians value may not all impress non-participating admirers as they do their competitive colleagues in the musical community. Still, the exacting demands of the musical community seldom disappoint the listener. That said, the listener often cannot appreciate the many subtle nuances musicians employ to meet the critical expectations of their colleagues. One must satisfy not only the well-disposed and under-informed customer, but also one's often ill-disposed and omniscient colleagues. Such overdetermination of the goal typifies many skilled trades and crafts.

One remaining concern about intention is this: the more detailed one's intentions regarding the sound sequence, the greater the skill required in realizing them. The more detailed my musical plan, the more ways it can fail. Overcoming greater risk of failure takes more skill than overcoming less. But this relativizes skill to one's intentions. Skill is surely a more objective phenomenon. Further, regarding players who formulate loosely-structured intentions while hoping for well-behaved spontaneous inspiration, the thinness of the intention neither diminishes nor boosts their skill.

Given the connections between skills, challenges, handicaps, and parties valuing the overcoming of challenges under certain handicaps, the complaint that skill is relativized to intention poses no worry. The objective quality of skill grows precisely out of an assessment of the challenges involved in consistently meeting the task at hand given the impediments to it. The detailed intention case seems riskier but only because the task at hand is described in terms of meeting those very risks. Musicians with rich intentions can always create their own challenges for their own undertakings. They may thus set up a skill acquisition race against themselves; for example, setting ever higher tempi for a piece which works well at a lower one. But their skill development plan cannot of itself be imposed as a benchmark against which the looser plan is measured. Rich and thin plans have no influence on assessments of relative skill requirements if the task at hand is conceived more broadly. As it happens, technical and interpretative conventions tend to be fairly spacious if not always broad-minded.

For example, instead of couching our goal as 'making the *Chaconne* sound precisely thus . . . ' (here follows a measure-by-measure interpretative schedule), we may set it as 'making the *Chaconne* sound sombre, noble, but serene'. The latter, though less determinate than the former, may portray exactly what the former aims to achieve. The methods employed – rich or thin plans – to achieve the end fade into the background so long as they are equally commensurate with the commonly adopted challenges and handicaps.

Causal limits, primary skill, and creditworthiness

Performance agency raises issues not only about causality and skill, but also about accountability and credit. Considering certain opportunities made available by electronic technology, performance proper requires that a player be fully in a position to take credit for the performance. To do so, it is not sufficient that the appropriate sounds merely be causally related to the performer's musical activities. We also judge what we take the performance exercise to exact fittingly from the player. Performances tend to be means-tested. They are activities the successful realization of which is in part determined by satisfying conditions attached to execution and the means of execution. Means-tested activities must not only reach specified ends but must reach them under certain causal limits. Agents are thus accountable for observing those limits. Concern about causal limits covers 'causal presence' involving the actual agents at work, and 'causal credit', or what the working performer really contributes to performance.

Concerning causal presence, performers must be causally central in music-making. One can always ask whether the alleged performer is genuinely the immediate cause of the performance. However seemingly gratuitous the demand that a performance be immediately brought about by the performer, fraud and deception do occur. Consider the phenomena of playing air-guitar and lip-syncing. Ignoring cases where singers lip-sync their own pre-recorded vocals (the common practice in rock videos), air-guitarists and lip-syncers are not guitarists or vocalists as such. When listeners are deliberately duped into believing that air-guitarists and lip-syncers are actually making the sounds presented, performance credit is violated. The call for causal presence may be dubbed 'the Milli Vanilli rider' in honour of a small and largely forgotten scandal. I will say no more about it here.

Concerning causal credit, the acknowledgement and praise that performers seek depends upon certain displayed skills which are acquired to meet certain musical challenges. Such skills are the prime virtues of the accomplished player. One can fake such skills or take various shortcuts, thus obscuring the real distance that otherwise separates those fully equipped with and those deficient in such skills.[6]

Just what must a performer do in order to take proper credit for a performance? The answer to that involves means-testing which pins credit upon legitimate performing resources. In the professional ethics of performance, what counts as playing something fair-and-square turns on a certain standardized causal environment. Were our options fixed, nothing much would be at stake. But as technology transforms the causal environment, customary standards are themselves accused of sustaining outmoded conceptions of accomplishment. Specifically, performers may, despite assuming an immediate causal role in the production of sound, lack the full responsibility for it we conventionally expect in performance. Let us consider such a case in some detail.

Suppose that one can offer a performance of a very difficult work by performing something which is very much easier to execute. Can one take credit for the more difficult execution? Must the audible sound bear some paradigm causal relation to what the performer causally contributes? Must a player directly execute the pitches and rhythms of some work as notated in order to perform it? Does a performance of that work require executing it as written within conventional margins for error and discretionary alteration? In response to a rhetorical: 'Well, how else can it be done!', consider a virtual device related to the 'ring modulator', a common input–output sound generating device, which complicates performance credit considerably.

Simple ring modulators have an internal oscillator set at a determinate frequency. On its own, the modulator's output is that of its oscillator; for example, a pitch with frequency 1,000 Hz. With an added input, the modulator gives as output two co-occurring frequencies which are simple functions of the oscillator frequency and the input frequency from the player; for example, the sum of the two frequencies (the sum tone or upper sideband) and the difference between them (the difference tone or lower sideband). For simplicity, I will consider only modulators that have as output a single sideband. Such modulators are called 'frequency shifters'.[7]

Suppose a player uses a conventionally tuned instrument (for example, a violin or guitar) to play a certain work. If the player wants a sounding of that work as output, but feeds the input as scored through a modulator, the output will not sound like the work. Why? If the player inputs pitches prescribed in the work's score, the modulator output takes each pitch and, say, subtracts the oscillator's frequency from it. To sound the work properly through the modulator, the player must input a sequence of pitches unrelated harmonically to the work's score but related mathematically; for example, by the subtraction function characteristic of a modulator which outputs difference tones. What the player actually sounds on the instrument to get some work as output is that work as scored plus the modulator's oscillation frequency. For each notated pitch n, the player must execute pitches of frequency $n + 1,000$ Hz to get the work as output. Call this revised pitch sequence when notated the 'shifted score'. If played from the shifted score without the modulator, the output sound is quite unlike that of the chosen work. When one plays from the shifted score through the modulator, the output sounds just like the chosen work.

But, the modulator's internal oscillator can be set at any frequency. Because there are an indefinite number of frequencies available on the modulator, there are an indefinite number of shifted scores of the same work which, when played as input into a modulator set at a given frequency, will yield an output sounding as the desired work sounds.

Such distinct shifted scores demand distinct patterns of execution and so will present varying orders of difficulty for a given player. Some will require virtuosic talents, others mere proficiency. For example, a modulator using a subtraction function and yielding difference tones requires that the player execute higher frequency pitches than those notated in the original score. Playing higher notes is sometimes physically more demanding than playing lower ones. One can reverse the difficulty by playing in low positions a work originally set in high positions via a modulator using an addition function which produces only sum tones.

In principle, for the sounding of any work, there exists a shifted score the execution of which falls within the proficiency of any player. Depending on the modulator, any player at any level of skill can execute any work with equal control, no matter how difficult in its original scoring.

Musical sensitivity is affected. Expressive subtlety comes increasingly under control the more one can take for granted technical execution. Some modulator can conceivably allow the expressively sensitive but technically weak player to shine as brightly as the sensitive, talented virtuoso and so achieve expressive parity with the virtuoso. Indeed, 'difficult', 'virtuosic', and other terms signalling great technical skill might cease to carry any weight. They become merely relational terms, relative to some pre-defined but ultimately arbitrary modulator. Such terms may even acquire a negative tone of inconvenience and nuisance, referring to pesky obstacles which can be corrected with the appropriate prosthetic modulator.

Someone is sure to object that to democratize proficiency thus runs afoul of lingering conventions about accomplishment. Isn't the modulator-dependent weak player like the runner on steroids? Isn't the player who demonstrates unassisted technical mastery somehow more honest to and with the work and thus somehow musically more creditworthy?

But what properly makes for creditworthiness? What exactly is involved in taking full responsibility for one's performance? It can't so much matter how hard the conventional player works. The modulator-assisted player may work just as hard. Furthermore, no one requires that every musician start from some state of equal skill or opportunity. Natural talent and social opportunity vary. Still, those short on facility cannot professionally compensate for their limitations with a machine, nor should expectations of hard work figure strongly. 'Virtuosic' does not precisely describe a species of difficulty. That term usually reflects only the actual distribution of abilities which may be improved overall through training. Just as yesterday's typical runner, for whom the four minute mile was 'impossible', would fall behind today's typical runner, so yesterday's flashy player might become today's struggler.

For a player to take proper credit for a performance, the performance must display the virtues of skill and expertise which professionally enable players to perform what they perform. In this sense, to take causal credit, one must be properly in a position to take full credit for what one has done under terms of appropriate agency. If results were all that mattered, no one could fault those who customized their modulators to enable the easiest input. Indeed, anyone who willingly chose a more difficult course would seem stubborn and appear to adopt the unconvincing air of a boastful show-off. On the other hand, if results-hardest-won are the prime objective, players would take the palm for the least facilitative modulator settings. One could imagine competitions where the contestants adopted increasingly nasty modulator settings for originally simple pieces. After all, if the game is to suffer yet survive, then the winner must suffer the most by surviving the worst technical trials. But if such masochism hasn't much to do with music, unassisted technical skill seems to become rather shallow a condition for creditworthiness.

Though imaginary, the modulator case is merely an extension of a very real, new breed of machines, the so-called 'intelligent' or 'smart' instruments.[8] Consider Joel Chadabe's interactive composing device (1984) which employs *Thérémin* antennae and special drumpads:

> Software translates [manual] gestures into high-level musical processes. With Chadabe's Solo system, a wave of the composer's hand can cause the tempo of a musical process to change and the harmony to shift. . . . The proliferation of inexpensive computers puts the capability of intelligent instruments within the reach of virtually every musician who wants them.[9]

This easy access facilitates expressiveness in ways hitherto unimagined. One's instrument becomes much more than an extension of one's body. It becomes virtually a collaborator:

> The intelligent instruments that already exist promise a new age of

24

communication in which the attention of musicians can be on their inner messages. Musicians need not worry as to whether the instrument will be powerful enough to represent the message. They need not worry whether they will be virtuosic enough to play the instrument. These concerns can be left to the instrument itself.[10]

Well then, what is amiss about using modulator enhancement? Why should attributions of creditworthiness favour the conventional player? Answer: using a modulator-enhanced conventional instrument to perform a work does not amount to performing the work itself but merely to being causally implicated in sound sequences as of the work. Being causally implicated in sound sequences as of some work is possibly necessary but is not sufficient for performance of that work. I must elaborate.

The modulator, though physically realizable, is just an abstract function over pitches. Score any sequence of pitches, and you can, in principle, define a modulator which takes this sequence as input and outputs the pitch sequence heard as *O Canada*. Any pitch sequence can, with its suitable modulator, represent any other sequence such that the former as input is sufficient for the latter as output. These scores bid the player to directly cause certain pitches – those of *Rule Britannia*, say – with the assurance that *O Canada* will emerge as output. Have I played *O Canada* by playing *Rule Britannia*? Scarcely. I have perhaps 'sounded' *O Canada*, but I've played nothing but *Rule Britannia*. Never mind what you hear out the end. Snip the cable connecting me to my modulator and *Rule Britannia* alone fills your hall.

Imagine a more graphic case for denying full causal credit for the output. All I can manage on a conventional guitar is a monophonic version of *Twinkle, Twinkle, Little Star*. A parcel arrives containing a mysterious device which I later learn is a sophisticated modulator. On the device is a dial with various settings named: 'Dowland: *Fantasy in G* (Renaissance Lute)'; 'Bach: *Chaconne in D Minor* (Baroque Violin)'; 'Weiss: *Passacaglia in D* (Baroque Lute)'; 'Britten: *Nocturnal Op. 70* (Guitar)'. The instructions read: '(a) Clip the device around the soundhole; (b) Set the dial at one of the settings; (c) Play *Twinkle, Twinkle*'. I set the dial to the Bach and, lo, as I go through the relevant *Twinkle, Twinkle* motions the room resounds with *Chaconne in D Minor*.

Have I performed the solo violin masterpiece? Absolutely not. Why not? Simply, because I cannot play it. I can't play the violin. And, anyway, even if I could, I've neither the skill nor the training, the talent nor the expertise for such a challenge. After all, one does not what one cannot do.

To count as a performance of the *Chaconne*, one must here ignore what I immediately do and attend only to the proximate results of that activity. But if the mere presence of some causal link between what I literally do (that is, *Twinkle, Twinkle* motions) and the *Chaconne*-sounding output is sufficient for my having performed the *Chaconne*, then any input can so count in principle, so long as one can define a function which will get one from one's immediate playing activity to the desired work-sounding output. Consider the typical player input for a given work; for example, a determinate sequence of hand movements on a conventionally tuned instrument under standard playing conditions. Abstracted, this constitutes a performance function for that work. Since no official requirement exists that there be one single performance-function (or family of functions) for a given work, isn't the door open for the player to define any function whatever?

But this is clearly absurd. Why? Because it legitimates the following performance-function for the *Chaconne*: (a) Retrieve a compact disc containing Pinchas Zukerman's *Chaconne*; (b) Place the disc in a CD player; (c) Set the player to the *Chaconne* track; (d) Activate the player. Talk about 'play-in-a-day'! (Suppose Zukerman himself clips on the device and follows instructions faithfully. Has he then performed the Bach? Despite his proven ability to do so, on this occasion we have no reason to attribute this sounding of the *Chaconne* to him. Because we cannot here appeal to lack of ability implies that, although such a lack may be sufficient to withhold attributions of accomplishment, it cannot be necessary. Zukerman has no claim here just because he has not done the right things, caused the right movements – at least as convention requires.) What matters is what musicians physically do rather than what listeners actually hear.[11]

Neither sameness of or difference in acoustic output – what the listener hears at the end – provide sufficient grounds for determining performance responsibility and creditworthiness. However necessary physical skill is for creditworthiness, one cannot, as a mere listener, read back from what is heard to the player's creditworthiness and hence skilfulness. Consider an analogy between moral motivation and physical skill. Just as one might argue that twins acting from different motives who produce the same result do not necessarily merit equal moral praise, so players whose activity results in the same experience for the listener do not automatically merit equal creditworthiness for that result if they employ different means. More contentiously, just as twins acting from the same motive might be equally praiseworthy or blameworthy, however different the actual results, so we cannot automatically deny equal creditworthiness to both players just because what the listener hears differs. If causal parity implies credit parity, then whatever one player can take credit for, so can the other in the sense of claiming equal skill. Like moral virtue, performance creditworthiness is not a function of results alone. Because listeners cannot decide differential causal credit merely on the basis of what they hear, listeners cannot judge on aural grounds alone who is the more skilled.[12]

This asymmetry of creditworthiness comes to life when we consider recorded performances. Whatever we hear on a recording is not itself sufficient to ground judgements of the player's real role and true merit. At most we can judge charitably that the player is as if creditworthy. Why? Because some players who make recordings may lack the skill in real-time to execute flawlessly more than a few measures at a time. Compare stage-acting with movie-acting. The stage-actor cannot rely on multiple 'takes' but must perform continuously throughout. A movie-actor with a terrible memory faces lethal danger on the stage. For the technically deficient musician, the recording studio like the film studio (read 'modulated environment') compensates fully, so such a player may have a successful recording career. Has any such 'bit' player ever actually performed any work having never played anything entirely non-stop? No long-standing traditions give one any reason for saying so. Whatever output the listener hears, unless two players can swap without noticeable effect the ways they produce such an output, they are not equally creditworthy within our present traditions of musicianship. Presumably, any non-stop player can change places with any 'bit' player. If the reverse is not true, the non-stop player holds a higher skill rank than the other and thus enjoys a greater degree of creditworthiness than the other. No mere listener would or could draw this conclusion.

But, one may retort, these very traditions are just that – mere traditions. Why must they count? Can't listeners just reject them? If they do so, what listeners respect in music becomes purely phenomenal. We will see in Chapter 2 that, for musicians, far from being mere traditions, they are deeply constitutive of musical practice which, unsurprisingly, derives its very nature from entire performance communities.

The listener standpoint detaches 'performance' from the player. Indeed, it creates an exploitable divide between phenomenal or listener-centred performance and agent or player-centred performance. Phenomenal performances can be distinguished and judged purely as acoustic phenomena. They may also be evaluated as acoustic phenomena which are as if caused by players under certain conditions of performance. Because, for centuries, phenomenal and agent performances have been directly and uniformly linked, judgements about the phenomenal performance have been taken comfortably to be transferable to those about agent performance.

Performance attribution and thus creditworthiness presuppose certain primary causal conventions which 'smart' instruments upset. Among these norms is the assumption that repertoire is rankable not only in terms of its musical value but also in terms of what level of player it demands. To perform such repertoire, one must not only sound it directly; one must sound it fair-and-square within the expectations of physical skill to which players tacitly subscribe. Such expectations occasionally face daunting trials. About his *Violin Concerto, Opus 36* (1936), Schoenberg warned players thus: 'I am delighted to add another unplayable work to the repertoire. I want the concerto to be difficult and I want the little finger to become longer. I can wait.'[13] Schoenberg here unequivocally, if mockingly, embraces the value of physical skill, one which is intrinsic to a long tradition of music-making.

As we will see, this long tradition has not gone unchallenged. Indeed, one can easily imagine this tradition succumbing finally to technological displacement. While it lasts, however, at its core is firmly entrenched the immediate unassisted causal primacy of the performer. That primacy underwrites creditworthiness.

Even though full performance (as discussed below) involves third-party listeners essentially, the centrality of physical action puts the listener's experience in a subservient place. Given that we must attend first and foremost to real physical skills, musicianship falls squarely within the craft tradition where it has been at home for millennia. Recording technology and computers are busy unseating that tradition. When it goes, phenomenal performance will be all that matters.

Intended audiences: the point of performance

Performances are not reflective activities savoured by their agents in solitude. Performances reach out for listeners. They are other-directed, or, in the idiom, 'given'. Unlike rehearsals, exploratory sight-reading, recreational practice, and other player-centred activities, performances are specifically and directly intended, designed, or meant for audiences. As purposive activities, their *telos* is to be experienced by those for whom the performer prepares them.

Rehearsals preceding the formal ritual of playing before an audience cannot be confused with the performance itself. The rehearsal is preparatory practice for performance. Performances rationalize and explain rehearsals preceding them. Any one performance may support many rehearsals, even though a performance and a rehearsal for it may be aurally indistinguishable. 'Indistinguishable' here means either something weakly descriptive like 'falls into the same class of related interpretations', or evaluative like 'provides no purely musical grounds for preference'. Rehearsals and performances not only may be, but often are intended to be, acoustically intersubstitutable. They are, however, functionally distinct. Playing episodes are rehearsals if and only if there is some further intended playing episode for which they are rehearsals. Rehearsals are thus dependent upon and subordinate to performances – at least, projected or planned performances. The final event may, after all, be cancelled.

As performances are for intended audiences, so rehearsals are for intended performances. Rehearsals must temporally precede performances. One rehearses to perform, and one performs (among other things) to be heard by an audience. Though the rehearsal is indirectly undertaken for the sake of the intended audience, it is never intended that the audience hear the rehearsal – though when things go well one might wish that an audience were present. Most non-participating listeners present during rehearsal (for example, stagehands) are not meant or expected to listen to what is played. If they should hear something, the player scarcely intends that whatever they hear is heard as (part of) the performance. Players use this to advantage. One can always renounce or re-take something in rehearsal. Errors in rehearsal are acceptable, excusable, and reversible even if rehearsals remain serious business. One cannot say of a big blunder: 'Oh, it only took place in concert' with the nonchalance of 'well, it's just a rehearsal' or gratitude of 'thank heavens, it's just a rehearsal'. Performance offers the agent no second thoughts or chances.

Anyone asked to judge a rehearsal is meant, obviously, to take note. Still, such judges are unlike audience members; for example, they may interrupt the playing to comment and advise on how to improve things when the formal event takes place. Importantly, the players are not playing to benefit their advisers as they do their audiences. From advisers they hope to gain rather than to give.

Rehearsals are playings which are purely means to other playings. Performances are never means to further playings. Thus there exists a teleological and temporal hierarchy among types of playing. This order reserves for performance a sense of occasion which ordinarily never attaches to rehearsal.

What of the full dress rehearsal? Drama, ballet, and opera are all performing arts, and dress rehearsals serve a purpose directly relevant to these artforms. Unlike pure music, these artforms are hybrid. They involve combined elements of music, dance, costume, set design, and so on. The dress rehearsal is often the last (and even only) opportunity a director has of combining all the elements together before the scheduled performance. This allows the director last-minute refinements, and gives the cast possibly a first taste of the whole production. With pure music, no corresponding reason exists to combine the elements. Players may wish to acquaint themselves with a hall's acoustics and general performing ambience, but these form no part of the traditions of music rehearsal, and certainly need not involve running through an entire programme in order, in tails.

Related remarks apply to the distinction between performances and largely informal activities like sight-reading, noodling, recreational practice, jam sessions, and the like. Such activities are self-contained and self-indulgent. Unlike rehearsals, they point to no future event, and, unlike performances, to no expectant listener. These are activities just for the player. Music-making boasts both its casual and formal sides, its self-directed and other-directed aspects. Performance and rehearsal bear, by dint of contrast, all the marks of the latter.

Why dedicate each performance to an intended audience? The question is not about player motivation which may vary as widely as motivation generally, nor does it reflect the interests of audience members which, too, may differ widely. In what sense is a performance for some potential group? Perhaps the listener is merely a target. The occasion of performance is incomplete without an audience. Performance is relational. The intended audience is the value that fills the third blank in the schema:

Performs (*player, work, audience*)

This analysis is consistent with describing someone as playing at an audience. Other equally inadequate analyses would stress positional expressions like 'before an audience', 'in the presence of an audience', 'facing an audience', and the like.

These substitutions disappoint because they neglect the normative flavour of 'for' conspicuous in expressions like: 'I did it just for you'. Players traditionally are responsible to their art and to their audience. The audience is not merely

29

the receiver, but a privileged receiver, a beneficiary of the player, the performance being offered as the benefit. Some good is supposed to arise from a performance, and only incidentally that of enriching or immortalizing the composer or performer. A classically Platonic theme, musicians in giving (offering, dedicating) their performances better (improve, benefit, constructively serve) their would-be listeners. That is integral to the craft of artistic entertainment.[14]

> The accomplished musician . . . must carefully appraise his audience, their attitude toward the expressive content of his program, the place itself, and other additional factors. Nature has wisely provided music with every kind of appeal so that all might share in its enjoyment. It thus becomes the duty of the performer to satisfy to the best of his ability every last kind of listener.[15]

Musical works

Performance requires skilled agents causing specific intended sound sequences for the intended benefit of an audience. In improvisational traditions, the sound sequences emerge from and as the performer's invention in performance, though they are often anchored in familiar harmonic, rhythmic, or melodic stereotypes. In the recent 'classical' tradition, such sound sequences typically relate to specific musical works which are often the invention of those other than the performer. Some think such works exist apart from their performances. The sound sequences are related to them by deriving from them.

Later on, I examine the relations between performances and works.[16] For now, let us accept that such sequences are meant to constitute instances or tokens of independently identifiable musical works. A performance of a work is an intentionally caused sound sequence constituting an instance or token of some musical work. Two broad sets of issues arise from this.

1   If performances are of works, how does this affect conditions for successful performance where the intention to perform the work may be frustrated? I consider sympathetically the view that one cannot have performed a given work without having intended to do so.
2   Works are independent of performers and come with bundles of properties. How is performance constrained by such properties? How is this constraint manifested? Which properties are to count? I support the view that the constraints works impose upon performances cannot be read off a priori from the scores of works. Such constraints, rather than being impressed upon performances through the works without the mediation of practice conventions, are, rather, encapsulated in changing sets of performance conventions (called 'constraint models') which are stable enough at a time to determine what passes as an acceptable reflection of the work in

performance. More contentiously, in Chapter 3, I present a case for works being collaboratively created in performance.

Works and intentions to perform them

The work provides a delimited objective for the performer (that is, what the sound sequence must instance) and one gauge of the performance's relative success for performer and listener. Being of-a-work, a performance may misrepresent a work by falling short of exact instantiation. Wrong notes are the most obvious failures.

Some performances fail to make the grade fully. Others fully fail to make the grade. Occasionally, the failure may be so dramatic as to compel us to withhold saying that the performance was of anything recognizable, even if we consider it an attempted performance of some work; for instance, the attempt at coloratura soprano solos undertaken by Florence Foster Jenkins. Concern about what exactly was performed, if anything, in a fatally botched recital presupposes strong reference to some independently identifiable work. Suppose that any performance must be of some definite work, and must be intended to be of that work. Under these terms, if the work was not, on any reasonable criterion, realized on an occasion, then no performance of it took place. If one asks: 'What happened?', one would have to resort to phrases like 'attempted', 'would-be', or 'alleged'.

Misfiring intentions create puzzles. Consider cases of mistaken attribution. Suppose a sound sequence of what was believed and intended by a performer to be Xavier's *Fourth Partita* is brought about. Suppose Xavier never wrote the piece but in fact Yalumba did, and that it was, to boot, Yalumba's *Third Suite*.[17] Obviously, there has been no performance of Xavier's *Partita*.

One would agree that, in the misattribution case, this very sound sequence was intentionally caused even if one key description under which both player and listener conceived such sounds – as of Xavier's *Partita* – cannot have been satisfied. Has a performance of Yalumba's *Suite* occurred? If we require that: P is a performance of some work W only if it is intended that an instance of W be played, then no performance of the *Suite* has taken place. Such a requirement brings out the agent-centred quality of performance.

Perhaps we want an extensional concept to allow comments like: 'Nevertheless, everyone heard the *Suite* whether they knew it or not', or 'Nevertheless, that's exactly what was played (executed, sounded) whatever anyone thought'. 'Perform' has an idiomatic role which legitimizes the inference: Player A performed sound sequence S, and S is an instance of work W; so, A performed W.

This intuitive use is more elemental and less specialized than the one being developed; hence my interest in making room for a primary non-extensional reading. The restriction may seem arbitrarily counter-intuitive. Consider again the player, Alphonse, who thinks all along that he has performed Xavier's *Partita*, but has in fact been playing Yalumba's *Suite*. Alphonse knows about both Xavier and Yalumba, and has views about interpreting their respective works. He reads an ecstatic review: 'Last night Alphonse gave us the most riveting performance of Yalumba's *Suite* ever heard!'. Alphonse will likely be shocked both about the information and the praise, and think himself lucky at best for having excelled at something he obviously had no plan to pursue. He has little reason to rank this as one of his successes. Indeed, he might even conclude that, had he known he was playing Yalumba's work and not Xavier's, he would have interpreted the work differently and possibly rankled the reviewer. No facile substitutivity is available. 'Performs' like 'believes' is referentially opaque.

As an illustration, consider Mexican composer Manuel Ponce (1882–1948) who composed, at Andrés Segovia's request, a number of faked pieces attributed to past composers like Alessandro Scarlatti (1660–1725) and Sylvius Leopold Weiss (1686–1750). One extended piece, a *Suite* in A major, published under Weiss' name, was for many years naïvely believed to be by Weiss, and was performed as Weiss. It was meant to have been a lute suite. To perpetuate the confusion, one 'modern' edition claims that it had been transcribed from the original lute tablature. Sincere players tried to reflect interpretively a Late Baroque North German *Zeitgeist*, fully appropriate had it been two centuries old. But this is twentieth-century music, written by a Mexican. Its real pedigree revealed, subsequent players infuse their readings with livelier Latin touches.

Works and constraints upon performance

Performances are not only shaped by the performer's plans; they must also conform to external constraints, for example, those imposed by the work of which it is a performance. Thus a performer must intentionally play a certain work under certain acknowledged constraints. These work-centred constraints are expressed in conventions adopted by performers. These conventions encapsulate what a given performing tradition holds to be especially important in respecting a work's proper nature; for example, most now accept obligations to adhere respectfully to the pitch and rhythm sequences specified in authenticated scores. Some faithfully follow the original instrumentation.[18]

Just how constraining are these conventions? Conventions vary with time and yield shifting boundaries of the work's so-called essential properties. Performance imperatives in one tradition may be discretionary in another. One risks elevating performance conventions to a metaphysical status far outstripping the standing they enjoy in performance circles. Performance propriety cannot be divined a priori by consulting an abstracted view of the work in some idealized historical setting. The ever-increasing influence of the accumulation of both new and re-discovered works and practices makes any notion of a fixed musical essence increasingly less viable.[19]

Interpretive constraints complement constraints upon performance instrumentation, conditions of performance, and so on. The full family of constraints takes in more than this. For now, call such external constraints, as they collectively influence the outcome of a performance, the performance's 'constraint-model' or

'C-model'. C-models encompass the properties of the work judged to be musically relevant at a time. Thus, C-models have more musical content than both notated works and individual performances in that they accommodate whole classes of interpretative options. Every work has at least one C-model at any time. Exceptions might include highly experimental, innovative works for which no detailed performance precedents apply; but even here, there will be some practice carry-over, however sparse, which forms the core of the work's C-model. Any given performance is judged to be of a given work and to succeed or fail as a performance of that work only if it conforms to the collective constraints constituting the work's C-model.[20]

The precise contents of any given C-model may be difficult to specify clearly and will depend upon the degree of rigour imposed upon performance within any given performance circle. Thus, there may be no standing essential properties for a given work over time as one follows the work chronologically through its various acceptable renditions. At many stages in performance traditions, far from strict adherence to some *Urtext*, performers were free to make revisions and amendments to works played. Notes, chords, dynamics and instrumentation may have been altered, repeats ignored, movements omitted, and more. At other times, certain historical norms and authorial directives are accorded overriding authority. There are no fixed criteria for correctness attaching to the contents of C-models, because there is no neutral standpoint external to any C-model regarding any given work. That said, any given performance tradition is constituted as a tradition by reasonably widespread acquiescence to norms of performance conduct encapsulated semi-officially for works in their C-models. These emerge self-consciously in pedagogy which, for its time, lays out the boundaries of what counts professionally as a rendition of some work. So, at any time, the C-model is a normative interpreter, so to speak, enabling one to convert what one has, say, notationally in score to allowable prospective performances of it.

The relationship between a C-model, a work, and performances of that work is music-specific and cannot be understood formally and abstractly in terms of mere instantiation. The language of types and tokens, kinds and instances, or universals and particulars helps very little, for there are many ways types (kinds, universals) can be represented by tokens (instances, particulars), many degrees and shades of what makes something count as a concrete example of a type, kind or universal. Whatever, then, makes some sound sequence a performance of a work neither illuminates nor is illuminated by analogous links between a statue and its casting, an etching block and its pullings, a design and its building, a poem and its readings, or a play and its stagings. Only at some formal level are these one–many relationships themselves much of a kind. Unfortunately, that level obscures the concrete operational links between the one and the many in each of these cases; that is, ignores the distinct mechanisms proper to each which explain how precisely one makes an instance from its model, and what latitude exists in each such mechanism for so-called departures from so-called norms. A 'misshapen' coin stamped by the mint may fail officially as legal tender and so officially be worth nothing because it is no member of the coinage at all. If, however, it escapes into the world, it become a numismatist's good fortune, but not before having led a modest trading life on the street where, for many people, a 'weirdly shaped' quarter still buys twenty-five cents' worth of bubble gum.

The role of C-models is best understood by examining what permits performances to be and forbids them from being instances of works. From the outside, a work's C-model is like a quality-control mechanism into which sounds are fed and from which only passable performances emerge. Whatever they contain has to make musical performance possible, an undertaking unlike whatever makes passable mintings, etchings, stagings, and readings possible. In conforming to a C-model of a work, a performance operates acceptably within the current tradition's considered view of the relevant internal limits imposed by the notated work and the ambient musical practices presupposed in it. Note that a degree of latitude often applies to any notion of acceptability to allow for performances of genius which indulge in just those departures typically limiting performance options. Sometimes, indeed, the work is no more than a medium to flatter performance genius. Let it be added, however, that what passes as 'genius' at a time also falls within broad conditions of acceptability.

The normative aura surrounding performance reinforces a truism that a performance ought to rise above a mere 'mechanical' recitation. What the constraints ideally promote are basic finished products rather than trial runs. One way of portraying the normative element in the concept 'model' is to call the performance a sample of crafted or shaped sound, or even sound sculpture. Skill echoes throughout. A typical performance relates not only to its cause but also to its C-model. Hence, a performance of a work is at least a humanly caused sound sequence intended and successful as a C-model of that work.[21]

Differences in how performances are conceived affect what we think standard or central. The central case so far is typical only of one delimited musical tradition where the musician plays from score under certain ritualized conditions; that is, the highly standardized twentieth-century formal classical concert recital. Clearly, an emphasis upon improvisation, central to jazz and Elizabethan performance, shifts the focus away from detailed, quasi-independent works and moves it towards sketch-like, dependent frameworks. As Chapter 3 suggests, creative classical musicianship involves continuously releasing and exploring the freer framework from within its classical work.

Performance integrity

Having considered various aspects of sound, skill, agency, and works in performance, we will now turn to some general structural conditions; particularly, those concerned with spatiotemporal continuity which contribute to the integrity or wholeness of performance. These integrity conditions provide a framework for coherence, unity, and completeness in performance, and also for performance identity and individuation. They contribute, as well, to performances as special sorts of occurrence.

Performance integrity depends in part on continuity regarding the work performed, the performance episode, and the agents of performance. These 'primary integrity' factors are structural, comprising the chief external spatiotemporal constraints on performance. 'Secondary integrity' factors are concerned with the continuity of the audience, aural experience, and musical interpretation.

Though not equally weighted, the integrity conditions collectively contribute to the distinctive continuity necessary for successful performance. This continuity lends performances their characteristically formal, ritualized, and ceremonial quality which distinguishes them from other goal-directed activities such as painting, reading, composing, writing, or speaking. Performance integrity demands an undisrupted ambience which sustains a ritual mood. One may say, only half jokingly, that successful performance hinges crucially upon strict adherence to the categorical imperative: 'The show must go on'. As will be seen, an essential feature contributing to this ambience is the non-serializability of performance.

Primary integrity factors

Primary integrity factors include continuity regarding the work, performance time, and performance staff.

Work continuity (complete presentation) Any performance of some individual work must present it completely. Within limits, everything in the work must be presented in any performance of it. In executing single works, the player cannot stop halfway through and be said to have performed it. Incomplete performances are not species of full performances, if they are performances at all. The boundaries of the work set the boundaries of performance.

What makes a presentation complete depends on accepted conventions; for example, completeness does not normally require a 'note perfect' rendition. Some notes may be wrong, some missing, some repeats left out, and, with larger works, whole movements may be cut, and yet we may allow that a performance proper has occurred. If a player leaves the very last cadence unresolved, we might complain about a failure to complete the performance, but if an innocuous bar or relish is omitted somewhere in the middle we might excuse charges of unfinished business even if the gappiness rankles.

Completeness must be approached cautiously. We accept performances of works known to be unfinished, but we still acknowledge therein an 'internal' completeness. A symphony minus a movement scarcely suffers as does a movement minus its final fifty measures. In our accepting performances of parts of larger works (for example, selected arias or movements), we thereby take such parts to be musically self-sufficient for the purposes of performance. That said, there are always limits to self-sufficiency however admixed with considerations of 'the purpose at hand'. Musical completeness is somewhat analogous to grammatical and narrative integrity. One may leave a story uncompleted – consider Kafka's *The Trial* – and yet have told a coherent tale. Missing chapters, like missing movements, need not wreck our sense of the novel's coherence. One cannot so easily leave a sentence awaiting completion, though the surrounding narrative often supplies enough to complete it. That said, even if I know what sounds complete an incomplete performance, as listener I scarcely complete the performance by humming the rest, whether in my head or aloud. I haven't that authority.

Temporal continuity (unbroken presentation)   A performance must present a work without temporal break. Complete presentation is thus not enough. Suppose a player starts, gets halfway through, stops, walks off stage, returns an hour later, and, taking up where he left off, completes his presentation. Though the complete work has been played in proper sequence, we do not have a proper performance of it. This presentation fails because a work must be presented completely in a continuous or unbroken episode in performance.

The strictures upon temporal continuity are not rigid. If a player has a memory lapse, stops, regains her composure, and resumes shortly thereafter from the break, we might allow that she gave a complete performance, but it becomes a flawed one.[22] What is temporally unacceptable in performance does not extend to all types of playing. Rehearsals and practice generally can, do, and often must involve incomplete presentation, temporal discontinuity, and even violations of order.

Some avant-garde pieces appear to reject utterly both work- and temporal-continuity. For instance, Christopher Hobbs disassembles and then randomly re-assembles classic works thus engaging in a 'calculated re-articulation of the classics'.[23] In *The Remorseless Lamb* (1970), a two-piano version of Bach's *Sheep May Safely Graze* was cut up. The right and left hand parts of each bar were separated and then randomly re-organized. To play these re-shufflings is not to perform the originals even if all the same notes are present, and even if a random shuffling happened to yield a version sequentially identical to the original. Further, once re-shuffled, the player must presumably play the notes in just that re-articulated order in the one continuous performance sitting.

Personnel continuity (steady staffing)   A performance must be presented by the same performer throughout. Consider a solo keyboard sonata. Player #1 starts playing, plays 10 measures, and then stops. Player #2 resumes on cue exactly at measure 11 and finishes the piece. This is aberrant. We expect in any conventional performance that a solo work be played completely, in order, in one continuous episode, by one performer.[24] Some stylized exceptions exist; for example, the practice of hocketing in some medieval polyphony and some seventeenth-century catches, but these pieces call for alternation among performers and thus are ensemble works.

Together, the three continuity requirements of the work, the episode, and the agent constitute the basic 'primary integrity conditions' for performance. Any playing episode is a single complete performance only if it meets such conditions.

Secondary integrity factors

Integrity hangs on certain less obvious factors as well. These include continuity regarding the listeners, the sensory environment, and the performance interpretation. Secondary factors emphasize the audience, the continuity of experience, and aesthetic expectations.

Listener continuity Any performance must be presented before the same set of listeners throughout. Normally we expect a player to present a work in one place before one audience. Though performances always take place in motion (after all, the Earth revolves), player–audience placement must be relatively stable. Thus arises the *Water Musick* (1717) dilemma where the sounds pass by the audience. Handel's suite was performed on a barge floating down the Thames. Imagine the audience stationed along the bank as the barge passed by. Though the 'primary integrity' conditions are satisfied, the total performance lacks a unified audience. As with parade marching band music, whereas everyone can see, no one can hear everything.

Consider a simpler case involving a player on a stage with a soundproof partition dividing two audiences. Suppose that only the player may pass through the partition. The player, unheard by audience #2, begins for audience #1. Halfway through, still playing, he walks through a door in the divider leaving audience #1 behind and entertains the second.

Neither audience witnesses the entire presentation, even though primary integrity conditions have been satisfied. Though any audience member could confirm after the fact that the whole had been presented, every audience member has experienced the aural equivalent of an incomplete presentation. So, for the audience, no performance proper has been experienced. Even if we agree that a performance transpired, the question 'For whom?' remains unanswered. Although the player experiences all, this is not the experience of either audience. If performance were typically like this, the only proper audience would be the performer. Of course, marching band music is meant to be marched to. The musicians and marchers occupy the same frame of reference. If most music, however, involved different frames of reference for audience and players, our conception of performance would change radically. The revised integrity condition must be: any performance must be presented before the same set of listeners, both performer and listener sharing the same spatial frame of reference throughout.

Sensory continuity Any performance must be aurally available to at least one listener in its entirety. Listener continuity requires that the audience and performance be co-present. But this emphasizes, not the quality of listener experience, but rather the engineering of audience placement. Is continuity of aural experience necessary for performance integrity? Typically we expect it. After all, 'one cannot "glance away" from a Haydn string quartet and then return to find it waiting . . . '.[25] In the *Water Musick* dilemma, no two members of the audience hear the same segment; nor does the audience taken as a whole hear the whole performance. One cannot thus aggregate individual aural snatches. Something misfires in a performance which lacks the opportunity for continuous aural experience of at least one listener other than the performer.

Interpretive continuity Any performance must exhibit appropriate interpretative consistency. What happens if the player changes interpretative course abruptly? Some examples: the player starts an eighteenth-century French courante with inequalities (*notes inégales*) and shifts suddenly to strict square rhythm; a cantata soloist goes suddenly from Baroque vocal style to crooner style; a player gratuitously goes from *fortissimo* to *pianissimo* bar to bar in a piece meant to be a uniform *mezzo forte*. Is this just tastelessness or a challenge to performance integrity? R.A. Sharpe views this matter seriously:

> we expect a conductor to present in performance a unified view of a
> work. . . . A performance must be throughout a performance of a single
> interpretation.[26]

For Sharpe, interpretive discontinuity can be as destructive of a performance's integrity as any breach of primary integrity.

Can this condition be sustained? The examples above reflect interpretative manoeuvres. Sharpe warns of the 'aesthetic repercussions' of such inconstancy, though such need not be fatal to performance unity. A stunningly tasteless performance of a work is just that. Such interpretive jolts are more like a sudden rush of gutter profanities at a diplomatic gathering than they are like the assassination of a diplomatic mission during negotiations. Tastelessness doesn't quite destroy the piece or the performance; however, it does wreck the mood.

Just how much interpretive inconsistency may damage performance integrity is unclear, partly because we lack any 'official' interpretive norms against which to gauge varying degrees of aesthetic shock.[27] However analysed, interpretive continuity could not be so crucial as to determine the unity (let alone identity) of a performance all by itself. After all, interpretation belongs to taste, not to structure.[28] That said, it is unlikely that anyone can lay down transparent ranking criteria to distinguish the degrees of upset caused to performance integrity by various kinds of disruption. If an unfinished final cadence kills the performance, what sort of lesser crime is perpetrated by interpretive ugliness? No clear line separates barely tolerable performances from no performance at all. At most, we might agree that less is at risk in an interpretive catastrophe than in a major temporal break-up of a performance – rather, perhaps, like the different impacts upon one's personal identity caused by losing one's career and losing one's mind.

Integrity and ritual continuity

Interpretive continuity is one of many mood preservers. If interpretive discontinuity can disrupt performance integrity, so too can other conditions which similarly distract. Consider: continuity of public calm – during a performance, half the audience gets restive and begins to hurl verbal and physical abuse at the performer (the English soccer match problem); geophysical continuity – during a performance an earthquake hits or a tidal wave strikes or a volcano erupts, etc. (for example, the 1989 World Series of Baseball disruption in San Francisco); mental health continuity – during a performance, the performer, while playing, begins to shriek, wail, and intone warnings of global doom. And so on. Any of these disrupts the performance, some to the extent of causing the performance to cease. All these factors jointly signal the general need for no serious distractions, interruptions, disruptions, disturbances, departures from some norm.

Performance is not uniquely vulnerable. Similar conditions apply to lectures, sermons, plays-in-progress, formal meetings, and ceremonies of many kinds like religious rites, official dedications, christenings, and marriages. These are all to varying degrees ritual or ceremonial occasions. They tend to be unspontaneous, scheduled, formally structured, sequentially ordered activities which are designed to capture and focus attention. All demand an atmosphere of decorum and order. Thus, they tend to invoke stereotyped procedures and behaviour, codes of conduct, designated personnel, pre-established protocol enjoying common acquiescence. Most have reasonably rigid boundaries, and are officially started and ended. Because their very nature demands a procedural strictness, their preservation demands an uncommon stability. Occasions are fragile creatures indeed.

As rituals, performances differ from other goal-directed activities. Though musical performances aim to present certain specified sounds, they are made ritual or ceremonial in part by having to accomplish this task seamlessly. Temporal continuity requires that one cannot break a performance into discrete bits. Performances cannot be serialized. Though this requirement can be ignored at will by any 'experimental' work which deliberately directs one to break off where one pleases and resume again *ad libitum*, one cannot perform any conventional work thus. Disruption clauses are not available interpretative options in performing a Bach violin *Partita*.[29]

Compare reading a novel or digging a garden. These activities admit temporal punctuation without loss of integrity. One can return to where one left off after a substantial break without sacrificing the very nature, purpose, and success of the activity. I may read *The Big Sleep* one page per day without wrecking the activity 'my reading *The Big Sleep*'. My reading the mystery can also co-exist with other activities. I can truthfully report that I'm now both reading *The Big Sleep* and composing an opera, even though I'm eating a popsicle and contemplating subversive acts this very minute.

Serializable activities are those which can get our utterly divided attention and survive. One can thus segment novel reading, opera writing, or garden digging. Certain sports officially divide into serializables and non-serializables; for example, those where the play is continually interrupted even in the middle of play periods (football, hockey) and the play clock stopped, and those where temporal continuity is maintained (soccer). One cannot 'call time' fifty metres down the track in the hundred metre event. Unlike performance, musical activities like practice and rehearsal are serializable.

Fine-grained distinctions in disruption complicate the overall distinction. Reading a long novel can sustain just so much fragmentation before it ceases to achieve its ultimate objective of acquainting one with the whole work. Reading one word a week will not do it unless I have an incredible memory, but reading a chapter a week might well suffice. Subtleties aside, the broad differences between serializable and non-serializable activities seem clear.

Music performance does not fit in completely well with lectures, sermons, and the like because of radically different serialization options. There are cases where continuity of delivery is of the essence; for example, in punchy or poignant speeches, addresses to the troops about to do battle, funeral orations. Some deliveries are intrinsically timely. These share much with musical performance, but can still endure small-scale punctuations which would prove disastrous in performance. As for my lecture on the late Permian extinctions, I can span two discrete sessions at will. I may even break off in mid-sentence and resume next Tuesday exactly where I left off, or recapitulate if I prefer. Content continuity seems more central to lecture integrity than temporal continuity. Why the difference? The matter of meaning divides the cases. The continuity of the sounds of a lecture is not necessary for the integrity of the lecture's content. A lecture's content is its meaning. Given workable tidings-over of meaning, the continuity of delivery reduces to a convenience. When a particular lecture is not itself an occasion, a special event, judicious serialization leaves the content unaffected.

Despite superficially attractive comparisons between music and language, musical performance embodies no quasi-linguistic meaning. Musical sound is not a carrier or vehicle for any musical meaning analogous to linguistic meaning. There is nothing but the sound to present, no 'acoustified' content, nor anything underneath the sound which can be carried forward in any silent non-musical gaps.[30] This sharply distinguishes performances from lectures despite their sharing various aspects of ritual and formality.

If one were to organize activities on a scale of relative serializability, it seems clear that performance will come as close to the non-serializable end as anything.[31] This marks it as highly ritual. Rituals create their own experiential mood. The point of some rituals just is to establish such moods. The success of the ritual rests on the maintenance of the mood. Though each ritual category sports its own disruption threshold, all operate on the need for procedural and experiential continuity and the absence of procedural, experiential, and external disruption. Such conditions as maintain the integrity of a ritual are thereby mood-preserving, the very effectiveness of a ritual depending upon a certain experiential atmosphere.

Performance integrity draws in places, times, works, players, audiences, and other matters not only because these figure as the focus of ritual attention, but also because they contribute jointly to mood. Ultimately, the wholeness or completeness of a performance is a matter of mood maintenance. Why must the show go on? Try stopping it, taking a break. Not much remains.

Listeners

It is time to examine the beneficiaries of performance by looking at live audiences and attentive listeners with a view to building into the model the requirement that performances be before present and attentive listeners. The notion of performance emerging makes it the central musical occasion at the very heart of the art of music.

Live audiences

Something aberrant haunts claims like: 'I've performed this work sixteen times, yet never before an audience'. Performance requires an intended listener, but merely having such an intention guarantees no appropriate course of action. With no listeners present, the sense of occasion in performance vanishes. Further, their absence makes the ritual of exposing oneself to external adjudication systematically avoidable.

Is the presence of an audience necessary for performance? When counting performances, one ordinarily includes a musician's public playing occasions only. These, besides, are typically the major playing occasions of general artistic significance. The accounts musicians and others keep of their performances are precisely records of staged public engagements. Accounts are not usually kept of practice sessions or purely personal entertainments as evidence of a musician's performance career. Thus, it is entirely fitting to say: 'Though I've played (rehearsed, practised) the *Partita* countless times, I've performed it only five times', or even ' . . . but I've never had an opportunity to perform it'. Implicit in these claims is the phrase 'before an audience'. These expressions suggest that performance is not merely intended for some listener, but that it also actually has some listener. In referring to one's past performances, the implication is that one had listeners present who were there to hear one play. (Incidentally, the phrase 'public performance' may not be as redundant as the analysis suggests. Having an audience is one thing; having a public audience another. One may perform before a private audience; for example, for a formal audition or jury, for one's close friends, or, as often in the past, for one's patron. Public audiences, though invited, are unselected.)

41

It takes two to perform. In performance full and proper, the listener and player must be distinct. What grounds exist for this? Certain non-musical performances clearly demand a second party. Consider magic acts or stand-up comedy. The magician cannot be deceived by his own tricks. He experiences no sense of illusion. Yet it is exactly the experience of illusion the magician is trying to create. Without that experience, no magical tricks have been performed, though they may have been rehearsed. To perform magic one needs a deceivable spectator. Further, to succeed in magic, one must have deceived someone. Similarly, comics do not tell jokes to amuse themselves. Much humour relies on various surprise juxtapositions which cannot (indeed, must not) come as a surprise to the performing comic. After practice, comics will not likely find their jokes personally amusing. To perform comedy one must have an amusable party at whom one's jokes are fired. In both cases, the rehearsal and the performance are dramatically distinct even though, on film, the events are indistinguishable.

Is the comparison apt? Magic and comedy exploit experiences of the unexpected. Neither magician nor comedian can be in that state. But the unexpectedness is not significant. One could just as well consider the village storyteller or orator, neither of whom needs to rely on surprise. The common factor involves the communicative quality of the activity; that is, action undertaken expressly in order to affect someone else who has chosen to be so affected. Lacking that target, the intrinsic other-directed quality of the episode is frustrated.

What of musical performance? Some think performing to be communicative, and even liken music to language and performing to speech.[32] The speech-act conception, however, is not crucial to communicativeness. Communication requires two functionally distinct units, a communicator and a receiver. Typically, these units are distinct parties. True, one can talk to oneself, but this is not like talking to others; and, in any event, the former is parasitic on the latter. Besides, it is not clear that talking to oneself is even a form of communicating with oneself (whatever that means anyway). At any rate, performing is no more like talking to oneself than talking to oneself is like talking to another.

Performers generally have intentions regarding their audiences which are absent when they play alone. Such intentions are integral to performance. The wish is to do something to and for that audience, to change it, to control its response, to work its feelings. None of this makes sense when playing alone. Here the unexpected may be pertinent. One cannot equivalently dazzle oneself virtuosically as one can a listener, nor lead on or surprise. Further, one cannot hope to reward oneself as one can hope to be rewarded by one's admirers. This asymmetry of effect makes a difference in other ways. Performers often aim to move their listeners to the verge of disturbance, to create overwhelming emotions in the hearer.[33] Players causing this in themselves could not play let alone perform under such conditions.

There is an acoustic asymmetry too. Performers never hear the music as their audience hears it because of the simple physical fact that performers direct their sound toward audiences. Performers stand astride or behind the immediate

42

source of sound, not in front of it. The sound sequence in performance is not just a physical commodity but a phenomenal one. Performers aim to generate phenomenal sound they cannot hear, sound designedly targeted for someone else. Players simply cannot do for themselves exactly what they do for their audiences.

Furthermore, performances are inherently subject to appraisal, judgement, and evaluation because they are designed to meet certain standards and achieve certain ends. At best, to judge oneself involves a conflict of interest. To play before no one leaves the question of communicative success or failure unsettled.

Ordinary intuitions may still resist. What's the problem with an unattended performance? Suppose Isaac prepares for a performance by working on certain pieces intended for some audience, and, finding the hall empty on the appointed evening, carries on regardless. In the sense suggested, Isaac has missed an opportunity to perform, even though he has, generously conceived, gone on with his 'performance' despite there being no audience. Isaac's persistence surely smacks of desperation. The act seems almost pathological without any listeners present. If Isaac has given a performance, the sense cannot but be charitable, parasitic, or even degenerate.

What of the would-be performance forbidden on pain of death; for example, a military ban on performances of *Finlandia*. Suppose Isaac proceeds in defiance before an empty hall, the would-be audience having been turned away by the occupying army. He is arrested and shot for 'performing' the prohibited work.[34] I am more inclined to rue Isaac's lack of a sharp lawyer than to suppose this a performance proper. Indeed, it is just as marginal and degenerate as the milder instance above.

Degenerate performances are not like regularly scheduled flights which depart and arrive on time despite the absence of passengers. Performances full and proper are more like murders. Not only must they have intended victims; they must have victims. Though empty hall cases are not like victimless murders, they remain wildly atypical. Very few musicians would ever undertake the tasks of mastery were the standing expectation that of either of Isaac's 'last stands'. In some respects, performances proper are very like lectures. Although a person may, in a way, deliver a lecture in an empty room, the idiom 'lecture to an empty hall' connotes the incompleteness and implied desolation. Lectures and performances alike look for ears to fill. Lacking the ears, nothing remains to fill save the room, scarcely a surrogate. Words are indeed spoken, but it would be peculiar to think that everyone had missed that lecture. One might classify the case as a lecture only because of dependently resembling features. No doubt, though, something pretty massive has gone wrong. So, typically, a performance must be of some work, intended for and actually presented to some third-party listener. Thus, another outward pointer is built into the model.

The attentive listener

Success conditions apply to listening too. The listener present must experience the playing episode as being intended for him and as presenting a certain work with thus-and-such musical qualities by attending to it in appropriate ways and entertaining various appropriate beliefs about it. I will call this complex listener state one of 'active concentrated attention'. This type of state makes possible and is partially constitutive of the listener's appreciation of the performance. I will not deal here with the precise nature of active concentrated attention – what and how listeners are to hear – as it concerns pedagogues interested in the skills of informed listening, or philosophers attempting to isolate special features of music appreciation.[35] Whatever the details of active concentrated attention, a player whose sole task is to supply background music and who succeeds by attracting no active concentrated attention of anyone before whom she plays gives no performance (except degenerately) even if the sound sequence is indistinguishable from that in a recital hall. Unless the intended product is experienced by the listener as a sound sequence with certain key aesthetic features, that sound sequence does not count as a performance.

Subtle wisdom prompts lounge, bar, and restaurant players to call their playing sessions just 'sets', groups of numbers. Some sets may freakishly aspire to be performances. Applause is one indicator that someone was listening, and that adds something to the player's output. It gives it a chance as a performance, so long as all the other conditions are met. However, the principal consideration, that the music must not interfere, kills all pretensions to performance. Lounge players do not so much play for or at the patrons as they do behind them, so to speak. In Cone's words, successful lounge music 'is not really music to be listened to, only to be heard'.[36] Performances are for the listener in distinct ways; as presentations to and for the benefit of the listener, and, less evidently, as sound sequences achieving a certain standing in the experience of the listener.

Does the required contribution of the listener's experience lead to unacceptable consequences? For example, mightn't the selfsame sound sequence count as a performance for me but not for you so long as we differ appropriately in our experiences? If so, how can we reasonably count performances? Are there as many performances as there are appropriately attentive listeners? Why equate the number of performances with the number of individual experiences of performances? Does the mere presence of at least one such listener suffice to meet this condition, the one applauding appreciator in a lounge choked with indifference? Suppose a bar pianist arouses someone's attention halfway through a number. Does the performance begin with the arousal assuming everything else to have been in waiting for the great moment? Is this half a performance? All this seems to be implied by the view suggested. So much the worse for the view.

Is it just absurd to make certain states of the listener preconditions for performance? Performances, strongly public occasions, seem now to depend for their lives not just on the listener, but on one who fashions a certain kind of sound sequence into a performance by attending to it in the appropriate way. Performances, supposedly the gift of the musician to her passive, receptive public, now become joint ventures, the listener critically and literally falling in as the silent partner without whose experiential capital the enterprise falls flat.[37] Is this where the performance model finally staggers off the world? Can we do without such a move, retaining the strong independence of the performance from the listener?

The joint venture view needs taming. Recall that sound sequences must meet many conditions, independent of the listener, to count as performances. The listener's experience itself depends upon their realization. Such conditions as the existence of musical works, skilled players, playing traditions, and so on, are scarcely peripheral. This should disable any enticement to exotic romances which cast the listener as the chief agent in the creation of musical events. Composers do the composing; musicians do the interpreting and presenting. Whatever the status of listeners, to place them on a par with music-makers is just crazy.

Listeners, though, have a central role. In our musical culture, attentive listeners contribute meaning and purpose to much otherwise free-floating musical activity. Music-making could survive quite happily without concerts, competitions, juries, and all other venues catering to non-participating auditors. Still, the formal auditor makes a difference by focusing the musician's attention on certain details of mastery. The very structured programme of preparation musicians follow is rationalized, in part, by its affecting the listener in certain ways. No musical subtleties would be worth the effort, if there were no listeners subtle enough for them. Players do not merely practise. The very elements of practice, the concentration, the revisions, the decisions, are influenced by the public *telos* of performance. In performance, the player's sound sequences take the shape they do in part because attentive listeners are capable of the experiences they have.

Performances are musical occasions of some moment for both player and listener. Their public nature betokens appraisal, exposure and vulnerability. That very nature burdens them with promises and expectations of success. One major indicator of a successful performance is the audience's positive response. For whom is this response primarily significant? Not the audience itself, surely. Audiences, like crowds, are mere fictions which decompose into a tangle of relations between individuals and the player. For any individual listener, then? But this would reflect poorly on such an auditor that he waited for the plaudits of others to assess the performance's success. Clearly, audience response influences a musician's assessment of her own success in concert. Though musicians can be contemptuous of their listeners, this arises when the listeners are judged inferior to the occasion; for example, unappreciative of the subtleties, or in attendance for all the wrong reasons.

When someone plays for others, something is meant to happen to those listeners. True, some players are indifferent to their beneficiaries. Others have misplaced interests; for example, to be popular with their fans. Still, if listeners attend, the imputation is that they are willing to and expect to exercise active concentrated attention. And if, despite such willingness, they cannot maintain their focus but, instead, drift to distractions like foot shuffling, whispering, general fidgeting, or even walking out, the musician, bereft of the rationalization of the 'dead house' hypothesis, will re-evaluate what she attempted and failed to do. Leaving listeners utterly unabsorbed can count even more against a performance than a catastrophically awful technical fumble which may, grue-somely, attract more concentrated attention than does flawless execution.

Suppose the player lacks attentive listeners because of having failed to engage and sustain the expectations they brought to the occasion. The player has dissi-pated the listeners' attention by boring them, rather as a bright and curious child can be alienated from learning by uninspired instruction. Under these circumstances, the performance has clearly failed. Musicians do not know if they have succeeded in performance unless certain responses are present, given, of course, the charitable assumptions that one's listeners are capable of active concentrated attention in the relevant sense, and that they are willing to exer-cise such attention on the occasion.

What of performances which fail by ruining the very conditions for being appreciated? One may be tempted to invoke the category 'attempted perfor-mance' just to distinguish these from the successes. Attempted performances are no more performances than attempted robberies are robberies. Although we typically call them just 'failed' performances, this can mislead by making it appear that some performance has nevertheless transpired. We can distinguish between failures in performance and failures as performances (or failed performances *simpliciter*). The former encompass performances falling off the standard; the latter non-performances with would-be performance aspirations. The distinction is meant to cope primarily with damaged-but-operational versus hopelessly-damaged functional items.[38] On the 'hard' reading, failed performances are no more performances accomplished than a failed mission is a mission accomplished.

A player's-eye view of the readied, then alienated, listener bolsters the idea that no performance ordinarily succeeds without the auditors' active concen-trated attention. It is another small leap to accept that failed performances are performances in name only, reminders of performances pledged but never deliv-ered. These two points support the claim that successful performance depends on the state of the listener. Performances, note, are elevated by this type of link into the best class of playing episodes; that is, they are those episodes which not only enjoy but sustain the active concentrated attention of their listeners.

In itself, this listener-dependent picture of performance does not seem outlandish given the link between performance and success. But the picture also implies that a performance can fail if it turns the listener off and that some failed performances fail to be performances. An air of oddity remains. Why? Here are two accounts reflecting the ways failure and the very existence of performances contribute to this sense of peculiarity.

1   The typical performance failure seems more objectively determinable than the picture indicates. It usually involves some involuntarily disastrous departure from the work-as-scored in the form of memory lapses, technical gaffes, loss of ensemble, and so forth. Here failure rides on damage to the identifying features of the work. That damage is determinable independently of any listener's response. Even if the listener immensely enjoys (through ignorance, charity, sadism, or whatever) a thoroughly botched rendition, the failure is still manifest.

2   Why suppose the existence or non-existence of a performance hangs on the effect a playing episode has upon listeners? Isn't it more fitting to conceive the performance as the output of the player received in common as input to the listeners, and to consider the listeners' response to it as an ambient condition of performance? This would capture the intuition that, however negative an audience's response, that never affects the status of the event as a performance.

Though both considerations might diagnose the sense of oddity, neither defeats the listener-dependent account because both hinge on debatable assumptions about the inadmissibility of 'subjective' factors in the assessment of principal performance failures and the very identity of performances.

As to failures, an indifferent or hostile response may be every bit as obvious as any technical blunder. Should such displays matter? Shouldn't one suspect one's responses? But surely, one may reasonably determine whether or not one is being appreciatively fair as a listener. Sometimes one can and should blame one's disaffection (or enjoyment) directly upon the imposed event itself. Playing causes changes in the audience. It is meant to. The player cannot be assured that all such changes in the audience will be either as intended or welcome.

As to the identity question, once we accept that performances are prototypically other-directed, one cannot just ignore the state of the audience. If the audience turns out by design to contain no involved listeners (as in a lounge), calling the playing 'a performance' must be by generous extension only. Certainly if nothing is artistically at stake and nothing is noticed, 'performance' seems merely honorific. If the audience turns out by misfortune to contain no involved listeners, that playing episode too must be 'performance' by the grace of superficial similarity only. Neither the lounge setting nor the alienated listener story satisfy all the elementary ingredients for performance full and proper.

These reflections ignore any puzzles about counting performances and, relatedly, when they begin and end. Fortunately, we can evade these by appealing to the other conditions of performance. The worry about whether a performance can begin halfway through is a non-starter because it ignores the requirement that any performance must be of some determinate work. There are no performances of half-works. Any performance of a work is thus dependent upon the completeness conditions attaching to the work itself, and not to the listener's state.

How many performances are there if there are many attentive listeners? This matter is most easily left with the identity of the sound sequence itself which has the potential of being received by many listeners. If a player initiates such a sound sequence, the potential for performance is present, all other factors being ignored. But increasing the number of listeners does not increase the number of performances, even though one might say that, all other conditions being satisfied, a single attentive listener may make all the difference between a viable performance having taken place or not. Note, though, if the player lacks all interest in playing for his listeners (that is, if he doesn't care whether he is heard, whether he makes mistakes, whether he finishes what he starts, etc.), no listener, dogged appreciation notwithstanding, can make a performance out of that.

Unfortunately, a fuzziness underlies the claim that the listener must be prepared for a performance to experience one, and that the player must be blessed with such listeners to render one. The significance of the attentive listener, however, is reinforced by the hunch that different musical events occur in the ambience of live 'muzak' and the recital hall despite their indiscernibility in recordings.

Differences in expectation exist. Should they matter? The lounge player expects nothing from the patrons, whereas the recital musician expects attention, appreciation, respect for a job well done. Similarly, the lounge patrons have but one musical expectation. The music must not intrude upon their conversational preoccupations. Concert audiences expect the performance, to which they agree to attend, to reward them aesthetically. Suppose expectation is mismatched in either case. Should that have any influence on whether or not some performance has occurred?

Imagine hapless Isaac once again. He has prepared for a performance, having been told by his shyster agent that he will play before a distinguished audience in a noble setting, the ballroom of the Ritz Snazzy Hotel. Isaac arrives early and notes uneasily that there are no chairs directed toward the stage but dinner tables instead, many of which afford no view of the player. He is treated by the hotel staff as the evening's hired help and told to begin at six-thirty, 'just a little after drinks'. 'Nothing too loud', he is cautioned. The patrons wander in, oil tycoons and executives for the annual Greaser's Ball, and get down to chatter, gossip, guffaws, and booze. Six-thirty arrives, and Isaac begins, determined, despite the humiliation, to give the performance of his rocky career. Not a dent does it make.

Like Isaac's gala before the empty hall, this event fails to make it as a performance except by generous extension. We might charitably consent to a counterfactual like: 'Were the audience prepared to attend to what Isaac played, they would have had any reasonable performance expectations more than satisfied'. But the fact is, they were not so prepared, and their expectations in the setting were fully satisfied in that Isaac's playing didn't interrupt their tittle-tattle.

48

Isaac's expectations were misdirected, his beliefs misguided. Nonetheless he played his very best. Has he given a performance despite this sad mismatch? What exact words we use here are unimportant. The question is whether this episode is different enough from those where everything works, to warrant our categorizing them differently. I think the differences are sufficient, if only because the case lacks systematically an ingredient taken for granted in typical recitals. By a 'systematic' absence, I mean that it does not hang on a freak misfortune as would a case where, just before a planned performance, the listeners are deafened by a high pitch squeal which disables their hearing throughout. Isaac thought he did perform, but no one else present did. So, he was wrong, alas, whatever he decided to do.

Taking stock

The discussion above traces out a series of conditions necessary for successful performance. I am uncommitted as to their joint sufficiency. In trying to expose the intuitive roots in each condition, I have at times stretched or departed from intuition by attributing to certain conditions a more integral role in performance than colloquy demands. That said, I have been concerned with the conditions under which everything transpires favourably. The model's strictures should help to articulate what is missing when performances are less than ideal. Here in outline are the conditions defined or implied:

P_1 is a model performance only if P_1 is (or involves):

- a datable sound sequence (that is, sonic event),
- immediately caused by some human(-like) being,
- the immediate output of some musical instrument,
- intended to be caused at a specified time and place, and in a specified manner,
- the exercise of skilled activity,
- the outcome of appropriately creditworthy physical skill,
- an instance of some identifiable musical work,[39]
- intended as an instance of such a work,
- successful as a constraint-model of such a work,
- intended as a constraint-model of such a work,
- intended for some third-party listener,
- presented before some third-party listener,
- listened to by some third-party listener exercising active concentrated attention.

Three items emerge as thematic undercurrents of the model of performance offered.

First, the significance of performance is strongly emphasized. The model displays the major musical constituents – musicians, works, sound, listeners – as converging upon performance, and deriving their musical purpose in and through it. Performance emerges as a complex activity which co-ordinates and focuses actions, skills, traditions, and works in order to define and create musical experience for the receptive listener. Should such defining and creating provide the *raison d'être* of music, performance rises from prominence to pre-eminence in the musical enterprise.

Second, performances can fail both by misrepresenting the work and by disaffecting the listener. However, the model implies that whereas performers have no categorical obligations to the composers of the works they deploy (for example, to do exactly as the composer bids in score), they have certain categorical obligations to their listeners. This gives the performer–listener axis more weight than the composer–performer pair. What performers will and must do for their listeners may appear to compromise or violate compositional directives; for example, changing instrumentation or dynamics to fit a larger hall, say. Different ranks in performance duties rationalize such relative accommodation of the listener and 'betrayal' of the composer. Performers need their listeners, but do not need any one (or even any) composer. Where works are intended as musical and not mere theoretical exercises, composers need performers. Performers are thus in a privileged position of musical brokerage regarding what counts as standard repertoire and how it is delivered. This brokerage role underscores the view that whatever arises in performance is most aptly conceived as the work of many conspiring, demanding, and collaborating hands.

Third, performance is action-centred. Music can, however, be conceived more abstractly as work-centred. A consistent model of musical performance can be constructed without appeal to independent works. In traditions where notated works gain prominence, performance may appear to serve a role subservient to them. The model presented is consistent with a more elemental notion of music as fundamentally a form of activity. This activity aspect is enhanced by subordinating the influence of composed works on performance. Such subordination comes out by absorbing compositions as components of performance constraint-models. These C-models are complex clusters of directives, specified and accepted by the performance community, which vary with and partially constitute performance traditions, and which accord to the notated work varying status. Constraint models set limits on and targets for performance. Included within C-models will be certain details of pitch and rhythm we commonly identify with notated musical works. The work itself, comprising one consensually adopted constraint among others, performs but one contributory functional role within the C-model. However central the influence of C-models, the notated works they enclose can never enjoy any special privilege. Notated works thus have no direct bearing upon performance. They are instead constituents of larger, more diffuse, regulative composites. The performance model thus stands on its head the view that performance is a means to the end of making the work manifest. Instead, the work, in action-centred conceptions, becomes one means of organizing and marshalling various skills eager, so to speak, to issue forth in acoustic gifts to receptive beneficiaries. Such a picture enlivens a regard for performers as creative artists in a primary and not a derivative sense, ones who deploy organized sound not utterly unlike the way painters use prepared yet modifiable pigments. By extension, performances become autonomous independent artworks, yet ones fully continuous with their makers.

2

SKILLS AND GUILDS

Introduction

Music performance requires skill. Below, I explore the environment in which musical skill is embedded. Approaching skill from its ultimate causal source, skills are elementally rooted in and flow from an agent's individual powers. Viewing skills as valued powers, many are defined, refined, revised and ranked from within larger structured organizations or traditions – practice communities, in a word.

Chapter 1 characterized having a skill (or being skilled) at some task as a special case of having the power to accomplish that task at will. The tasks at which skills are directed are regarded as challenges. That some task is recognized as a challenge depends upon recognizing that certain specified handicaps can hinder its achievement. Certain tasks become challenges just in case certain acknowledged handicaps are present.

Considered neutrally, to have a skill at doing something is to be able to overcome at will the challenge of achieving it under some specified limitation. This makes having a skill as objective as having any ability. But this reading fails to rule out silly cases like having a skill at eating spaghetti under thirty feet of water without scuba gear. Further, it trivializes skill through indifference to the common supposition that having a skill is something interesting, enviable, laudable, valuable, admirable, and the like. Because skills are positive attributes, skill attributions are normative. Considered normatively, there has to be an acknowledged value or point in overcoming the challenge. Otherwise, no one would be prompted to praise let alone try to acquire any skill. To recognize that value, one need not accept it as one's own. Still, one must acknowledge that something is a challenge to those for whom overcoming hindrances to achieving it has positive interest. The dinner-down-deep challenge can have its followers and thus escape universal silliness.

This chapter embeds the normative account within the organization and tradition of music-making. Part I – Skills, primary causes, and primary crafts – examines skilled agency in music. Two questions predominate: (1) How are skills marshalled in making music?, and (2) what kinds of skills are ultimately involved? Regarding (1), music-making involves the global organization of many independent skills. Regarding (2), music-making skill paradigmatically requires the immediate causal intervention of the player. That immediacy provides a basis for determining and assessing performance handicaps. Instrumental skills are essentially and broadly manual; vocal skills are essentially glottal. This type of direct control embeds performance within 'primary craft' traditions. Valuing performance skill is an instance of valuing results in the primary crafts

Part II – The Guild tradition – examines the institutional context; that is, the traditional, conservative musical communities which determine what counts as musical accomplishment. Such communities now face new challenges to their authority. Certain electronic means make the achievement of otherwise difficult musical ends relatively easy. Would or should any musician resist such shortcuts to facility? On what grounds could any community rationally reject such new-found facility? Below, musical communities are typified as traditionally organized around the instruments of music. They are likened to Guilds which define their own conditions for membership and rank. I argue that Guilds systematically resist instrumental innovations in order to preserve their own structure which requires the establishment and maintenance of a skill hierarchy based on handicaps legitimized by the Guild.

Part I: Skills, primary causes, and primary crafts

How skill contributes to performance

Performance involves causing and expressively shaping ordered pitch and rhythm sequences, all of which requires many distinct skills. How are these skills identified? In preparing for performance, players fragment the entire sequence into a set of distinct sub-sequences. Such sub-sequences represent isolable challenges or musical objectives for the player. Sub-sequences may overlap. They need not be dealt with in any fixed order nor require equal attention. One player's sub-sequences need not be those of another, nor need any one player concentrate on the same sub-sequences each time the piece is practised. Two consecutive chords may form one sub-sequence, the technical challenge being a smooth transition. A melodic fragment may be isolated to focus control over the expressive effect of hanging on a phrase. Sub-sequences may be as short as a single chord, or as long as a protracted grand finale. Early on in musical training, the sub-sequences of concern to novices tend to be more uniform than those of seasoned players. This reflects the relative consistency of general technical desiderata and the contrasting idiosyncrasy of fine interpretive details. Since each sub-sequence presents a distinct challenge, subduing each challenge may call for a distinct skill. I will not worry here about individuating skills. Once musical hurdles are identified in practice, practical schemes arise about how to clear them. When activated, those schemes constitute the exercise of a skill for that hurdle. Traditionally, *études* address certain generic hurdles; thus their value in fostering the acquisition of widely applicable skills.

There are both technical and interpretive playing skills. Though these categories are not rigorously distinct, they have a few distinguishing features. Technical skills involve causing objectively determinable and (often) quantitatively measurable acoustic effects. Many skills connected with instrument-specific technique belong to this group. Hard directives like metronome markings and softer directives concerning accentuation and shading also belong; for example, *staccato, marcato, sforzando, un poco forte, pianissimo, crescendo*, and *ritardando*. Staple measuring devices like metronomes and tuners are accorded authority regarding tempo and pitch. Though kindred devices – for example, to measure dynamic aspects of loudness and pace – are not currently used, measurement is possible in principle. Disputes about whether a crescendo really did build up consistently or whether two players began properly together could be decided mechanically as surely as any photo finish.

Interpretive skills involve aesthetic effects for which no obvious quantitative measure exists, and typically emphasize 'expression', the details of which are often matters of irresolvable dispute. Typical interpretive skills include being able to infuse sound with affective or imitative character. Traditional directives draw upon many dimensions: for example, emotional disposition (*amoroso, giocoso, furioso, malinconico*), general deportment (*con grazia, nobile, violento, robusto*), elemental movement (*con fuoco, con moto, energico*), not to mention the weather (*calmo, tranquillo*), and the subtleties involved in *religioso, innocente, pomposo*, and *meditativo*.[1] To explain how to make a passage more *rustico*, a teacher may summon indirectly suggestive means like humming, singing, gesticulating, dancing, or resorting to meta-metaphors. For instance, cellist Paul Tortelier once chastised a master-class student for playing a passage in 'too bourgeois' a fashion. The skill, all along, is to control the qualities of sound to fit one's musical plans, whether one matches one's acoustic goals against a metronome or against a more impressionistic measure.

Once local sub-sequences are under control, the player turns to building up sets of such sequences. The new higher-order units may impose new problems which summon further skills. The process is guided by, and yet influences along the way, the ultimate rendition or interpretation. Performance preparation thus constitutes a co-ordinated and systematic form of building or construction. The audience enjoys a final product generated by the methodical fragmentation and reconstitution of sound sequences. The process of dividing the project into problem elements, applying localized skills to these elements, and re-assembling them into a unified whole is common to many activities; for example, the business of sculptors, painters, weavers, luthiers, and carpenters.

Primary causation: how skills are deployed

Having a skill is knowing how to do something which is *prima facie* a good.

Performance is a form of making, that is, music-making which requires sound-making skills. Performance skills neither explain, justify, confirm, prove, nor primarily enhance one's understanding of what one does. They are purely practical. They serve to get things done, and only to get things done.

Sound production requires that sound waves be transmitted through a transmitting medium. Sound waves result when something flexible such as a reed or string is physically distorted so as to oscillate or vibrate. In musical instruments, the vibrations are amplified in resonators such as pipes or soundboxes. Traditional sound-making requires an agent to create vibrations in a device by blowing air through it or striking it. The relevant body parts (lips, fingers) are causally in immediate physical contact with the vibrating object (reed, string). The chief handicaps comprise the limitations and constraints imposed by the sound-making devices.

Exercising musical skill involves physically altering something directly. Every musical effect stems immediately from some physical control the player has over the vibrating object. Performance requires an intimate acquaintance with the sounding properties of one's instrument as well as ways of using parts of one's body to exploit those properties. Music-making calls for 'contiguous hands-on control' over sound.[2] I call direct or immediate physical causation of some effect by an agent 'primary causation'. The skilled primary causation of sound I call 'primary skill' for short.

The exercise of primary skills stamps the details of the agent's actions directly into the emerging effect. Each nuance of sound reflects some physical manoeuvre. Other artforms also rest upon primary skills. When a painter lays pigment directly onto canvas, each patch of colour is an immediate signature of some movement. As one can reconstruct a conflict from fossilized footprints on an ancient delta, so the physical (and occasionally even psychological) movements of the artist may be reconstructed from the painting's distinguishable features, ones which are isomorphic with the spatial displacements of the artist's hand. With exercises of primary skill, we can regard the work as a crystallized three-dimensional re-enactment of a dynamic four-dimensional sequence of creation.[3] Performance being temporal, we have the entire causal dynamic preserved.

The craft tradition

In deploying an organized complex of primary skills, music-making fits within a larger category of pursuits, the Craft Tradition, a dynamic schema for which involves:

agent using *means* applies *skill* to (*raw*) *material* for *result*

In performance, the means are the player's tools, the instruments. The skills include both the general instrumental and musical proficiency required to use the means and those specialized powers addressing local problems. Deploying skill, the material given in score is transfigured by the agent using an instrument to yield the result, the polished performance. Unifying the means and skills is a methodology, a systematic complex of information about and procedures for creating the result and dealing most effectively with the means specified.

Practices such as music-making, sculpture, weaving and carpentry share not only the basic craft structure but also a critical regard for primary skills. As predicated upon skilled primary causation, they are all primary crafts. The terms 'primary craftwork' or simply 'craftwork' are occasionally used to refer to the result of a primary craft. Performance can be viewed from two perspectives as a primary craft or as a craftwork.

Because of their immediate focus upon the physical world, primary crafts have an elemental self-sufficiency. In any simple 'last survivor' case, one could conceivably be a practising potter, electrician, cook, engineer, physician, or musician (though not a performer). What that lonely world cannot have is a practising politician, administrator, policy analyst, professor, manager, staff sergeant, accountant, salesman – anyone whose occupation vanishes without other people. This perhaps reflects the fragile quality of the non-primary occupations which depend largely upon words and not upon things.

A spirited champion of the crafts, Socrates elaborated the notions of *technē* and *aretē* – the ideals of craftsmanship – and stressed the connections among intention, action, training, skill, expertise, and real results.[4] Socrates reminds us that, if humans get anything right at all, this success is most strikingly plain in those trades underwritten by explicit methods, demonstrable skills, and well-defined physical goals. The routines of craftsmanship, illustrated through relatively earthy vocations, tellingly served as the paradigm to which allegedly grander enterprises like politics and moral life itself were to aspire. Socrates includes a wealth of hands-on practices under *technē* – cuisine, sport, medicine, navigation, horse-training, music, and so on. That we now distinguish the fine arts, crafts, trades, and professions probably reflects little more than our shallow sensitivity to social and intellectual status. What some now call 'professionalism' merely re-affirms the unity of practice, method, and skill (or virtue) once expressed by *technē* and *aretē*. That music performance, painting, and sculpture are crafts implies the distinctiveness of skill and training involved in them.[5]

Practising a craft competently and proficiently minimally requires certain foundational skills. Those with more complex and refined skills have expertise or mastery. Competence, proficiency and expertise are measures of accomplishment in a craft. Those with expertise or mastery not only typically have more skills than those with competence or proficiency; they are often more reliable in the exercise of whatever skills they share with the competent. Some skills can be reliably exercised even in sub-optimal circumstances; for example, any reasonably competent player should be able to play simple scale passages reliably under such unfavourable conditions as having cold hands or a headache. Other skills require highly stable background conditions for reliable deployment. Having a grasp on a given skill comes by degrees. Those sharing a skill will vary in the range and number of conditions under which they can reliably deploy it. Favourable conditions will enable some to repeat the skilled action more accurately and over a longer period. Those with mastery typically achieve superior results more efficiently and reliably than those with mere competence. Expertise shows in its results.

Physical expertise figures centrally in the primary crafts. We noted above that the results of primary skill are direct records or signatures of that skill. The thing made shows its making. The products of primary skill are things-as-thus-made, inextricable unions of process and effect. Given this, whatever value attaches to the result should attach, in part, to the process creating that result. This is indirectly supported by the call for perfection in the crafts. Two necessary conditions for perfection are that the result be flawless, and fashioning it be flawlessly done.

Perfection is the highest aim of certain handcrafts. Consider, for instance, the lute-maker's preoccupations. Lute soundboards have soundholes with intricately carved designs called 'roses'. Mastery in rose-cutting is highly regarded among luthiers. Given two intricate roses, indistinguishable to the eye, one may nonetheless be better than the other. How so? In one case, the luthier made no mistakes, never had to repair, never had to preserve appearances. In the other, the luthier's knife slipped and a clever patch had to be improvised to make everything seem flawless. If the wood cracked cleanly along the grain, and if the summer wood was not compressed, one could, with careful gluing, hide the error even from the most discerning builder. Only chemical or X-ray analysis would turn up the patch. The second luthier might have spent overall less time on the job than the first. Still, the first rose is better because it was made better, even if the soundboards are never X-rayed and the flaw in the second instrument never detected. The first rose is objectively a signature of superior skill. (Note, 'better made' does not here imply 'functionally superior' or 'better suited to the purpose'. In fact, good glue joints are often stronger than the natural bond. Further, repair is a high craft itself in which the second luthier may achieve perfection.)

Imagine a parallel in performance. Suppose a pianist cannot manually master (or bother to master) a technically demanding passage in an otherwise manageable piece. To compensate, the player rigs the piano with a device which, when activated, automatically executes the passage. This 'cruise control' gadget fits in so seamlessly with the rest, no one can tell when it is being used. The pianist performs flawlessly, but, alas, subsequent exposure leads to disgrace. Even if the expert listener's aural experience is indistinguishable from cases where the player performs conventionally, fellow performers and, likely, listeners would regard the rigged performance as worse. Why? The seeming skill signature in the sound is forged. The player has cheated.

The case is little changed if the player actually sounded the right note sequence but achieved it through sheer luck. Suppose the player is highly unsure of his ability to play a passage after consistently botching it in practice, but performs nonetheless without error. The credit for such accuracy cannot go fully to the player, as he will avow. Good fortune steered his fingers when skill failed. If truthful, one will confess that one likely could not do it again. Though an audience might accept the 'one-off' result with the same satisfaction it would otherwise experience had the execution been truly confident, the player must match himself against the standards of the performance community. Against any fully informed judge, his performance has a strike against it and will not be judged equal to the fully masterful execution. The legitimate, fully skilled performance is objectively a record of greater mastery. If that legitimacy does not figure in the value vested in performance, the differences in the legitimate and rigged concerts would be irrelevant. Perfectionism in performance, however, requires that the result be both flawless and flawlessly given.

What of perfectionism in the plastic arts? Patch jobs in sculpture seem to come very close to the lute-maker case. There are likely equivalent cases in painting. Curiously, efforts to match the performance-cheating case in the plastic arts may backfire. Suppose a painter wishes to include a representation of printed text in a work, but cannot paint text properly; and so sneakily glues in a page from a book instead and no one ever notices. For example, suppose that arch-realist William Michael Harnett had such trouble painting the sheet music in *Music and Good Luck* (1888) that he finally opted to glue in a real sheet copy of 'Saint Kevin', the music featured in his painting. Is this cheating? Though typical expectations and beliefs are foiled here, this case is not as clear as the performance case. In collage, for instance, such kinds of attachment form part of the accepted technique. Musical 'collage' of sorts is routinely employed in recording studios by splicing together bits of different takes to assemble the best composite. Unlike their visual arts colleagues, however, performers cannot splice in a taped passage played by someone or something else into their own rendition.

Perfectionism is common enough in the primary crafts to warrant the claim that the value attaching to the displayed product depends in part on the value attaching to the maker's activities. The value we place in the latter is expressed in our respect for expertise. Valuing a result is valuing the mastery it shows. Our respect does not properly attach to appearances of mastery, but depends upon the fact of mastery. Were it otherwise, art and mechanical manufacture become indistinguishable, and our inclination to place greater value in hand-made over machine-made items, supposing they are visually indistinguishable, would be compromised.

Certain performances are specifically fashioned so that the activity outshines the result itself. Many virtuosic works, musically trite in themselves, succeed as showcases for awesome technique. These works, if none other, must be watched in progress to gain the full effect. But these pieces distract one from the fact that primary skills are displayed in every performance and are no less the bearers of value despite being inconspicuous. The result-as-done-masterfully-well is the object of ultimate value in musical performance, an object which most manifestly is as someone does.

Value in and valuing the crafts

The chief benefits attaching to a regard for skilled action are: identification of a skill gives one a reason to single out the action or agent for positive or negative regard; and valuing skill provides a clear basis for comparative evaluation.

Many people can discern certain items or actions as resulting from uncommon exertion. Some do so after having failed at efforts to accomplish something that an inner sense of self-confidence alone would not deliver. Sometimes, observation without trial offers the same message. Discerning something as the result of uncommon exertion partially involves regarding the activities embodied in such products as *prima facie* difficult to master. Most people willingly respect accomplishments displaying such difficulty and exertion even if the products are otherwise thought unimaginative. Why? Recognizing difficulties overcome, one acknowledges that skill must have entered in. (Note that even sheer brute strength is usually never alone enough. One must persevere, however strong one is, and that, if nothing else, betokens a kind of self-mastery.) Identifying skill in a result thus provides a reason, however slight, to respect the agent and the undertaking. Why should one thus have a reason? Acknowledging skill in a result, one tends to accept that: the result did not arise accidentally; the agent was not merely lucky in having achieved the result; the result is not something anyone can do merely by deciding to do it; and, the agent was probably in sufficient control of the result to be able to repeat and/or vary it at will. These amount to perceiving the result as something difficult done designedly. Skill displays human agency in top form. Though one may think certain skills trivial, no one is indifferent to skill as such. Skill is displayed most evidently in the physical control we read off the products of human hands and in the intricate discipline we read in action itself. I think this no surprise. It's primordial with us, the blood ancestry of *homo habilis* locked deep within *homo sapiens.*

A simple contrast illustrates the case. Compare mouthing the words to *White Christmas* and imitating Bing's version. However banal each exercise, the latter displays skill far more palpably than the former, and, hence, provides more occasion and greater latitude for evaluation. To judge the imitation worthy, room must be set up for skill to be displayed, for example, is it as mellow as Bing's, as comforting, as evocative? The singer's would-be skills are thus isolable, his degree of craftsmanship a matter of comparative assessment. The lip-sync case is too ordinary in too many ways to undergird such evaluative niceties. If nearly everyone without any demonstrable effort can succeed as a competent *White Christmas* lip-syncer, no reason exists for thinking anyone worthy for having done it at all, let alone well. One can contrive so-called challenges, but if no uncommon exertion is called for in meeting them, why describe them thus?

The ease an agent finds in producing a result does not itself debase the product. Some prodigies have remarkable facility. What they accomplish is no less admirable, but fullness of ease is merely a blessing, a case of good luck.

Though facility may indeed contribute to fine musicianship, it cannot obviously be a virtue required of any musician akin, say, to musicality. (Interestingly, while 'facility' has a positive tone, 'facile' does not; as if in displaying the former, one risks, through smugness, giving the appearance of the latter.) Musicians lacking inborn facility are, in that respect, none the worse as musicians than their luckier gifted colleagues. Further, abundant facility can never be made a requirement of artistic success. The whole institution of training and practice exists precisely because most artistic trials are seldom overcome effortlessly. Indeed, they are not meant to be. Systematic effortlessness is resisted in the craft tradition because it cheapens skill.

The recognition of skill in a result places that result in a normative space by providing a basis for determining how well something was done against a benchmark of how much better it might have been done. If a result signals the skills behind it, we have thus reason to think well or ill of it, relative to those skills. Further, we have grounds for comparative judgement of results displaying the same skills. The unskilled commonplace, by contrast, fails to merit inclusion in any normative space. The ordinary is neither good nor bad.

The primary craft tradition is a storehouse of primary skills. Because of their directly physical nature and their roots in the most primal human agency, we are able in many elemental and spontaneous ways to appreciate some of the challenges they address and the extraordinary marvels they seem to draw out of our often graceless human anatomy. The extraordinariness flows in part from the fact that no natural selective advantage could have accrued, say, to the isolated ability to move one's fingers swiftly over a keyboard. Some humans learn to perform certain physical actions we just weren't specifically designed to do. However untutored in the details, we are directly aware of the physical dexterity in the musician, dancer, painter, athlete, and luthier. Our respect deepens as we descend to the microscopic subtleties, as we learn how very finely honed physical manipulations can and must be.

There is no trickery in these primary skills. They get right down to the world and its very real resistance. In spirit with the dark message of the philosopher parody, Jean-Paul Ventre; namely, 'Les choses sont contre nous', to fashion such physical phenomena as sound, a prehistoric tradition has had us physically work to set the air in motion. Howsoever we 'construct' our conceptual worldview regime, physical demands remain physical. If the value of a result is a function of the value of the primary skills making the result possible, we choose our basis for judgement wisely. Until we forsake appraisal and respect altogether, we need to rely on determinable standards of achievement which make success meaningful and failure a possibility. Primary skills embody the least arbitrary and capricious basis we have for evaluation and evaluative comparisons. Their traditional centrality in performance provides some insurance against liberal universalism where everything counts equally, and also against clubbish forms of exclusivity grounded largely on the formal approval of people with make-believe titles who run make-believe institutions. (This is not to deny that such make-believe can destroy. It most assuredly can; but what it destroys are prospects. It cannot destroy skill.) Primary skills thus provide the most transparent basis for respect for artists, art-making, and works of art. There's a physical world out there into which we were evolved and in response to which we first develop our primary skills. Not unlike trying to outrun a cheetah, making music well is difficult and making it splendidly is remarkable, period.

Part II: The Guild tradition

So far, music-making has been characterized as a primary craft with emphasis upon the critical status of primary skill in performance. Those skills derive from and also define a primary craft community. Part II examines the regulative nature of skills among musical practitioners. In particular, such skills embody the demands and desiderata of performers devoted to specific musical instruments. Groups unified under an instrument, a body of technique, and a standard repertoire I call 'performance communities'.[6] The community of musicians dedicated to developing and advancing instrument-specific skills act somewhat like professional trades Guilds. These communities establish membership credentials, regulate standards of proficiency, and ensure consistency in the recognition of differential merit. Above all, the Guild maintains the craft's skill-centred exclusivity, and aims to ensure that its exceptional practitioners find and enjoy their properly earned and established rank.

Innovation and conservatism in performance

Performance communities share with many structured institutions their conservatism and gradualism; that is, their reluctance and resistance to change. They do not speedily adopt radical innovations in instrument design, repertoire, evaluation procedures, pedagogical methods, or basic technique. The successful introduction and entrenchment of whole new instruments is exceedingly uncommon.

Many innovations are rejected.[7] When change occurs, it affects other community standards. Here are three examples: (1) The changeover on the violin to the brighter, louder, more strident steel E string from nutty, mellow gut impelled changes in bowing technique and interpretive options; (2) When guitarists adopted right-hand fingernails, techniques affecting tone colour, loudness, and execution speed changed, which, in turn, made players receptive to the more tough, stable, but less warm-sounding nylon treble strings which replaced gut in the 1940s; (3) and, of course, the adoption and addition of keys on the woodwinds and valves on the brass transformed the very repertoire of those instruments. More globally, mass production of instruments and the use of cheap, reliable plastics has made musical instruments vastly more accessible to many more would-be players than ever before. This abundance has its inevitable spin-offs in teaching opportunities, music publication, and interest in performance, live and recorded. Technological innovation invariably wreaks widespread and often unpredictable change.

Innovations in instrument design usually create timbral and technical novelties. Redesigned or enhanced instruments never sound just like their predecessors nor do they play in the same ways. Musicians typically exploit the technical and timbral novelties in emerging repertoire. Despite this, design change does not usually compel any wholesale reassessment of the accumulated standard repertoire. Early works, conceived for now surpassed instruments, are just 'ported over', and executed on the new devices. Dowland's lute, Bach's clavichord, Marais' viola da gamba, De Visée's theorbo, Haydn's baryton, Mozart's fortepiano – all these 'obsolete' machines did not take their repertoire to the grave and thus deny it to latter-day guitarists, cellists, and pianists.

Though proponents of authentic performance have successfully stimulated the reconstruction and use of old instruments for early music, the ultimate effect is incomplete. Players of modern instruments are generally willing neither to master what amounts to a different instrument nor to abandon a cherished repertoire just because it was composed with an earlier instrument in mind. Modern pianists have good reason not to relinquish Bach, given that their proficiency with Bach's major works determines in part who counts now as competent pianists. Further, pianistic tradition has determined on its own authority that what counts as Bach's work proper is entirely preserved for musical purposes on the modern pianoforte. Players of modern instruments may even regard them as superior to, because they are improvements over, early instruments. History backs this somewhat. Many innovations were often accepted, even encouraged and commissioned, because they offered something more valuable than traditional options.[8]

The ultimate synthesizer: an offer one can't refuse?

Performing musicians must acquire sufficient skills to produce intended results on specific instruments. Precise control over such devices dominates much of the instrumentalist's concerns. The instrument is seldom altogether a co-operative medium of expression. If it were, rigorous drill and practice would be redundant.

What motivates instrumental innovations and their acceptance? Because an instrument may limit a performer's technical ambitions or expressive plans, and because certain design changes facilitate both technical and expressive operations, such innovations may become very attractive. Such became apparent in our consideration of 'smart' instruments in Chapter 1. Their adoption may entail the loss of some valued features (for example, timbral idiosyncrasies), but these are often amply compensated for by new advantages and opportunities. The innovations may even be just better all round.

If offered superior means to achieve performance ends, wouldn't it be irrational and irresponsible to reject them? Historically, the conservatism described has not been stagnant but cautiously progressive. Instrumental changes are adopted because they improve musical opportunities. These adoptions often reflect approval of technological advances; for example, better materials, better construction techniques, advanced applications of the physics of sound and engineering acoustics, and so on.

Consider a related case in instrument-making. A modern luthier who chose to cut purfling channels with a seventeenth-century style of purfling cutter would be merely eccentric when the job can be done faster, with greater ease, and more cleanly using a power router spinning a tungsten carbide bit at 30,000 rpm. We may fully admire and respect those who, in the past, laboured under adversity, but, in admiring such work, one scarcely recommends thereby the conditions under which it was done.

Shouldn't one use the best tool for the job? Respect for technological innovation flows from our regard for technology as the prime source of functional improvements. This respect should presumably stimulate the design of increasingly improved instruments. Consider that our century offers the bravest yet of the new instrumental worlds. Shouldn't we rejoice in the prospect of finally supplanting chronically flawed acoustic designs with their fully reliable, unimaginably versatile electronic successors? Current synthesizers have compelling virtues:

> they are often more portable and less expensive than their acoustic counterparts, and they usually require only a minimum of keyboard technique, rather than the years of complex training required to skilfully play most acoustic instruments. For these reasons, synthesizers are accessible to more people, and that is probably the key to their success over the past two decades.[9]

Consider the next step up in this hard sell for the 'ultimate synthesizer':

> Count your new blessings! For you winds, no more spit to mop up, no more bursting lungs, no more chafed lips. For you bowed strings, no more wrecked backs and chins, no more wolf tones, no more hassles with tuning and intonation. For you plucked strings, no more calluses, no more buzzes and squeaks. Best of all, no more years of practice! David Munrow's joke was on him when he snubbed the harpsichord as a 'mechanized psaltery'.[10] Name a harpsichordist who hankered after a psaltery? Who would look back?

These new instruments promise a vast facilitation of the results traditionally sought with conventional instruments. What are the implications? Pianos replaced harpsichords, guitars replaced lutes, violins replaced viols.[11] Not many complain. We may now face a revolution which sweeps away woods, pipes, membranes, strings, and, with them, centuries of hard work. Sticking to acoustic traditions may become merely dated, stubborn sentimentality. Will progressivism welcome the new electronic panacea, or will our enthusiasm be dampened by the conservatism described above? Are there limits to the acceptable degree of facility promised by new technology? Might the changes in store be just too 'perfect'?

I would guess that even a player fully convinced about the advantages would hesitate. This is no light gesture. In many ways, technology is to practice and the achievement of purpose what scientific theory is to knowledge and the achievement of truth. If theory answers our drive for better understanding of the way things are, technology responds to our need to improve our chances of getting what we want. Consequently, to shun an effective new technology may seem very like reluctance to welcome and accommodate a new theory which promises to get us closer to the truth. Consider, for example, what resisting much of modern medicine and water purification would imply. If such resistance to better theories is irrational (and so prone inadvertently to frustrate our ends), so too is walking away from superior technologies. So, if one wilfully rejects such technologies, then, *prima facie*, one is obliged to justify or, at least, explain one's rejection. Below, I examine misgivings about the new technology, thereby making explicit features integral to the conservatism of skill-based performance communities. In the end, explanation steps in where justification flounders; for the conservatism is just that, a tendency to preserve certain means of operation in order to sustain certain established values, when it is just those values that are under fire.

Resisting the ultimate synthesizer

Arguments resisting radical technological substitution which appeal to empirical or essential properties prove ineffective. One may complain on empirical grounds that the trained ear can always tell them apart, but this is a red herring. Aural indistinguishability as such has never been a historical requirement. Modern violins scarcely sound just like their Baroque ancestors. Most technical improvements in instrumental design predictably coincide with tonal and timbral changes. In some cases, these very changes were the initial objectives which stimulated design changes; for example, demands for greater volume, sustain or dynamic range, or a richer complement of upper partials. All avowed distinctness aside, precise synthetic replication is attainable. It is just a matter of engineering. 'Given enough oscillators, any set of independent [sound] spectral components can be synthesized, and so virtually any sound can be generated.'[12] So, from the listener's perspective, the acoustic effects from two radically distinct sources of sound may be phenomenally indistinguishable.

The argument from essential properties is more intricate. One is a violinist just in case one plays the violin. Since the ultimate synthesizer is not a violin, its players are not violinists. Therefore, no one *qua* violinist can accept the synthesizer as a violin substitute because it is a different instrument altogether. If the piano is scarcely an 'improvement' over the violin, neither is the ultimate synthesizer.

Musical instruments are effectively tools used by operators performing certain roles or jobs. Some tools are literally 'tools of the trade'. Such tools stand in a special relation to the job assumed by their users. Indeed, certain role names essentially invoke the tool employed. Following the craft tradition pattern, typical craft-centred roles have four focal points:

skilled action – means/tools – material – result

Most roles have specifiable material upon which certain actions, using specific tools, are undertaken so that a specifiable result obtains. Many role designations highlight these focal points, thus suggesting distinctive role categories.

Material (object of attention)   Some role names refer to the object upon which the agent's specialized activities are directed; for example, dentist, veterinarian, podiatrist, fireman, glazier. The role title answers the question: 'Upon what is the agent's attention focused?'

Means (tool or instrument)   Some role names feature what the agents typically use in the exercise of their role; for example, guitarist, drummer, gunner, X-operator (as in lathe- or crane-operator), telephonist. The role title answers the question: 'With what tool is the job undertaken?'

Skilled action   Some jobs are described in terms of the agent's activity; for example, baker, pipe-fitter, teacher, painter, preacher, cook. The name answers: 'What does such a one do?'

Result (product)   Related to but distinct from 'skilled action' is the reference to what the role results in; for example, musician, novelist and roles commonly described by the form X-maker (violin-maker, cabinet-maker, etc.). The name answers: 'What is produced by the role?'

Any role might have been characterized in any one of these ways. (Further, many roles are identified merely by rank; for example, vice-president, colonel, senator, etc., or by position as in sports; for example, right-wing, forward, fielder.) Given that craft roles have their characteristic activities, objects of focus, typical results, and customary means, it may just be a linguistic accident that certain roles fall into existing categories. We might have named surgeons after their scalpels or bakers after their cakes. Roles do not differ in kind just because their names fall into different categories. All violinists are musicians. However, given the category a role name falls into, certain features of the role attach to it unaccidentally.

Regarding 'means', naming a role after its tool suggests that the tool is no more incidental to it than the activity is when that is used in role designation. Explicit reference to the tool warrants taking it as a tool of the trade. (There are analogous activities, results, and objects of the trade as well.) These come in two sorts; typical and essential. A typical tool of the trade is characteristically but not necessarily used by the role-bearer; for example, hand chisels are typically used by cabinet-makers even though they may be forsaken in favour of power routers. Essential tools of the trade are those whose use is necessitated by the role in which they star. Guitarists have no option but to use guitars; cyclists must use bicycles.

One who does not and cannot play the lute cannot be a lutenist. The tool becomes definitive of the role. Since tools themselves have essential features, to supplant any tool of the trade in the category of means isn't quite as innocuous as the switch a typist (properly so called) makes from a manual typewriter to a wordprocessor. No violins, no violinists.

Perhaps all that happens is that the designation 'violinist' vanishes? Why shouldn't we keep the name 'violinist' just to mean a musician who produces sounds of a certain quality; namely, like those that come from a violin. 'Violinist' would retain a vestigial flavour akin to calling those police officers who have never been nor intend to be on a horse 'Mounties'. Why not call the new electronic devices 'violins'? Still, this is not quite innocent for it involves changing the very meaning of 'violinist'.

Does this help the resistance? If being a violinist is to be a violin-player, then, *qua* violinist, one must use a violin as the tool of the trade. But if a violin is an instrument with such-and-such qualities, then no one who uses a synthesizer which merely shares its sound with a violin can be a violinist. What are violins? Descriptions of characteristic sound will have to be supplemented with general design features and causal properties to mark off acoustic from non-acoustic families of instruments. For one instrument to be the same kind as another it is not sufficient that their outputs are indistinguishable to the ear. That's not even a necessary property.

The differences in causal properties between modern and Baroque violins are superficial compared with those distinguishing any violin and any synthesizer. Synthesizer 'violins' are not bowed, have no soundboxes, strings, fingerboard, bridge, tailpiece, nut, pegs, or scroll. Modern violinists know more or less what to do with a Baroque violin; most modern violinists wouldn't even recognize a synthesizer 'violin' for what it is let alone know how to handle it. Without implying that any or all of these typical violin features are essential, it is pretty hard to confuse violins with synthesizers. As mimics of acoustic instruments, synthesizers are parasitic upon them. Violins don't synthesize – make up out of simpler elements – the sound of a violin. As mimics, synthesizers cannot be confused with the original. Thus, a player who forsakes the violin for a synthesizer ceases to be a violinist. *Qua* violinist, no one can prefer a synthesizer to a violin. (This oversimplifies somewhat. Synthesizers were designed to expand sound horizons dramatically beyond conventional acoustic capabilities. As a source of sound, the ultimate synthesizer is a superset of the class of acoustic instruments. Whether that alone makes the synthesizer a violin of sorts is at issue.)

Although this trades heavily on mere names, significant distinctions within the musical world coincide with distinctions among instruments. Whatever we call violin players or violins, what they play makes them what they are. Whatever synthesizers are called, they are not uncontroversially continuous with whatever we customarily call 'violins'. Synthesizers share some typical violin features like sound quality, but that no more makes them violins than the fact that lions and tigers can interbreed makes lions tigers. Safety must lie in the identity conditions for violins and thus violinists.

The appeal to essential properties falters once one notes how indeterminate those very identity conditions are which purportedly relieve anyone *qua* violinist from having to choose between an acoustic violin and a synthesizer. Some progressive shifts have already been made; for example from gut-strung, low-bridge to steel-strung, high-bridge violins. Why are these not distinct instruments? What stops us from altering bit by bit those features of violins, until we get something dramatically distinct from our starting point and yet very much the same instrument by dint of the continuous, gradual improvements approved over the years?

But, surely, the accumulation of gradual changes will eventually transform the violin into something else. Can we accept saying 'The changes to the violin are manifestly well displayed in the following' and be pointing at a synthesizer all the while convinced that we are referring to a violin? Compare: 'This creature manifestly demonstrates the changes that have gradually occurred in fish' as we point to an amphibian, taking it all the while that we must be speaking about a fish. This is dreadfully un-Darwinian. That said, regarding violins, no one can specify in advance where we should or will draw the line, particularly if we are confronted with a seamless sequence of modifications. For instance, some modern electronic guitars have neither soundbox nor head. Some don't have strings. They look and sound like Star Trek weapons, but they're guitars. How so? In some respect, because those who play them identify themselves as guitarists and are so identified by their peers and fans. Further, they regard themselves as heir to the guitar's tradition of transition, from the unamplified, to the amplified, through to the fully digital electronic variants of our time. Speaking taxonomically, it is as if, historically, 'guitar' first named a reasonably primitive species which, through adaptive radiation, spawned a whole cluster of distinctive offshoot species among which is included the new electronic family which co-exists with the acoustic cohort. We have already accepted a fundamental meaning change; namely, whereas 'guitar' once named a distinctive species of acoustic instrument, it now names a whole genus or even family of instruments and has become semantically closer to such terms as 'the winds' or 'the bowed strings'. As the semantic breadth for 'guitar' increases, predicates like 'flat-backed' or 'gut strung' become increasingly less prototypical and increasingly more local in significance.

As a last resort, we might distinguish between improving and displacing a tool. Improvements occur within a type, not on it. A tool may be improved and yet remain essentially the same. Consider changing the bevel edge of a chisel or improving blade steel quality, or adding valves on brass instruments. Improvement presupposes the continuation of the same tool family. Not only is the general function retained; so are the primary features which make it identifiable as being of the same type. Tools may also be displaced. An entire tool type might be supplanted by a new type which does the same job under a broad functional description but employs distinctively different design and/or operating principles and may demand quite a different technique. Wordprocessors have obviously displaced typewriters though few changes of operational technique have occurred. The displacement of some hand tools by power tools has required substantially new operational techniques. Can the essential differences between traditional instruments and synthesizers warrant the claim that instrumentalists need not consider any displacement substitute (whatever the benefits), though they ought to consider some substitute replacements?

Unfortunately, none of this helps much because of the residual dynamism and lack of fixity attaching to identity conditions for instrumental types. Instrumental types are purely conventional. The conventions tend to change over time, and tolerate a good measure of flex. But despite problems about type boundaries, why not insist that a legitimate choice between the violin and the synthesizer is forced upon us? It is useless to point out that 'violin' now typically refers to thus-and-such wooden boxes. Look at the historical semantics of 'guitar' and one learns a lesson about 'violin'. This wordplay is not quite idle because of the radical implications for performance of 'smart' violins. After all, suppose the newcomer makes violinistic life in particular and musical life altogether easier. If one violin-thing is better than another, one would be a fool to turn it down, no? Because essentialism for instruments just doesn't help, we lack any non-arbitrary conceptual grounds for delimiting acceptable technological improvements.

A socio-historical perspective: performance and Guilds

Arguments resting on sound quality or traditional functionality do not justify the cautious conservatism of performance communities. Can we at least explain why we do not quickly cede entrenched instrumental traditions to radical technological innovation? The discussion below does not 'prove' the conservative point; rather it clarifies what is at stake by supplying more details about conservative commitments. That said, the synthesizer is upon us, here to stay, and needs locating in performance practice. It is not just another instrument, nor just another instrument type. It represents a revolutionary opening move in the unification of music-making categories. How so? In brief, the synthesizer can supply all sounds to all people with a single increasingly accessible universal *modus operandi*. Therewith, categories like 'baritone', 'pianist', and 'guitarist' become superficial, literally surface fluctuations. Once this happens, artistically ancient and deep-flowing distinctions between vocal and instrumental music and their associated traditions crumble.

The argument in outline

The resistance to electronic encroachment is best understood by recognizing that musical instruments are not mere tools for their users. Their value to their users is not exhausted in the sound output considered in isolation. Performance communities value their instruments partly because of the handicaps they impose between player and result. Such handicaps are deliberately chosen and accepted. Why? Performance communities, like any Craft Guild, recognize and value mastery and a hierarchy of skilled practitioners. Instrumental challenges ensure that such hierarchies of skill survive. Performance communities further their instruments in part by maintaining an exclusivity of skill. These themes are elaborated below.

What displacement technology threatens

The synthesizer was conceived as a displacement technology. Resisting it seems like a response to a perceived threat; namely, the debilitating impact of technology on human skill. What effect does the synthesizer have? It facilitates playing to the point where the results are dead easy to achieve. Cheap electronic keyboards supply simple examples; for example, automatic arpeggiation and rhythm boxes. More costly ones allow complex tone control. The impact is severe. It gives anyone with minimal effort and skill the power to create the very results for which the musician has spent years in training. This seems to cheapen the musician's skill. Furthermore, if society values musicians largely for their results, the value of musicians declines. The skilled musician is thus displaced along with the displacement of the instrument. This threatens redundancy. We have here a familiar instance of the human price of technology.

In automation cases, humans are displaced with relative ease because the jobs themselves are often manifestly mechanical, routine, and stereotyped by nature. Some would add, the tasks are beneath human dignity because of those features. Certain human activities are removed for ever by technology. The blacksmith went, and the thatcher. We now witness the end of human mail-sorting, type-setting, arc-welding and car-assembly. Apart from social and political resistance, those working at these jobs must eventually concede that the machines provide all the reason needed to step aside.

Displacement technologies are generally valued because they make certain tasks easier to do. This greater ease comes by removing skill requirements altogether thus reducing the task to a purely mechanical process, or requiring much simpler skills to achieve the same end; that is, skills which take less time, training, and effort to acquire, and which thereby can be acquired by many more people.

Displacement technology carries the disturbing message that the human skill, expertise, and dedication which go into the result are not special, and are just further mechanical functions. The engineer can scoff: 'Anything you can do, I can do better – and more cheaply, safely and effortlessly. It's the results that count, that's all.' Machines destroy the point in acquiring such skills. Tools are great levellers. They level those activities formerly monopolized by the doomed aristocrats of high skill. Technology's democracy will not enfranchise an upper class.

Why not all skills are threatened

Is the player's reluctance really rooted in the fear of being displaced by technology? Are traditional musical skills rendered pointless by technology? Consider chess, putatively a game of subtle inferential skills. Has the last grandmaster to go down in flames because of some programmer's project, and been handed notice as brutal as that given out to assembly-line workers? Is chess beneath human dignity? Would we wish to liberate chessplayers from their empty pursuit? Should orchestra players be freed from their bondage because some technician-cum-synthesizer can do it all in a dust-free studio over the weekend? Do chess and music machines provide good reason to stop playing chess or music? To all, I think not.

Why not? Suppose we appeal to the creativity in chess and music; that is, the ingenuity, concentration, intensity, imagination, and skill involved. These cannot be grouped with mechanical activities like mail-sorting. Unfortunately, any distinction between 'brute' and creative enterprises must acknowledge that technology may offer both. Chess programs are scarcely simple-minded arcade amusements. Suppose we stress the resident individuality of the creative sphere; that is, even if a machine can stand in for a human, the human's performance will still be distinct. The human's performance will not thus be exactly replicated by the machine because every performance, the machine's included, is distinct and so has value. But this rests the case on empty minutiae and makes humans no less dispensable than machines. The machines alone can drown us in all the individuality anyone could ever hope to admire.

What of dedication? Players invest much time and effort learning how to get what they want out of their instruments. A devotion arises out of the acquisition of mastery over a recalcitrant object. The respect of their peers derives from an appreciation of this very victory.

Is this simple sentimentality? If sentimentality it is, it is hardly simple. People consistently continue to accept and do battle with predictable aggravations even though they can taste the ease at hand. We not only revere our musical past; we wilfully and almost proudly sustain it in technologically obsolete ways. This cannot be dismissed by facile appeals to inertia or plain cussedness.

The entrenched dedication in performance to certain families of instruments makes sense when the exercise of any skill using specific means is made the object of value despite the functional superiority of alternatives. Sometimes, we even infuse less value in what is done than in the manner of execution. Thus, unlike many functional enterprises, those crafts wed essentially to traditional primary skills cannot be simply oriented towards results.

I will call 'action crafts' – to contrast with 'output crafts' – those which, first, do not suffer loss of participants because technology is available to displace human agency in achieving certain desired results, nor second, necessarily review or abandon traditional primary skills and instruments dedicated to those results just because there exist new technological means facilitating the achievement of those results. This plays upon a variant of the essentialist reflections considered earlier. Performance is stereotypically a primary action craft as are many traditional handicrafts. (Chess is only by courtesy a craft, but is, as such, an action craft though not a primary one. Housepainting is typically an output craft.) Respect for action crafts does not grow out of a taste for ease, efficiency, and economy.

Rituals of victory

The deliberate retention of traditional devices for certain purposes reflects the value invested in the activities involved in using such devices. If easier means are ignored, the obstacles and difficulties facing the participant are by extension also deliberately retained. It cannot be part of the procedure to eliminate the difficulties, for, if it were, the use of new facilitating means would be encouraged. Such obstacles instead must be overcome. These obstacles are deliberate handicaps. Overcoming them under accepted artificial constraints becomes a ritual requiring skill. Agreement to attempt to succeed in such a ritual signals one's interest in becoming a member of an exclusive community.

Music and other primary action crafts are structured to achieve their ends under contrivedly traditional restrictions. Under such terms, one is forbidden from deploying means which otherwise maximally facilitate the desired result. These restrictions and the community of participants which preserves them define the tasks which, when overcome, result in skill and expertise.

Such skills have much in common with the virtues in the old-fashioned sense. In those respects, performance shares much with exploring and athletics. Specialized gear notwithstanding, ardent mountain-climbers do not typically solve their challenge by blasting and bulldozing so as to furnish level terrain where once there were cliffs; nor do they hasten ascent to the peak in helicopters.[13] Being an accomplished guitarist is in part being able to subdue confidently the treacheries of the guitar. That does not open the option of re-designing the instrument to eliminate the snags. They've got to be there. The chess grandmaster need not feel belittled by the computer which has beaten him nor even obliged to recognize what he's been trounced in as chess. 'Ah! Computer-chess', he may say with possible contempt, thinking of it all along like earthmover-mountaineering and synthesizer-violinistics. At the very least, chess programmers rely intimately upon a vast infra-structural corporate-technological universe. Chess grandmasters do not – nay, cannot – get there as members of a strategic policy and planning team.

There is a risk of parody here. Immense skill may be required to remove a cork from a bottle if one is deliberately equipped with tools which are radically unfit for the task. But that does not vest in decorking any ritual of victory. On the other side, just because it may be easier to play a violin work on a synthesizer, one would not describe violins as obstacles to the playing of violin sonatas.

The account offered leads to neither result. Merely because any given activity may be made difficult and skilful does not make it just like guitar-playing, say. It could become that way, but that would involve the many historical and social factors which sometimes coalesce into an organized practice. Though difficulty and skill lie at the core of such practices, these alone are inadequate to organize and unify a practice. Second, violins are not impediments to violin-playing. The language of obstacle and handicap is meant to highlight two notions: (1) a normal condition in violin-playing is the requirement of often uncommon primary skill, and (2) the demands imposed by normal violin-playing do not warrant use of any means whatever to facilitate one's efforts.

Explaining allowable innovation

Earlier we considered that innovations are acceptable only if perceived as improvements. But only some types of innovation in instruments or procedures are allowed; not all or any types. What determines the range and choice of improvements? Do approvals of acceptable improvements rest on arbitrary standards? These questions conceal a cluster of problems. Some are historical, some technological, and some about the abstract connections between membership in performance communities and the constitution of such communities. In what follows, I consider a few responses which lead to a sketch of performance communities as rank-preserving Guilds.

As a principle regulating the introduction of new means and measures, one may require that the acceptable improvements do not make anything possible which would otherwise have been impossible. This deeply conservative view implies that if one removed every improvement and returned to some primeval instrumental or procedural state, one would be able to sustain everything else like repertoire, technique, skill requirements, and so on. This just seems false.

More weakly, one may allow any improvement provided that, if it were subsequently removed, the craft itself would not be debased. Music-making would be as rich and inspired as ever even if short of certain options. Although this may be acceptable, it is also very nebulous. If it means that musicians now would feel their art complete even if deprived of post-Baroque instruments and techniques, the verdict could go either way. If it implies that at no time in the craft's history has performance been less demanding, that is likely true. That is, no acceptable improvements can ever make performance noticeably easier than it has ever been.

The last reading implies that choice of acceptable change is governed by the preservation of standards. The restrictions might be framed thus:

> For every facultative improvement admitted in instrument design and procedure, there are overlaid new handicaps to mastery which preserve (a) the equal need for skill acquisition, (b) the equal relative amount of effort required to gain skill, and (c), the relative proportions of the most highly skilled to novices in the community of practitioners.

The last item suggests that the performance community maintains an equilibrium in the proficiency of its practitioners such that an aristocracy of skill is maintained; that is, performance communities work to sustain their own social structure. This will become prominent in the following.

Aspects of performance professionalism

The notion of a skill aristocracy can be illuminated by contrasting professional and artistic training traditions. Regarding the professions, high minimum standards are wanted and required in medicine, architecture, law, accountancy, engineering, etc., because bad results can impoverish or kill. Such a desire for standards is internal to each profession and supported by the general public. One wants the most modern, advanced procedures and instruments to be employed. No one wants surgeons to operate in the old-fashioned way with whisky and pocket knives, no matter how fantastically skilled they are. No one demands historically 'authentic' surgical performance. (Even historically 'authentic' architectural practice is not fully demanded judging by the enormously sensible and legally required use of chemical fire retardants in the materials used for the reconstructed Globe Theatre.)

Nothing about these professional fields rules out universal excellence as an achievable and desirable professional objective. Our professional communities can sincerely endorse an optimistic directive aimed at producing indistinguishably superb practitioners. The best a profession can ever promise is that those seeking professional services may indifferently select any professional practitioner and expect as a matter of course the same superb level of skilful service. This may never happen in law or medicine, talent being where you find it. That there are in fact those who are distinguishably the very best in their respective fields is a contingent and scarcely ideal condition. That said, no one fears or shuns the prospect of an army of generals in medicine or engineering – at least, in respect of skill and expertise. To the extent that there remain manifest differences in skill in medicine, medicine is professionally deficient – unless it settles for the more achievable option of having only to ensure indistinguishability among practitioners at the level of basic competence.

In those artistic traditions where manner is king, universal excellence cannot be countenanced where that entails the indifferent substitutability of practitioners.

This does not just rest on the greater significance of and interest in style idiosyncrasies. Some practitioners are much better than others. This skill distance between practitioners is not only acknowledged, but encouraged and preserved. The range of proficiency is not a contingent (and even regrettable) quality of artistic communities, but constitutive of them. Universal excellence could never happen in principle in performance because the ongoing community design is to maintain a structure of skill ranks in the performance community. This deliberately sustained skill hierarchy is what distinguishes it as a community. ·

Both the professional and artistic communities are unified by what is generally called 'professionalism'; that is, roughly, association with and dedication to a specific set of methods and objectives undertaken with respect to certain accepted minimum standards and respected ideals of achievement.

A number of principles underlie the professionalism of artistic communities which relate the acquisition of skills to the goals of competence (proficiency), mastery (expertise), and virtuosity. The systematic endorsement and enforcement of these principles goes a long way toward defining and unifying a performance community. I consider some elementary principles briefly.

The skills called for in artistic communities are designed to respond to challenges people are not natively equipped to overcome; at least, not with reliable proficiency. Any community-specific skills must be acquired or learned. Furthermore, they cannot be learned adequately by unstructured 'experience'. They are not 'life' skills, but the fruits of relatively formal and structured training. Training establishes certain minimal standards the reliable skill at attaining which gives one competence or proficiency. Full professionalism or mastery is not achieved without time and effort. Some never achieve it. Some achieve a status of exemplary professionalism. Schematically, these notions of acquisition and rank can be thus presented:

Native versus acquired skill No one comes born with skills sufficient to overcome successfully the challenges recognized by the community.

Challenge Proficiency is a product of the use of skills acquired to overcome certain obstacles. There is no competence without skill or obstacles.

Training Proficiency comes with the acquisition of skills formal training for which is necessary and for which there is no dependable substitute.

Mastery is the hard-earned goal of those whose skill takes them beyond minimal proficiency.

Virtuosity   is, in turn, the pinnacle of mastery.

Armed with these broad principles of skill placement and hierarchy, one can add dividing principles which underwrite distinct skill class quotas:

Exclusivity There is no minimum limit on effort or education such that, once exercised, any person acquires skill. Some will never acquire skill, no matter how much effort is exerted.

There is always room for the bottomless category 'doing such-and-such poorly' or 'being mediocre at such-and-such'. Such would-be participants are not regarded by those with more than 'official' minimal proficiency as belonging to the community but merely as aspiring to belong. Amateurs, dilettantes, hobbyists – as these terms are used somewhat disparagingly – fall outside the community.

Comparative skill Skill is a matter of degree. For someone to have greater skill than another involves the capacity to produce a greater range and variety of results more reliably under a broader range of circumstances.

This principle allows that not everyone reaches the same standard, and yet allows them inclusion in the same community. The community tolerates an achievement band. How broad it is will depend on how exclusive its influential participants want it to be.

Perfectibility Whereas there is a lower base threshold to skill there is no accurately pre-established or predictable upper limit (within sheer biological possibilities).

Proficiency represents a minimal achievement in a community, one which is definable with some accuracy within the training wing. So, satisfying certain training requirements, one can say fairly that one has skill at some task. The highest end, however, is not so defined. One may recognize that certain participants, the virtuosi so-called, are separated by a considerable gap from the next group of those with mastery. But this means neither that such virtuosi are recognized as such precisely because they have achieved certain specific new skills, that is, there is no minimum virtuosity threshold as there is a minimum proficiency threshold; nor does it mean that any virtuosi represent the highest possible degree of accomplishment and skill in the community (unlike saying that those with mere proficiency represent the lowest degree of skill).

We cannot tell in advance just how amazingly good some practitioner may become, how far beyond present high standards someone will venture. The really great virtuosi of a generation tend to astonish their contemporaries even though they may not astonish themselves. Unlike proficiency and not unlike fame, virtuosity tends to be highly mercurial. It is far easier to lose one's virtuosic rank than one's proficiency rank. Virtuosi always stand to be outclassed by those who astonish even more. In contrast, the entire training schedule might have to change radically before someone, already deemed proficient, might be declared no longer competent.

Constitutional aristocracy There can be no artistic community where everyone with skill is equally a virtuoso, nor can a majority or even large minority be virtuosi. Virtuosi are the community aristocrats.

This feature distinguishes music doctrinally from medicine, say, as communities of practitioners. As mentioned, universal virtuosity is systematically disallowed and thus made impossible in artistic communities. Conveniently, as humans differ from one another, one expects differential achievement in any reasonably demanding enterprise. The facts of human nature provide for such skill aristocracies which, though unfortunate in medicine, are required in music.

What happens when, relative to the key objectives of a community, more and more can achieve them virtuosically? To compensate for the imbalance and to reach a new equilibrium which reflects the same previous optimum proportion of aristocrats to commoners, the community's minimum standards get tougher. That is, the old proficiency requirements and standards of mastery are superseded to ensure the appropriate ratio of virtuosi, masters, and the competent. What makes a given ratio appropriate is determined by complex social, historical, political, and even biological factors. Suffice it to say, we do not seem very effective at willingly accepting anything but the smallest slate of 'winners'. We steadfastly keep that slate small, even if it means attaching significance to fractions of time which we cannot even identify without prosthetic instruments, as is the obsessive practice in many sporting events.

Such homeostatic controls regulating proficiency classes have been implemented in golf circles. The main golfing association, the PGA, decided to ban a new technological innovation – the square-grooved club. Why? Such clubs improve everyone's chances. This should have made them unobjectionable, but they damage a delicate equilibrium. Apparently, while improving the game of amateurs evenly, and maintaining the same skill gaps at that level, they tend to narrow considerably the gaps between the top professionals. Here differential virtuosic status at the very top of the skill aristocracy is important enough to the golf community to warrant a ban on a facultative but rank-destabilizing technology.[14]

Performance communities as Guilds

The context which best accommodates the limits and conventions associated with performance communities I call the 'Guild tradition'. Here is roughly how it operates. Becoming a violinist is tantamount to earning membership within a unified club of skilled specialists. This so-called club, the Guild, is a construct of sorts, although associated with it at any time are many concrete, interacting institutions which collectively set and maintain surprisingly uniform standards and expectations. Among the features constitutive of the Guild are various schools of pedagogy, the identification of standard core repertoire, the standardization of instruments and tunings, rankings of conservatories, common and ranked competitions and masterclass circuits, specialist magazines and newsletters, local instrumental societies and concert series, and so on – whatever might, at any one time, be included in 'the guitar scene', or 'the piano scene', etc.

The qualifications for gaining and maintaining membership centre round the acquisition and demonstrated mastery of two related clusters of skills; namely, musicianship and musicality. Musicianship takes in technique, the mastery over physical hurdles imposed by any instrument. Musicality encompasses interpretive sensitivity; in particular, adding novelty to the traditional repertoire without destroying its links with a seamless interpretive tradition, as well as extending the repertoire by reviving forgotten works or championing new ones.

The highest rank of mastery is virtuosity. Consummate virtuosi are ones never impeded in any exercise of musicality by any limits to their musicianship. Within the Guild, there is never room at any one period for more than a handful of virtuosi who, each generation, define new horizons of skill and thus new objectives for the remaining membership.

The Guild determines membership by establishing prescribed handicaps which themselves grow and evolve within the traditions. The core repertoire sets one bound upon membership. To achieve membership one must master certain pieces; to achieve advanced membership one must master certain advanced – difficult – pieces, ones that stretch both musicianship and musicality to significant limits of control. As the repertoire grows, it adds new challenges to standing conceptions of virtuosity. With the growth of repertoire, not only are certain new challenges imposed, but certain traditional requirements are displaced; for example, the ability to extemporize an enormously complex cadenza (skills now surviving in Western music largely within jazz tradition).

Another handicap is the means of performance, the stock-in-trade instruments of the Guild. That the Guild favours certain designs, worships certain builders, resists certain alterations is a complex function of historical passage and inertia, conceptions of virtuosity, internal properties of the repertoire, traditions of pedagogy, audience expectations, standards of the instrument-makers, and more. Why any instrument became entrenched over long periods – many didn't like barytons or bandoras – and what exactly fuelled acceptable and subsequently embedded alterations in instrumental design cannot be answered without looking closely at the social conditions of music-making. Suffice it to say, entrenchment did occur in our culture so that instruments like the violin, the piano, the oboe, and the guitar have already enjoyed centuries of stable, gradual, development. That said, the nature and rate of design change in the various instruments has not been uniform, nor have all changes of a facilitative nature gained acceptance. Indeed, history does not warrant a generalization to the effect that functional improvement alone explains design change.

What message does this have for the ultimate synthesizer case? The resistance to synthesizers from those within entrenched acoustic traditions derives largely from their historical and normative independence. They lack the right pedigree. Synthesizers have not emerged and evolved within the continuous traditions of the standard Guilds. Further, synthesizers don't respect or even address the primary challenges imposed by the Guild. A synthesizer-violin master cannot thus rank as a violin virtuoso. Indeed, such a master will not rank at all within the violin Guild, any more than a computer chess program gets to enter the hall of fame of the grandmasters. This lack of rank or standing is partially a function of the utter lack of criteria by which to peg the level of musicianship and musicality of the synthesizer-player within the violin Guild. Such alleged absence of criterial overlap makes for further Guild exclusiveness. Consider, for instance, the boundaries created by so-called 'styles' where classical guitarists come to believe they have less in common with flamenco or jazz guitarists than they do with concert flautists.

There is another limit as well. Suppose that certain synthesizers make traditionally difficult performance tasks so simple as to be within the reach of beginners – the promise of 'play-in-a-day' finally realized. The Guild is so structured as to make it impossible for all such players to enter the ranks of virtuosi. The Guild, indeed, will not abide this coarse democratization of expertise. If the repertoire cannot exclude the masses, then the instrument is used to do so. Ironically, then, the very 'dysfunctionality' of the conventional violin relative to technological possibilities is exactly what the Guild values about it. This dysfunctionality demarcates the zone for those specialized skills which constitute violin-playing proper for the Guild. No one accuses the ultimate synthesizer of failing expressively, and we agree that it overwhelms by its technical facilitation. Its chief fault lies in its snubbing and thereby undermining the Guild structure. The synthesizer is no mere alteration in the traditional sense; it is an upstart technology, a new class of instrument. Hence it is understandably, and perhaps reasonably, shunned by those for whom the standards and demands of the Guild constitute the *raison d'être* for respecting and attempting to acquire Guild-ridden skill.

The synthesizer, of course, is no mere lackey awaiting admission and acceptance by the ancient musical powers. Unlike them, it rides the winds of our time, and, far from self-protective entrenchment, it enjoys the adventure of rapid, imaginative development. But, if it is a musical instrument at all, it too will inescapably, almost organically, have organized around itself a synthesizer Guild, driven by its own handicaps and hierarchies, until it forms its own tradition with its own anointed virtuosi. This synthesizer Guild will, no doubt, eventually encounter and shun its upstart competitor, the trans-ultimate synthesizer.

The future may guarantee faster Guild turnover, but the internal structure and dynamic remain the same. The message here is simple: however universally facilitative an innovation seems at the time, someone is sure to arise who makes a new mastery out of it. Once that seed is sown, skill is called out of retirement, and the tradition of tradition-building gets yet another new start.

Part II

CHALLENGES TO THE MODEL

3

PERFORMANCES AND MUSICAL
WORKS

Introduction

Are composed, notated musical works primary in the musical enterprise? Are performers and, derivatively, their performances in some sense subordinate or subservient to the notated work? One strong expression of the subordination of performance to the composed work is phrased as a near commonplace in the venerable *Harvard Dictionary of Music*. In the entry on 'Interpretation', after locating the performer as 'middleman' between composer and audience, performance is assigned its humble role of obeisance:

> A personal interpretation is the performer's great privilege, granted him by the composer. A really fine performer is always aware of the responsibility toward the work that this privilege imposes.[1]

Skill and craft give prominence to agency in music-making. If music is that primarily which is given, and if music-making thus radiates out from the performer, primacy of performance is assured; however, the notated work vies for equal, if not greater, musical standing.[2] Strongly put, the subordination view takes notated works as primary, and performance as functionally and ontologically subordinate to them. Why? Because, functionally, performance serves primarily to instantiate the work for listeners; and, ontologically, because the existence of much performance is contingent upon the work's existence.[3] Notated compositions, in Chapter 1, were embedded within constraint models. As components therein, such notated works set certain parameters for performance, but ones not singularly more significant than the others. Have composed musical works been undervalued? Has their true role been misrepresented?

Below, I examine the dominance relations between musical works and performance. Unless otherwise specified, by 'work' I refer to compositions as fixed or set in notation. Though this is not the only way compositions may be presented, it is, in the Western art music tradition, the most typical way most players become acquainted with a composition. Because players nearly always work directly from relatively fixed notated scores (very few working personally with composers), the musical work for them is most directly associated with the notated score.

This chapter examines the subordination view and finds it wanting. Not only does it over-value the status of fixed works; it underplays the fact that notated works massively underdetermine whatever emerges in performance. Underdetermination takes many forms. Notated works do not underdetermine performances quite on analogy with schematic diagrams in electronics which permit a limited range of substitutions but which nevertheless manage the critical details of real circuits. Better, perhaps, to conceive them in the way fossilized bone underdetermines the creatures the palaeontologist reconstitutes, all the soft tissue, the physiology, the behaviour, the very life demanding the palaeontologist's creative intervention. But this is not quite right either unless the musician's task were largely reconstructive of past musical life, and so largely a matter of fitting hypotheses to the elaborated facts. There is a truth the fossil bones bespeak. Music-making is not a form of truth-seeking or hypothesis testing. Better yet to conceive notated works as being frameworks, like story lines, scenarios, or scripts awaiting completion through collaboration by players and the receptive approval of the musical community and its audiences. As such, notated works are neither like types nor archetypes, but more closely resemble templates, sketches, outlines, or guides which, when consulted within the bounds of conventional approval, hold promise for workable and working music. If music is that which is made, works are that which is musically workable.

How would the subordination view affect what performers do? Supposing that the notated work dominates performance by imposing certain limitations on it, what might these limitations be? I consider two forms of limitation: first, the work limits the performer's creative options; and second, the work as relatively fixed creates tensions in performance because of possible conflicts in the performer's obligations to present the work both accurately and interestingly.

Regarding the former, I examine contrasts between improvisation and score-guided performance and conclude that, although creative options vary, they do not vary enough to suggest that score-guided playing is distinctively limited by works. If creative options do not vary significantly, and if improvisation is not, *ex hypothesi*, creatively limited by works, then neither is score-guided playing.

Regarding the second, the subordination view characterizes the work as autonomous and fixed, and yet performance practice demands variety and novelty. How is variety under fixity possible? Variety under fixity is made possible by the work's underdetermining its performances. Once we consider various types of underdetermination, the work, if fixed, may be less dominant and domineering than supposed. Indeed, the degree of variety invited in performance points to a sense of the full work veritably emerging in its performances, a condition typical of practices like story-telling. Interesting parallels between story-telling and music-making suggest that the performer becomes a collaborator in the full work. If so, then once again, the notated work fails to limit performance significantly.

Taken full strength, subordination makes performance an optional aspect of music, as secondary to the musical enterprise as reading novels aloud is to the present literary enterprise. I raise a number of concerns about unperformed 'readings' as supposedly adequate performance substitutes. Because of the many allusions to communication and language, the chapter sketches a critique of a speech model of performance, and closes with a picture of performing as a multi-faceted activity dedicated to a number of diverse ends.

Improvisation and score-guided playing

The subordination view gains credibility if improvisation and score-guided playing are significantly distinct; notably, regarding the control and authority the player has over the resulting sound. By reducing opportunities for perfor-mance creativity and invention, scored works presumably dominate performance. Assuming that composition and performance are distinguishable,[4] and that improvisational playing involves no scored work, we can conclude that the subordination view affects only score-guided playing.

What constraints are there on improvisation and score-guided playing? Do they differ significantly? Improvisation seems more immediate a form of music-making. Unlike improvisers, score-players make sounds in accordance with and because of external directives given in score. Ideally, improvisers fashion from their own inner resources a sequence of sounds *de novo*, owing little, if anything, to any other artist. This immediacy resembles painting's in many ways. It portends complete control over and freedom with the result, full accountability for its result, and full expressive individuality. Regarding the free (that is, impro-vised) fantasia K.P.E. Bach writes: ' . . . nothing more is required than a display of the keyboardist's skill . . . [I]n a fantasia the performer is completely free, there being no attendant restrictions'. For Bach, these free pieces are aesthetically special because they are 'expressive not of memorized or plagiarized passages, but rather of true, musical creativeness'.[5] Presumably, in using a score one's playing is tantamount to being expressive of 'memorized or plagiarized passages'. Further, though determinate melodic and chord sequences anchor much improvisation (for example, *My Funny Valentine* or *The Spanish Pavan*), improvisation is compatible with risk-taking.

By contrast, score-playing, as dependent upon and subordinate to some independent work, is primarily interpretive. Scores express what the composer wants the player to do. The player's skill is thus put at the disposal of the composer's will.[6] Further, performance success and failure are bound by the achievement of a correct rendition, a restriction foreign to improvisation.

This conception gives the absurd impression that score-playing is to improvi-sation as painting-by-numbers is to painting from blank canvas. In fact, nothing said above divides improvisation and score-guided playing so utterly as to make them stand in radically different relations to the music made. Consider that: scores invite performance discretion which generates extreme novelty even for the composer of the piece; as scores close off certain options, the creation of novelty becomes more difficult; this inspires players to exercise that much more ingenuity and to expand invention in areas remaining open for musical elaboration; because composed works are often musically more sophisticated and extended than the results of much impromptu playing, the former actually offer surplus opportunities for expression and novelty over the latter; the 'completely free' players whom K.P.E. Bach praises are constrained not only by standard musical conventions – one isn't free to make musical nonsense – but by their own musical imagination which may be singularly dull; and, anyway, there is considerable overlap between highly disciplined improvisation and highly discretionary score-guided performance.[7] So if works subordinate performances, that cannot come from systematically imposing creative limitations which are always absent in improvisation.

Fidelity, musicality, and instantiation

Notated works may dominate performances by creating tensions in them. Score-players assume two obligations between which conflicts can arise: to render the work (1) accurately, and (2) creatively, interestingly, imaginatively. Notation fixes many details. Creative playing involves adding novelty and variety to performance. Tensions between the work's fixity and performance variety complicate the relation between works and performances.

Such tensions between stricture and licence re-surface in the conception of performances as instantiations of notated works.[8] The work-performance relation is often analysed in terms of couples: type-token, universal-particular, or kind-instance. Though these couples are distinguishable, works are generally considered abstract entities; performances are concrete particulars.[9] Since notated works typically pre-date most of their instantiations, and since much music-making is undertaken in order to instantiate works, notated works constitute a standard for their instantiations. Instantiation is an achievement, a mark of having met some standard, but success is neither monolithic nor absolute. Consider the normative aspects of fidelity and musicality: does the performance succeed as an identifiable instance of a given work? Is it faithful to the work as scored?, and, is the performance an aesthetically interesting instance of the work?

Clearly, fidelity may be met where musicality fails, and not every musically successful performance need be exceptionally accurate; so, 'A given performance instantiates a given work only if the performance meets all the fidelity and musicality conditions for the work', is excessive.

The success of an instantiation depends upon its purpose. Compare instantiation for the purposes of faithful exemplification and for musicality. The conventional benchmark for exemplification is thorough fidelity to the score, the prime virtue being note-perfect execution. But successful exemplification does not guarantee a musically satisfying rendition. Further, obsessive preoccupation with exemplification can detract from musicality. This is reflected in complaints about awesome technical playing which comes off as mechanical. At times, musicality may even demand breaches of exemplification to improve the original's aesthetic potential. Two cases prompt exemplification breaches: (1) composers sometimes write strictly according to the abstractly theoretical harmonic and melodic demands of the passage, ignoring instrumental idiosyncrasies; and (2) composers familiar with one set of instruments write for other instruments in the idioms typical of their favourites. Violinists may have to abide pianistic structures, or oboists violinist structures.[10]

Musicality depends upon the notated work and practice conventions, but extends beyond both to the player's creative contribution. Creativity cannot typically create problems for performance. Though a competent rendition may be musical, the height of musicality (in contrast to exemplification) requires some departure from routine. This makes specifying exceptional musical success in advance as impossible as predicting the most remarkable inventions of the next decade. While the most successful exemplifying instantiations display maximum mutual resemblance, the best musical instantiations display prominently interesting variation. This is because exemplification seeks uniformity to match what is fixed in the work, while musicality displays the player's individuality and imagination.

Though one cannot achieve musicality wholly at the expense of exemplification without jeopardizing the identity of the work, exemplification and musicality can conflict, especially if the fidelity conditions close off many interpretive options.

The fixity of the work

However fixed the notated work, its details cannot interfere excessively with variability in the instance. Otherwise performing works would be akin to minting coins. On the other hand, musicality scarcely requires that one use only the immediate resources of one's imagination. Just how compromised is the discretion available to the score-player? This is basically to ask: How is variety under fixity possible? which, in turn, prompts the question: What is the nature of a work's fixity? Whatever the answers, notated works must allow highly varied instances to meet the expectations in performance.[11] Notated works which tolerated a single type of instance would not be works-for-performance as we know them, but would instead satisfy certain composers who have turned to electronic instantiation precisely to avoid the variety typical of instantiation by so-called 'interpreters'.

The work-performance relation can be conceived as a one–many relationship between types and their tokens. Performances are spatiotemporally delimited events; works are abstract entities. Though made by human beings, works seem not quite of this world. They share theoretical space with patterns, structures, designs, theories, schemas, and other abstracta. Some regard works as autonomous fixed entities, particularly after the death of the composer. What sort of fixity is this? Though scores can be edited and revised, the underlying object of these operations may be thought to survive. One may always revisit the work, the contents of which are definitively determined by its author operating in a precise context of creation.[12] Thus conceived, works cannot be destroyed the way spatio-temporal particulars can. Left alone, a painting is fixed as a work, but mutilation can change paintings utterly. No abstract design lurks behind the piece of coloured cloth ready to bear the standard should its 'en-canvassed' instance fall in battle.[13]

The fixity of musical works embraces both precise security of details and immunity from change. However conceived, the fixity of the work must typically be consistent with the opportunities for novelty expected in performance. This makes the work's fixity quite unlike the definiteness of general abstracta such as formal logical structures or unlike the unalterability of the past, say.[14] As will be argued, a more fruitful comparison is with stories, parables, legends, and jokes. That a tale is fixed in structure, plot, or theme, and yet admits instantiations which add local colour is familiar enough. Such works effectively are frameworks. This mode of variety under fixity will later be considered as a fruitful model for musical invention.

Underdetermination

What is it about works that makes possible their enjoying many distinctive instances? It must be either the paucity of detail in the scored work, and/or, the permissiveness of the work regarding its allowable instances. It is essential to works that their instances await creation rather than mere realization; that is, exactly what any instance will be like must be inaccessible from acquaintance with the work alone. Certain features, musically central to performances, are not specified in score. Hence, the scored work only partially determines what counts as an adequate instance. In brief, notated works underdetermine their performances.[15]

Are these 'extras' there all along, implicit in the practice conventions of the period of composition? However we unpack historical conventions, these still must be compatible with the very instantial variety expected when these works were new. Whatever one builds centrally into the work, some performance aspects will remain undetermined. Otherwise, there could be only one acceptable interpretation. How might we characterize underdetermination? Given that works are typically represented as scored, scores underdetermine performances in two ways; namely, regarding musical content and musical directives. Such content and directive accounts are examined below.

Structural content accounts

Works are sometimes described as 'structures' or 'patterns' to emphasize their organizational nature. Structural content accounts stress the musical materials constituting any work. Since the critical constituents are ordered pitches, we may consider scores as primarily depicting abstract acoustic structures.[16] On this account, underdetermination comes down to the score's systematically falling short of furnishing a complete acoustic musical description of whatever happens in performance. There is both a structural incompleteness here and a related epistemic gap. Knowing a score well is insufficient for knowing everything musical offered in performance.

Further, the work underdetermines the performance causally in that the score fails to supply a complete explanation of any performance. The score might explain why, as a performance of some work, this performance consisted of thus-and-such a pitch sequence. But one would be at a loss, relative to the content in score, to explain why a certain passage was executed with a peculiarly aggressive *marcato*. Both descriptive and explanatory underdetermination fall under the structural conception of works.

Directive set accounts

Structural content accounts depict the work as an object with parts. One may also consider the work as a directive (or imperative) set; that is, an ordered set of instructions or commands rendered thus in score. So, a black dot on the top line of a staff with treble clef and without sharp signs tells a guitarist at least this: Stop fret #1 on string #1. For players, pitch notation often might as well be tablature which is overtly directive. This fits both traditional and avant-garde music well.

Underdetermination here has negative and positive aspects. Negatively, the work fails to direct the player in all relevant respects. The score is thus an incomplete instruction set. Typically, far from being taken as a deficiency, one simply regards the directive gaps as brute facts about notation, and indicative, perhaps, of the composer's interests. Had the composer really cared about precision regarding certain parameters, instructions could have been invented to cover them. That composers accept certain stock interpretive options saves them the nuisance of having to clutter their notation. It also suggests that these options are adequate enough, however unexclusive. For instance, many eighteenth-century composers settled for a few generic symbols to indicate a trill here or an appoggiatura there. By contrast, J.S. Bach was uncommonly thorough in writing graces out in detail. His contemporary Johann Scheibe complained about Bach's cramping people's playing style: 'Every ornament, every little grace, and everything one thinks of as belonging to the method of playing he expresses completely in notes . . .'.[17]

Positively, the incompleteness of the directives reads as an open invitation to discretionary collaboration. The player is entrusted to complete the work in sound as if the composer were saying: 'I have taken you this far. You, player, must now create these further aspects of the work'. The undirected aspects become the *ad libitum* domain of the player. Here compositional underdetermination is complemented by and effectively demands player self-determination.

Though the structural content or directive set accounts are compatible, each reflects a difference of perspective about the relative importance of works and performances.[18] To suppose that works are abstract sound structures reinforces the view that works and performances belong to distinct ontological categories. Strikingly, performances are simply unnecessary to music abstractly conceived. The existence of a work is not dependent upon its ever being played. Performances from score live entirely borrowed lives. This ontological hierarchy thus attributes a 'greater degree of reality' to the work than to its instances. In contrast, taking works as directive sets, we diminish their abstractness and thus collapse the ontological hierarchy. Instruction sets are ontologically humbler than content structures. This ontological demotion of works and promotion of performances flows from the sense that commands to make sounds haven't quite the fullness of real sounds made. An ignored directive is pretty hollow. A law no one obeys is just words; a symphony no one plays just dots on yellowing paper. Just as authority hangs on obedience, directives gain credibility in being satisfied. Thus, an imperative does not live independently of its satisfaction as a structure can of its realization. The 'degree of reality' is reversed. An accent upon directives fosters the particularization of the work by having it live only through its living instances.[19] Though one may speak of the autonomy of directives, it is more awkward to talk of the existence of a command which will never be obeyed than of a structure which will never be constructed. Unlike structures, directives necessarily link to agents. Given a directive ('do thus-and-such'), one assumes the existence of a commander and a follower. Commanders command only when followers listen and obey.

Whichever account chosen, structural or directive, both depict the work as intrinsically underdetermined, skeletal, and incomplete.

Musical instantiation as invited variety

Underdetermination remains a negative characterization which signals a gap between works and their instances. To say merely that works underdetermine their instances does not specify how those instances relate to the work, nor does it warrant in itself any belief that the instances will display variety. Underdetermination merely enables the variety under fixity special to performances and works. Many contexts of underdetermination permit variety and novelty, but most are unhelpful. For example, pure randomness, emergentism, and biological variety all involve the underdetermination of occurrences. Unfortunately, none provides for the agency, deliberation, and appraisal called for in performance.

Musical instantiation is a goal-directed activity undertaken by agents intending to make representatives of the type. What counts as a passable representation varies from case to case.[20] Humans deliberately fashion copies according to some prototype in many ways. Not all tolerate instantial novelty to the same extent. Where only 'exact' copies are acceptable (typical in minting and semiconductor manufacturing), any instantial novelty signals a flaw. Sometimes, variety is tolerated within limits; for example, in industries like logging and agriculture where some latitude exists for departures from the 'standard' log or pumpkin. In other cases, novelty and variety are openly sought and positively virtuous. As an individualist art, making musical instances is distinguished from passive, routine, predictable forms of instantiating as occur in mechanical replication strictly governed under the aegis of a determinate stereotype. (Note that creating instantial variety is not a virtue in individual orchestral players. All the players of a section must play alike, the instantial variety of that unified sound being the responsibility of the conductor.) Creative music-making falls at the liberal end of instantiation and, thus, requires a context of underdetermination conducive to substantial discretion, control, and variety despite the fixity of the type. Summarizing some of the special qualities of musical instantiaton:

A performance is an acceptable instance of a work only if it involves actively making passable instances. Performance instances extend beyond passively, accurately and obediently matching sounds to notated works.

A performance is an exceptional instance of a work only if it involves actively making creatively novel instances.

Because the work underdetermines its instances, nothing conclusive in the scored work alone can determine that a given instance is exceptional. One learns and even decides what the work is like through making some of its instances.

Music-making as instantiating involves understanding and interpreting the work.[21]

These stress not only the calculated distance between work and instance, but also the contribution instantiation makes to giving and not merely revealing the full work to us. Musical instantiation is a form of initiation and intervention without which the work type has no more than the spectral quality of a promise of music. Indeed, the scored work alone is, in many ways, nothing more than possible music.

Often, the score is all that remains of the work, and represents, for us, the composer's final word. Though one learns something about the work through its score, this knowledge is, alone, as skeletal as the knowledge one has of a person through a biography. Knowing a work is not merely theoretically to anticipate its progress. To know a work is at least to know how to make it, to participate in its very progress by making it sound. This is because the work fully emerges only through its performances. Musical works, if types at all, are dependent types; that is, types the existence and qualities of which depend upon their instances.[22] The dependence of the work upon its performances is another way of describing a work's interpretive potential, the capacity of a work to sustain and be sustained by an abundant variety of performances. This two-way sustenance shows itself in the ongoing interest shown by players in the performance options left open for them, and in the continuing interest of audiences in hearing yet more instances of the same work. The work survives through the continuing diversity of its instances: 'It is the renewed vitality of each performance that keeps [Mozart and Beethoven] alive'.[23] The instantiation style which is most conducive to performance freedom falls within a broad category containing diverse forms of creative communication, and which involves a form of bilateral contribution.

Is performance necessary?

I have indicated sympathy for a participatory notion in which the full work emerges in its instances. Contrary to this is the view that 'hearing an instantiating sequence of sounds is no more strictly necessary for acquaintance with a work of music than hearing an oral reading is for acquaintance with a work of literature', the appeal here being made to forms of 'silent reading'.[24] Though raising the theme of music as communication, the analogy with reading fails in the following ways.

First, as Descartes noted regarding mental images of thousand-sided figures, there are limits to inner soundings. A work with a thousand simultaneous parts cannot plausibly be an object of inner sounding. If 'acquaintance with X' means 'non-mediated sensory experience of X', score-reading will often fail to acquaint the reader with the work. If 'acquaintance' means just 'theoretical understanding', this is as distant from the work as biochemical information about humans is from an appreciation of them as living animals.

Second, if the work is conceived for an instrument the sound of which one has no experience of, one cannot form any such idea a priori. To be acquainted with the work as a baryton trio, one has to conceive it thus. One cannot do so without ever having heard a baryton.

Third, on the silent reading view, music is only contingently a performing art. It is as if music performance were a stopgap, convenience, or optional amusement. This does not follow just because music has an independently 'readable' notation. If it were so, we need never bother realizing drama scripts, cooking recipes, and labanotation in theatre, food, and dance. But this is eccentric. The readability of a notation does not make of it a form of frozen speech capable of being played back in the mind without remainder. That one can hear in one's head an imaginary performance is uncontroversial. That what one hears replaces a performance is as odd as saying that the imagined taste and smell of a dish read off a recipe satisfies one's hunger. Furthermore, such a view makes meaningless the banal observation that some works are virtuosic, some elementary. Does it take greater skill to 'audiate' very fast scale passages rather than slow ones? If this is a skill at all, it is not musicianly skill. Why would anyone bother with the latter, if musical equivalence were to hand in the mind's ear?

Finally, performance always faces the risk of failure. One may get the notes right but quite misconstrue the work. One can discover one's problems and then correct them. Private 'audiations' are systematically insulated from the ambient environment critique performance lives in. If becoming acquainted with the work in one's head involves the same demands as becoming acquainted with it in public, presumably one can get it all wrong. How might one know this? What constrains one's inner performance? If a reading is not at all like an inner performance, how could it simulate internally all the necessarily acoustic qualities of performance?

For these reasons, 'readings' of works in score cannot substitute for 'hearing an instantiating sequence of sounds' as a means of acquainting oneself with a work. Further, merely hearing such a sequence can never inform one about a work as fully as instantiating it. This is surely because the unperformed work is systematically incomplete.[25]

Performance is more than the player's subservience to the composer. It demands a collaboration between the scored work and performer, the details of which are constrained by various limiting agreements which determine outer boundaries of discretion. Talk about agreement is akin to talk about contracts. Informally, such agreements are embodied in the various constraint models in play at any one time, all of which are subject to ongoing re-evaluation and re-negotiation. Often, all we possess are the notated skeletons and fragmentary evidence about practice from old instructional manuals, recordings, paintings, and reviews. We choose the flesh to clothe these skeletons. But, we are no more bound by these particular constraints than we are by the relics of protocol in social interaction. Talk of collaboration may even suggest too mutual an interaction between player and work. Sometimes, the scored work is rather more the silent partner in the business of performance which carries the message: 'Here is some musical capital. Run with it. Invest and profit'.

Making the type: performing as story-telling

In performing, more occurs than someone's making a formal structure audible through compliance with an instruction set. The scored work benefits in its instantiations, as do all dependent types. A group of familiar practices exemplify this dependency. Consider the story-teller, the reciter of legends, the comedian. Each draws upon a story, a saga, a joke, as material for recounting. The story, saga, or joke is not completely captured within notational structures because these are too determinate. Unlike theories, stories are not analogous to structures of true propositions, independent of their articulation, and somehow answerable to the external world. Stories, jokes, and legends are completely within the ambit of and controlled by people. We decide what stories there are, what distinguishes them, and what they are about. Such Anglo-Saxon perennials as *The Legend of Robin Hood* are not ossified enough to boast an embalmed authorized version. The elements of the legend may include reference to a time, a place, a few supporting characters, some character traits and exploits, but we have here nonetheless a skeleton, a modest story frame. Even where so-called authorized versions exist, it is unclear whether anyone has any categorical reason to abide by someone's claim to authority, since one may always question by whose authority such versions have been sanctified. Of course, there must be some stable elements, but exactly which ones take precedence will be subject to negotiation and debate. Here's one famously unauthorized version:

'Do you know Robin Hood, Huck?'
'No. Who's Robin Hood?'
'Why he was one of the greatest men that was ever in England – and the best. He was a robber.'
'Cracky, I wisht I was. Who did he rob?'
'Only sheriffs and bishops and rich people and kings, and such like. But he never bothered the poor. He loved 'em. He always divided up with 'em perfectly square.'
'Well, he must 'a' been a brick'.
'I bet he was, Huck. Oh, he was the noblest man that ever was. They ain't any such men now, I can tell you. He could lick any man in England, with one hand tied behind him; and he could take his yew bow and plug a ten cent piece every time, a mile and a half.'
'What's a *yew* bow?'
'*I* don't know. It's some kind of bow, of course. And if he hit that dime only on the edge he would set down and cry – and curse. But we'll play Robin Hood – it's noble fun. I'll learn you.' [26]

The same tales and jokes are recounted in different guises. Since replication is possible, we should be able to state the identity conditions, and also to assess the acceptability of the instances. What counts as telling the same tale or joke can be couched in both a strict and an indulgent way.

Strictly speaking, telling-the-same-joke reduces to the-same-telling-of-the-joke; that is, with no verbal or even intonational variation. This imitative con- ception of jokes, friend to a die-stamp conception of instantiation, would guarantee the death of humour. No such stringency could be taken seriously unless one deliberately built in stringent limits within the prototype, for example,Woody-Allen's-joke-about-the-pet-ant-just-as-Woody-did-it-in-his-show-on-May 3rd-1965. Anyone held to that routine would be bound as an impersonator and not as a comedian. Such is the sentence passed on those slavishly devoted to the letter of fidelity.

Indulgently speaking, one acknowledges that successful comedians not only vary instances of the same joke in their routines; they often calculatedly invent new approaches to old material, cleverly reworking and thereby sustaining humour in an otherwise stale gag.

Stories and jokes not only admit of but are often improved by inventive elaboration where no accountability to the truth intrudes. Detail may be added which owes little to reality. Whereas the embellished police report amounts to falsifying evidence, the newly redecorated story wins praise. Fictions firmly anchored in reality cannot be stretched as broadly as can looser flights of fancy. If Sherlock Holmes lives at 221B Baker Street in 1885, he has a shorter walk to Regent's Park than to Charing Cross. To confound this vitiates the point of giving his address and forces upon the reader a gratuitous revision of London geography. Where one lives by the truth, therein is one constrained by the truth. There is no escaping it entirely. Fictions lacking all anchors would be unintelligible.

Anchors to the world impose external constraints upon fictions. Fictions are bound by internal constraints as well, but these may shift and wander. One may set the story of Robin Hood in modern times with differing villains and adventures, yet the story continues. One might have only to retain a central protagonist who 'robs from the rich to give to the poor'. Robin Hood, the ruthless mobster who runs protection rackets might never convince, though that never dampens curiosity about the 'other side' of Robin Hood. Is this the mere retention of a name for gimmicky purposes? But why should anyone accuse thus, as if there were some HRM Robin Hood Official Standard Measure. If we welcome the Dark Side of Robin Hood, that suffices to give Robin his badge of Satan. Sherlock Holmes has recently joined just such schematized DIY figures, who, having burst free of his Doylean shackles, busts bad guys guilty of perversities no Victorian raconteur would dare to have conceived.[27] One must take make-believe seriously for what it is. Are we just extending a character rather than a story? Yet the character could be the story.

What can change without loss of story or character identity is often a function of what we want to change, or what change we tolerate. The identity of the legend, story or character is profoundly flexible; hence, a story may evolve over time. This could be crucial in keeping the story alive for later generations. Thus it both grows and strengthens in change. The prototype itself undergoes modification through the novelty of its instances. 'Some stories just cannot change!' one might protest. But stock, quasi-fictional, legend-laden, Western figures like Socrates and Christ have enjoyed centuries of varied invention in art, literature, television and film. Fresh lore emerges constantly and invites elaboration. Relatively recent durables include Wyatt Earp and Al Capone who already enjoy numerous incarnations, especially in film and television, the public story-telling media of our time. The late Princess Di may well enter the sphere of hardy tales and legends. Nor need the inventory exclude the purely fictional if we consider Philip Marlowe and James Bond who have quite overgrown the compounds of their mortal makers. It takes a real effort to keep a good story still; none at all to get it moving. This prompts reconsideration of the notion of types and, correspondingly, their fixity. Detailed fixity strangles the potential for new instances, and likely strangles itself thereby.

93

Good story-telling demands leniency regarding the prototype or frame. Stretching the truth gets to become a lie; stretching the fiction breeds new and sometimes livelier fiction. Successful replication of jokes or stories demands invention. A joke instance which succeeds will avoid loyal fidelity to some prototype, distinguish itself from all other copies of the same prototype, and be adroit at taking liberties with the expected. Jokes and stories, unlike police reports and research papers, are exactingly judged on their ability to survive second tellings. A joke religiously repeated after a short interval fails to be funny. Faithful word-for-word replication is just boring, a tedious mimicry of some past delight which, in virtue of its very fidelity, kills all future prospect for delight.[28]

The baseline story itself is never enough, and may be hardly anything at all. It is more a frame for a full story, fully told – a veritable framework. This places great responsibility upon the story-teller who must both maintain continuity with the story expected by the listener but also entertain and move by not boring the listener with a glut of the expected. To be able to remake the same story interestingly each time it is told is to exercise a craft. How recreating is accomplished will vary from person to person. The finer details make up the tricks, secrets, and genius of the trade.

All this has a bearing upon musical works and their performances. The activities run parallel in many respects, particularly regarding the call for varied instances, the communicative point in creating the instances, the skill employed in accomplishing such variation, the deep underdetermination of the instance by its type, and the general grounds for accepting and appreciating any given instance. This should come as no surprise. The practitioners are all performers, each one obliged to do something new for someone listening. The performer intentionally brings about something which cannot be just a chip off the old block of the work itself.[29]

Are the parallels between the musician and raconteur undermined by seemingly major differences between scored works and familiar tales? The traditional tale or joke is extremely flexible and seems to tolerate all manner of modification and embroidery. Though some elements must persist, tales do not impose such rigid constraints upon their instances to match those imposed upon performances by typical scores. The scored work seems far more fixed and final.[30] On this misgiving, a few reflections.

One might suppose that, for the performance-work pair, translation from one language into another is more fitting an analogy. After all, translators are bound to a fixed text and more beholden to that base than the story-teller is to a storyline. All considered, translations themselves run along a spectrum from the literal to the free. Nothing in the original in itself decides which translation style is ultimate or privileged. The many incarnations of Homer's work have, each one, borne the stamp of its interpreter and its age. It is not as though there is a fixed semantic bedrock awaiting the translator's removal of surface detritus. Especially with poetry, some translations emphasize the structure and metre; other translations aim to preserve the gist; still others, to free the spirit.

Because music notation has no semantic underlay, its rendition in sound must be at least as open to elaboration as any text is to its translation.[31]

Stricture and licence come by degrees. Stories, legends, and jokes do not exhibit equal looseness. Some seem to demand more consistency across their instances than others. Story-telling happily incorporates play-acting which, when offered as formal drama, owes as much or as little to any written script as performing does to any scored work.

Scored works differ markedly in their detail, some being vastly less restrictive than others depending on the period and composer. Whatever allegiance is owed to the score, the historical range of tolerances in scores is very broad. Nothing compels us to regard the more constraining scores of the common practice period as typical of anything but their own conventions.

That musical works are fundamentally spare and flexibly structured, and that they are invitations to collaborative elaboration comes out forcefully in practices like transcription and arrangement. Most scored works allow great instantial variety even if we follow the notation and instrumentation literally. We frequently alter the scored work's literal bounds to allow further instantiation opportunities. In transcriptions and arrangements, both instrumentation and textual content are themselves varied, as if the strict details of the scored work have no more definitive hold on practitioners than the hard, real life details had on the *Lives* of Plutarch. Transcriptions willy-nilly open a solo oboe work to pianists, cellists, trombonists, whole orchestras. How very different in kind is this from having Sherlock Holmes track down Nazi sympathizers in Washington? Note that transcriptions do not stand to scored works as do performances. This complicates matters, but not unintelligibly; for scored works can clearly have as instances both concrete particulars like performances as well as dependent types like transcriptions and arrangements. Still, if an acceptable performance of a work is an instance of that work, so, by parity, an acceptable transcription of a work is also an instance of that work. And if musical blood-lines count, any instance of a transcription of a work is also an instance of that work, once removed, so to speak. That the transcription itself is a work is immaterial. What is significant is that works, like stories, are structurally flexible enough to spawn genetically related but often strikingly different looking offspring.

Taking stock, story-telling was introduced as a model of instantiation for the relationship between works and performances in order to give prominence to the high degree of creative variety we attribute to and value in musical performance. This creative variety seemed headed for conflict with the presumed dominance and fixity of the musical work, thus leading to tensions between obligations of strict fidelity and of innovative musicality. No tensions arise once we re-assess the so-called dominance of the scored work. The story-teller mode removes any threats of tension between type and instance by making deliberate variation a priority. This variety is neither optional nor risky once one respects that stories and musical works are dependent types, or frameworks. The very substance of a story grows out of its telling; its depth and longevity hang entirely upon the creative ingenuity of its tellers.

The story-teller mode fits musical instantiation well. Specifically, the aspects of invited variety, the notion of participating in determining the nature of the full work, and the primacy of presentation all square nicely with the activity-laden notion of performance endorsed throughout. The story-teller mode also emphasizes the value of skill in performance, the high demands and virtues of control, and the communicative element in performing. Finally, this view of the relationship between works and performances puts the former in their proper musical place primarily as vehicles and opportunities for the latter in the larger business of making music.

4

COMPUTERS, READYMADES, AND ARTISTIC AGENCY

Introduction

In Chapter 2 performance was portrayed as a primary action craft, a category attaching intrinsic significance to a craft's skills and methods. Results are acknowledged and valued only if they are achieved using specified means under specified handicaps. The recognized means and handicaps are regulated and appraised by a Guild-like community through various pedagogical and competitive institutions. Such communities are constitutionally conservative. The fundamental ways musicians now make beautiful noises on their winds, strings and drums have not varied much in millennia. The primary machines of music are still run on elemental human physical energy, however coated with a veneer of valves, plastics, and gears. This inherent conservatism displays itself in the face of new designs to radically facilitate practice. This chapter examines further certain ways in which two foundational assumptions for primary crafts have been by-passed in recent developments in the arts, and what implications this has for performance traditions.

Two challenges to agency

Computer-assisted music, musical quasi-readymades, and experimental music challenge the centrality of immediate agency. For those with a stake in the traditions, it is worthwhile to expose these developments as neither threats nor alternatives to performance paradigms. Instead, at their best, they represent new enough ways of dealing with sound as to merit consideration as new artforms, much as photography and film have become.

In the first two parts below, I consider cases where primary causation or skill is absent and how this affects any primary craft model. Examples of these are drawn from computer-assisted arts and readymades. In 'Challenging primary causation', I argue that when primary causation is absent, the notion of performance undergoes major change. When based on indirect causation, a distinctive synthetic form of art-making emerges. 'Challenging skill' argues that when skill is no longer essential, so many value-regulating mechanisms are thereby abandoned as to force a re-consideration of the very nature of the artform itself.

Any primary action craft centrally involves primary causation and manual skill. Traditionally, both music and the concrete arts (painting and sculpture) belong to this category. Is this status integral to them? Aren't there viable types of music and painting which do not summon primary causation or manual skill? In the concrete arts, don't computer art and readymades display just the features we seek? Thus one might claim that:

• the use of computers in painting and music changes basic agency relationships. There is a non-primary causal link between agent and result because immediate control over the product may be absent or vestigial. Skill, however, is still required.

• Regarding classical readymades like Duchamp's *Fountain* or recent beach art such as Harding's *A Piece of Driftwood*, the artist's skill is not displayed in the object displayed. The object may have been made by some stranger for some utterly distinct purpose, or fashioned by the forces of nature. *A fortiori* such cases eliminate primary causation.

Might this worry about skill miss the mark? Doesn't the Romantic view of immortal art declare any concern with skill, training, and the soiling of hands incidental to art's true generative processes? Isn't the artist guided by otherworldly forces? Isn't art the fruit of inspiration, creation arising *ex nihilo*? Some nurture misty images of the artist possessed whose work erupts magically and spontaneously from the smoke and fury of chaos. Romantic tales abound about the demonic frenzy of Paganini in concert. Who can avert the glowering stare of the leonine and ever-angry Beethoven, frozen in countless ceramic busts, scowling down titanically from the craggy heights of the neighbourhood teacher's upright?

However seductive, such accounts overlook the dead ends, the re-takes, the rehearsals, the horse work. They are prone to confuse passionate, obsessive dedication for magic. Nor can these fantasies explain the bedrock of consistency and reliability one reasonably expects from good artists. Inspired touches survive only atop a disciplined base. If Paganini, frenzied, could play brilliantly twice in a row, the frenzy was either for the paying guests or an inadvertent epiphenomenon.[1]

Challenging primary causation: indirect causation

Remote control

Primary causation involves direct control. Not all causation is primary. Causation is indirect when what the maker does skilfully is at a significant procedural remove from the final effect. Indirect causation is standard in computer art and music. I will call the process 'remote control'.

'Significant remove' involves more than a matter of degree. An extra-long paint brush places a painter at a great but not significant remove from the painting. Direct control allows hand tools and thereby does not require literal hands-on procedures. However, contiguous hands-on control occupies a privileged place. Traditional tools are conceived derivatively, their ancestors being primary physical manipulations. As extensions of the body, they yield results no different in kind from those available to the unassisted limb. Hand tools are used to strike, puncture, shear, sever, shape, mix, dig, and spread the very materials the hands would otherwise contact contiguously. These are all primitively manual options which tools are designed to facilitate. What about soldering or brazing? Again, these employ heat to materials in order to bond them. Nothing vastly different goes on when I soften a piece of wax in my hands. Lasers are different. Tools refine manipulation not only by protecting the hands; they also often allow greater control over fine or gross detail.

Marginal cases exist; for example, manipulation of microscopic objects or hand-work on extremely massive or hard items. One cannot etch a 'very large scale integrated' circuit by hand nor carve the Great Sphinx with one's fingernails. These, however, reflect little more than degrees of physical scale rather than kinds of process. A tiny human could hand-embroider a silicon chip, and a giant could hand-maul a stone deity.

One cannot, however, hand-fire electrons at a phosphor-coated screen, physically move binary code into a memory register, or manually transmit electromagnetic waves. One cannot do any sort of manual job at these, not even a sloppy job. These are veritably out-of-body processes.[2] Though the boundary is not absolute, in some cases the tool clearly extends the body, and, in others, the tool clearly transcends the body. When I speak of a significant remove between maker and work, and of remote control only, I have in mind the use of tools for results no even unrefined version of which can be manually accomplished.

Remote control in the arts

Causally indirect art-making processes using computers are commonplace. Because computer processes must intercede between the user and the result, these processes are indirect avenues to the result from the perspective of the agent. Hence, computer art involves remote control.

Should we place any store in remote control? Won't remote control seem like direct control if we ignore the distinction between hardware and wetware? After all, our brains intercede between our movements and what they result in. Perhaps we're conceiving direct control too primevally. Though computer graphics artists don't make images by applying coloured stuff, surely they use programs and computers just as painters use pigments and brushes or sculptors use rock and chisels.

We must be cautious. Any temptation to merge the nexus of computer, software, and digital drafting devices with that of the complex comprising brushes, pigments, and canvas should be scrutinized. The computer 'painting' is an electronically generated image which dies with voltage drop. Stored on disk, it is less like an image than it is a directive set magnetically etched in metallic oxide. Computers produce code, not colour.

The same applies to the relation between computer music and the simpler complex of player and instrument.[3] The audible sound caused proximately by a computer comes immediately from an amplified playback system, just like the sound from a CD. Computer music is not performed; it is played back. The music exists on file as a decodable magnetic pattern. One processes the code through a sequencer program. The code, which is the ultimate source of the sound, can be created, accessed, and made meaningful only via a program.

Even if the causal process in making computer art and music is indirect, one might think that remote control leaves everything else where it was. The use of indirect causation may have no more impact on the artform generally than, for example, the acceptance of new materials like nylon and acrylics or new tools like spraycans. After all, the value of skill and the ideals of craftsmanship survive in computer art even though immediate physical handicraft is displaced by a form of design skill.

The similarities between manual and computer painting are, however, superficial. Remoteness of control breeds a remoteness from the primary crafts. The skills deployed in painting and computer art differ in kind. The painter's skills include knowing how to control the display of colour. This translates into knowing how one's body enters into one's work. Primary craft skill exemplifies self-control. The computer artist's skills include knowing how to control the machine's electronic display. Some machine controls may even simulate aspects of real painting (for example graphics tablets), but no one fusses about the physical idiosyncrasies of the pigment. Anyway, the type of computer input device is completely optional. One could use voice control, or even another computer to supply input to the first.

In Chapter 2, a work of primary craft constituted a spatio-temporal 'signature' of the artist. This skill signature influences our attribution of worth to a work. Crafts dedicated to perfectionism appeal to this signature to distinguish results which are otherwise indistinguishable. This skill signature never emerges in an electronic medium. Computer images are not the immediate products of the artist's hand and hence record no story about the artist's immediate physical intervention. The work's physical qualities are detached from the artist's physical activities. This might explain their often seeming to have no identifiable earthly source.[4] No observation of the computer-generated image reveals what the artist physically did in creating the work. Anyway, such information is of no special interest in computer art because masterful computer technique requires no manual dexterity.

Primary causation belongs to those primordial acts of labour Locke thought essential to human nature which flow from our need to control the material world and thereby make it part of us.[5] Remote control is a form of making by analogical extension only. It is an intellectual design strategy having none of the immediacy of daubing pigments on cloth. The computer's internal functions have no clear counterpart in the world of brushes and coloured pastes. They are not neurological stand-ins or brain substitutes. We don't build and program our brains in order to alter canvas.

The respective technical virtues differ. Manual skills such as steadiness and exactitude play no role in computer art. Computers are uncommonly forgiving. One can always take back mistakes, indeed anything, on a computer with an utter invisibility unknown to manual operations. Computer technique instead involves facility with command sets. Because input options vary, good computer technique partially calls on the ability to exploit fully the opportunities provided by the software used.

Why even classify computer art along with primary art? I suspect little more is at work here than vestiges of meaning and some sentimental associations. Computer art is no more a species of painting than photography is. Computer cases are associated with primary crafts because of a reminiscence of common creative construction. Computer artists do something akin to bringing new objects into being from some elemental materials no prior examination of which could reveal the final outcome. But computerized bringing-to-be and handling of the elements are distantly metaphorical. However similar the creative foreplay, not much else is.

The use of computers in music is even more remote from traditional performance than computer art is from primary painting. Computers are not musical instruments as keyboard synthesizers clearly are, nor does the use of sequencing software constitute playing of any sort. The remoteness of control bears no likeness whatever to the elementary agency of performance. Sequencers are sound-processors, akin to word-processors in storage, editing, and related data functions. Just as no one would call the creation of a drama using a word-processor 'computer acting', so the creation of music using a sound-processor is scarcely 'computer performance'. But we have here more than a fancy composition typewriter. Sequencers provide direct and authoritative playback. To hear what one has sound-processed, one opens the file which directly delivers a sound sequence (and optionally a visual display of the sound using colour, graphs, or any other scalar representation). Suppose, in using a word-processor to write a play, one could assign to each character part a unique computerized voice. Suppose, further, one could precisely modulate such computer-voices for each word and sentence so that one could play back one's script in voices, exactly as one wanted the lines to sound. That's what sequencers do.

The computer sequencer is a comprehensive composition-playback tool which allows the operator to bypass performance altogether and to create an immediate, definitive sounded version. Computer use thus 'liberates' the composer from the performer and the limits of conventional instruments. If, so to speak, the composer is first-person to the work as the player is its third-party, computers rid the composer of all third-party intervention. The result means the elimination of performance as such and its displacement by 'pre-cast' or 'presented' music; that is, playback which has been utterly and finally set up in advance.

The hunger for such first-person independence goes back decades. Lecturing in 1939 at the University of Southern California, Edgard Varèse addressed the frustrations and hopes of the composer:

> We composers are forced to use, in the realization of our works, instruments that have not changed for two centuries. . . . Personally, for my own conceptions, I need an entirely new medium of expression: a sound-producing machine (not a sound-reproducing one). . . . Whatever I write, whatever my message, it will reach the listener unadulterated by 'interpretation'. It will work something like this: after a composer has set down his score on paper . . . he will, then, with the collaboration of a sound engineer, transfer the score directly to this electric machine. After that, anyone will be able to press a button to release the music exactly as the composer wrote it. . . . Here are the advantages. . . . Liberation from the arbitrary, paralysing tempered system; the possibility of obtaining any number of cycles or if still desired subdivisions of the octave; unsuspected range in low and high registers, new harmonic splendours obtainable from the use of subharmonic combinations, new dynamics far beyond the present human power orchestra; a sense of sound projection in space by means of the emission of sound in any part or in as many parts of the hall as may be required by the score.[6]

Going a step further, Leopold Stokowski prophetically anticipated freedom from notation, and expressed the dream of the composer working directly in sound. In a 1932 address before the *Acoustical Society of America* called 'New Horizons in Music', Stokowski rues conventional notation which denies to composers the means to 'express all the possibilities of sound'. He predicts

> a time when the musician who is a creator can create directly into TONE, not on paper. . . . Any frequency, any duration, any intensity he wants, any combinations of counterpoint, of harmony, of rhythm – anything can be done by that means and will be done.[7]

We have arrived. However, instead of supplanting traditional performance, computers have given composers something new to do. These new prospects are not unlike those made available to playwrights and directors who moved from the stage to film. Now that pesky stage-prop limitations have been overcome, the next obvious move is to engineer the virtual TV or movie star – unageing, untemperamental, pliable, versatile, drug-free, and cheap.

Computers: assimilating sound and colour

Electronic imaging and composition are more like one another in processes, resources, skills, and problems than are their manual predecessors, 'hard-copy' painting and hands-on performance. Neither computer form demands manual dexterity nor registers any physical input traces in the output. Both require coded input, the mediation of a coding–decoding machine, and, intriguingly, allow the seamless inter-translation between aural and visual media. It is computationally straightforward to map sound onto colour, colour onto sound. Computer-assisted music can be made by creating computer graphics, and vice versa. By mapping shapes and hues onto sounds, one can 'perform' by 'painting'; and, equally, 'paint' by 'performing'.

Both machine performance and machine graphics involve retrieving and decoding for sensory access the same sort of information. Electronic music is essentially a form of sound display, a direct counterpart to electronic visual display. By contrast, plucking twisted gut, thumping stretched skins, and blowing through hollow reeds are procedurally independent.

The isomorphism of sound and colour display is a function of the highly delimited options for computer input and output. Every input, whether for sound or colour, is reduced to the selfsame machine code. Every output is precisely the input processed centrally and decoded from the same language for uptake and interpretation by human sensors. That a processed output goes to a screen or a speaker is all one to the computer. The uniformly quantized machine-accessible input suggests a hard information-reductionism for all outputs. Output is merely code which happens to be transfigured into sound or colour via add-on plugin playback machines – screens or speakers. By such means, the otherwise unitary output is made sensorially distinct for the benefit of the drab beasts whose information receptors are limited to detecting sounds and colours.

Painting metaphors are commonly used in traditional music description; for example, in our talk of musical shapes, colours, contours, and textures. We probably resort to painting metaphors because, biologically, sight is our most subtle and powerful sense. In computer contexts, these metaphors may merit upgrading to portrayals of real supervenient properties which share a common unifying foundation. Mark, this works in the currency of information theory only, which makes units of abstract information the fundamental particles of reality, their coded representation becoming the one common referring language. This monistic information-reductionism takes the superficially distinct dimensions of sound and colour and their respective artforms to be one at bottom.

The use of indirect methods does not upset the significance of primary crafts in the arts. With indirect causation, primary skill might become a fleeting reflection of our past. Remote control, however, does not intrude upon performance. Instead it presents a new way of exhibiting sound. Given the fundamental basis in information, that sound or colour is displayed is epiphenomenal compared with the fluid commerce the computer permits between what we (contingently) decode via our distinct modes of sensation. This trans-sensory free-trade zone signals the revolutionary character of computer art and the underlying unity of all computer arts. Primary crafts and their arts, on the contrary, will always be distinct because of their uniquely varied forms of causal intimacy. This categorical pluralism of the primary crafts is quite alien to the 'universal machine'.

Challenging skill: readymades

The products of primary causation are primitively describable as something-done. The products of primary skill are primitively describable as things-done-a-certain-way. Take away skill or prevent the artist from deploying it, and the intended result might never happen. Given this, how has the acceptance of certain 'found objects' as artworks affected the primary craft tradition? This development emerged most clearly in the concrete arts. Later on, I consider its implications for and applications to performance.

The readymades challenge

Need an artwork be an immediate product of skilled and trained human hands? Though painting and sculpture evolved and prospered as primary crafts, opposition was raised in *Fountain* (1917), a work by Marcel Duchamp (1887–1968) consisting of a standard white porcelain urinal. *Fountain* was joined by *In Advance of a Broken Arm* (a snow shovel) and *Bottlerack* (yes, a bottlerack). Nature's inventory supplemented that of industrial origin in Suzanne Harding's *A Piece of Driftwood* (1980). These works, aptly dubbed 'readymades', are now accepted as artworks and have significantly influenced modern conceptions of the arts.

Readymades are works of natural or industrial origin put forward as art by artists none of whose conventional physical training, skill, and dexterity accounts for the existence of the object displayed. No physical feature of readymades can be traced to any particular physical manipulations of the artist. I will call such artists 'readymakers' and what they do 'readymaking'.

In the primary crafts, 'the artist made the work' entails 'the artist primary-caused the work'. With readymades, the question 'Who made that?' invites a counter-question: 'Which? The bottlerack or *Bottlerack*?' For my purposes, whereas the readymaker readymade *Bottlerack*, he did not make the bottlerack. The existence of the readymaker is incidental to the existence of the physical bottlerack, ultimately displayed (if transformed) by the readymaker as art.

Basically, the process of readymaking consists in declaiming through exhibition certain objects to be artworks. Principally a presenter, the readymaker is more like an impresario, curator or retailer than a painter or sculptor. Though readymakers contribute titles to their objects, skill in naming is not a form of primary causation called for in painting, sculpting, or performing. Title-concocting requires intellectual imagination, but no bumping up against the world.

I speak here of pure readymades, though hybrids and mixed categories exist. Duchamp's adding a moustache and goatee to a print of the *Mona Lisa* and offering it thus as a new work suggests distinctions in levels of primary contribution. What links this more with pure readymades than primary craftworks is the indifferent manual skill employed by Duchamp in his creation of *L.H.O.O.Q.* Though one may think *L.H.O.O.Q.* conceptually provocative, one cannot appreciate it as a display of Duchamp's dexterity, however one admires the dexterity in the *Mona Lisa*.

Some crafted works incorporate found bits of the world. The figures in Duane Hanson's *Couple With Shopping Bags* (1976), though shaped from polyester resin and fibreglass, are fitted out in snappy K-Mart garb. Chunks of industrial waste are welded together as in Richard Stankiewicz's *Construction* (1957). The categories of primary crafting and readymaking thus do not exhaust either the types of makers or works available, but they do have their paradigmatic pure forms.

As an activity, readymaking is largely a passive (or even negative) process, marked by an indifference toward (or even contempt for) any primary skill traceable to the artist. If controlling the work requires that one determine the manifest qualities of the work, readymaking involves neither direct nor remote control. To label and exhibit a shovel may indicate daring and cleverness, but one's success hangs on no prior manual training. The object's native properties remain intact even after undergoing a category transplant to artworkhood. The readymaker, of course, is neither out of control of nor lacks control over the readymade. Such descriptions more aptly fit primary craftsmen gone berserk or randomly generated graphics which come as a novelty both to the programmer and spectator alike.[8]

In severing links between artworks and skilled handicraft, readymaking creates a gap not only between artist and artwork, but between the artist and regulative practice communities. To create readymades, no manual training is necessary. One is not answerable to external canons of achievement. There are no pedagogues, institutional controls, and professional ranks – no earning of professional standing. Instead, the baptismal designation of some object replaces the art-making authority that traditionally was vested in the professional environment responsible for the preservation of standards pertaining to the craft.

Implications, repercussions, further questions

Readymades upset a number of traditional conceptions of the arts largely because of what they leave out. For example, to accept naturally occurring items such as driftwood as artworks, one repudiates:

• the assumption of human origin; that is, that all human art comes from us, not directly from the earth;

• the ancient view linking art with the process of primary causation; that is, driftwood is not so much made into art, as 'discovered' by being declared to be art; and,

• the status of art as a technical pursuit, a process of crafting; that is, institutions dedicated to preparing art-makers for art-making become incidental or even obstructive.

To allow mass-produced items (manufactured independently of the artist's knowledge, will, and interests) to stand, physically unaltered, as art by that artist marginalizes handicraft. Readymades thus challenge:

• the status of the work as the artist's handicraft and so create a gratuitously peculiar attribution problem; that is, it is like displaying someone else's aesthetically indifferent production as if it were (suddenly) worthy of aesthetic attention, as one's own display; and,
• the notion of taking credit for a work; that is, credit for the creation of a work goes to a person whose history never intersected with that of the item's making. Normally, in the arts, one does not credit the discoverer of an artwork (hidden, say, for centuries and then unearthed) as one credits the creator of that work. With readymades, the difference between archaeology and creativity evaporates.

Readymades, further:

• eradicate the classical bases for classification and ranking; that is, since conventional artistic background is unnecessary and never deployed, no discernibly significant differences among artists exist regarding their individual styles, or the predominant influences upon their present work. As to rank, it becomes strained to talk of better or worse readymades or readymakers. If ranking criteria exist, they cannot reflect properties internal to the works – yet, if somehow they did reflect internal properties, ranking differences could not be attributed to any readymaking virtue; and,
• throw into confusion general principles concerning the essence and identity of artworks, as if the damage to fundamental agency and responsibility for works were not enough. Individual handicraft provided a clear causal locus for identification and individuation, as did the makers' determined stamp of individuality. Remove these and the question 'What makes this thing an artwork rather than just a bottlerack?' is going to be asked. More annoyingly, the question becomes complicated. If the bottlerack counts as an artwork, the status of artworks in general becomes unclear. Puzzles arise from cases of easily mistakable identity. This toothbrush lives to clean your teeth; that otherwise indistinguishable toothbrush called *Toothbrush*, though forever unfulfilled in its essential functional life, will be studied fawningly by flocks of cognoscenti.9

However engrossing these puzzles, my concern here is with the tendency of readymaking to trivialize primary skills in art. Let us allow that readymakers are artists in the same evaluative category as their primary craft colleagues. By this, I do not mean that what immediately makes for a good readymade also makes for a good craftwork. I intend something more general; for example, that, within the domain of the concrete arts, a readymade may be as worthy of aesthetic attention as a craftwork. (The readymade may be aesthetically worthy due to complex relational properties; for example, its making a valuable contribution to or being a powerful influence in the history of art.) Primary skill is irrelevant in readymades and so does not count in favour of the readymaker. If readymades and craftworks are aesthetically commensurable and comparable, and if dexterity – traditionally the hallmark of the accomplished artist – is abandoned, what compensates for or replaces the expectation and appreciation of primary skill? In brief, if, at one time, one could differentially assess art objects in part on the basis of the quality and type of skill required in their making, and, if such skill no longer figures as a common denominator for such judgement, whatever we use as the new common denominator – once we accommodate readymades – will rule out primary skill as evaluatively salient just because readymades require none of it. Primary skill is thus rendered aesthetically indifferent. As indifferent, it is dispensable. As dispensable it is trivial.

Alas, residual respect lingers about skill, one grounded in a primal sense of the bond between art and obstacle. Further, like nothing else, skill provides public grounds for positive appraisal. When primary skills count in artistic ranking, skill differences break deadlocks. If primary skill doesn't count, an evaluative vacuum appears. Readymades do not move us to forsake regard for primary skill in other contexts. Skill remains stubbornly entrenched, which explains perhaps why readymades are vulnerable to scorn, ridicule, spoof, and dismissal.

The lingering status of and regard for primary skill and its abandonment in readymades betokens an attitudinal tension. Despite their intellectual acceptance in art circles, readymades never mingle quite unnoticed. They smell of contrivance. Because of its relative clarity and traditional centrality, primary skill unifies some common artforms. It binds various enterprises as being of a sort, and, as a membership test, excludes would-be glaringly unqualified invaders. Readymaking, by dismissing the aesthetic supremacy of skill, upsets the coherence of any notion of unity in the arts.

Computers in art-making do not disturb the centrality of primary causation in traditional performance and painting because they usher in a new artform which offers 'inter-media' potential to dissolve boundaries between sensory modes. Readymaking, however, tests any commitment to artistic skill by seeming to offer the most casual participants whatever capacity makes readymakers artists proper, free of charge. If readymaking is a genuine artistic *modus operandi*, the craft tradition's status declines unless we declare an aesthetic divide between display-works and craftworks, marked by different evaluative criteria, status rankings, and training procedures, analogous to the massively independent worlds of rock and classical music. But such declaration would be altogether *ad hoc* and artificial because the readymade emerged fully within and in response to traditional concrete arts. Readymades are integrally part of classical art history.

107

Tellingly, readymaking has been concentrated in the concrete arts where it has been taken seriously. The willingness to accept readymaking and thus put aside the primacy of manual skill in the concrete arts stems from a number of possible causes; for example,

1   one has, always, something to show for it, a marketable physical object with a title and a message;

2   viewers have become generally accustomed to an increasingly relaxed display of technical dexterity in the concrete arts;

3   the concrete arts present rich opportunities for expressively effective work despite the absence of primary skill;

4   non-artists with some aesthetic sensitivity have a tendency to display at home, say, certain natural or manufactured items like shells or glassware for aesthetic purposes, so it is a reasonably small step to have them accept like items in official venues like galleries;

5   the concrete arts community is inherently less conservative than the musical world, say. The difference in degree of conservatism may have much to do with the relatively larger number of co-ordinated forces needed in music-making. The institutions of performance may be much bigger, more complex, and more intricately organized than those of the concrete arts. Thus they will be more prone to resist even small changes, because any change will have significant effects throughout the structure.

Whatever its impact in the concrete arts, what influence has readymaking had on music? The influences, though manifest, have been indirect. In the next chapter, I examine a number of experiments in music-making, ones which draw upon central readymaking themes and which, on analogy, raise questions about what sorts of sounds count as musical and what sorts of sound-makers count as musicians. To these matters, I now turn.

5

EXPERIMENTS WITH MUSICAL AGENCY

Introduction

In Chapter 4, I claimed that, whereas computer-based art leaves the primary craft tradition in peace, readymaking does not. Computer-based painting and music already exist as fully-fledged autonomous arts which converge at bottom upon a unitary artform; that is, one which treats sound and colour as merely distinctly accessible properties of information, the one underlying substance. Readymades give us art-as-display rather than art-as-made, and thus prompt revision of our conception of works, artists and art-making by endorsing options the primary crafts exclude.

How has readymaking affected music-making? That there are no exact performance counterparts to readymades is not surprising. The more music-making forsakes direct control, the less such music counts as performed, however, the more readymade-like the music becomes. Eliminating control utterly leaves bare sound; while restoring direct control destroys the standalone quality and autonomy of the sound object. All that said, however, various categories of experimental music selectively deploy clear-cut readymade themes which raise issues about the traditional nature and role of musical agency. Among such themes are:

1   the employment of non-traditional display objects;
2   the causal independence of the display object from the artist's hand;
3   a relative indifference toward the background and skill of the artist;
4   the absence of the basis for an evaluative scale against which works may be compared within and across categories; and, incidentally;
5   an element of surprise or of the unusual.

Unlike the impact of readymades in the concrete arts, however, experimental music seems not to have seriously upset tradition with its quasi-readymades. Briefly summarized, the argument elaborated in this chapter is that many species of experimental music either fall quite outside the sphere of performance practice, or fail to free themselves from traditional expectations. Those falling

109

entirely outside the sphere of performance practice challenge traditional practice no more than does computer-based music; that is, they set up alternative artistic forms of manipulating sound. Within performance practice, where experimental music involves 'performers' whose primary skill is minimized, such music either falls uncontroversially within the traditional performance framework, falls afoul of the traditional framework, or allegedly forces revision of the traditional framework. If it falls compliantly within or afoul of the tradition, any putative challenges to tradition miss the mark, or at least are compromised. If it allegedly forces revision of the traditional framework, we have *prima facie* a challenge to the need for musicianship as conventionally conceived. But we can turn this challenge back on itself by questioning whether the newly conceived musical participants – whom I call 'sounders' – are plausibly identifiable as musicians.

If sounders are acceptably identifiable as musicians, many of the Guild traditions apply to them – with largely unflattering results. If they are distinct from musicians, then what they do is different enough to place them in a category which doesn't so much disturb the central place of primary skill in performance as provide an alternative rationale for musical participation and experience. For example, in some experimental variants, music becomes a distinctive form of socializing – even of self-discovery or therapy. Such experimentalists do not so much displace traditional music-making as they assign different priorities to the point in making musical sound. Some of the more daring variants deliberately give us music without musicians. If this is music at all, it is so by virtue of selectively isolating certain frames of reference which bear some resemblance to traditional terms and conditions. So isolated, these frames are, relative to the context from which they are drawn, musically truncated. In Chapters 1 and 2, performance is a centrally situated part of a complex functional process. Remove or radically re-fashion performance, and the survival of the whole requires functional re-adjustment of the remainder. But what survives is a very different creature. If this is a fair analysis, we have not so much a clash with traditional models as a parallel mode of musical occasion which understandably must revise the conditions of participation.

Preliminaries

To explore quasi-readymade themes, I consider a few examples of experimental music which I divide into three categories: (1) snip-n-mix, (2) found sound, and (3) fancy-free pieces. Each category is characterized, with emphasis upon any implications for the action craft view of performance.[1]

To start, however, I must discuss *musique concrète* – arguably the closest musical counterpart to concrete readymades – only to note its identity as a species of the genus including computer-based music which, as we have seen, runs parallel to and not in conflict with traditional performance practice.

Musique concrète involves the selection and presentation of common sound. In the quasi-readymade cause of making art out of everyday objects, the French

110

composer and ex-sound effects technician, Pierre Schaeffer, recorded and then fashioned complex collages of familiar sounds such as bells and trains on tape. By these means, he and his colleague Pierre Henry created the *Symphonie pour un homme seul*, an 'opera for the blind'. *Musique concrète* significantly influenced the development of electronic and computer music. The use of the tape recorder as an 'instrument', and as an editorial and compositional device raises intriguing questions about what counts as composing music, about what composition aims for, and about the essence and quality of music and musical sound.[2]

Unlike readymaking, *musique concrète* demands a high degree of acoustic engineering skill. Raw sounds are massively modified with respect to attack, decay, duration, order, and speed before being grouped and displayed. Further, even though *musique concrète* and readymaking both use common ambient materials, the former challenges no performance conventions because it was never meant to include any role for performers. The *concrètiste*'s immediate product is a master tape. *Musique concrète* pieces are not performable. They admit only of 'soundings', the aural counterpart to the 'viewing' or 'screening' made possible by the film projectionist. As noted in Chapter 4, much of computer and electronic music is meant for unperformed, uninterpreted display over which composers have complete control.[3] Far from challenging the role of primary skill in performance, *musique concrète* is no more a comment on performing skill than fashioning three-dimensional computer images is a comment on chipping marble.

Quasi-readymade experimental performance

Snip-n-mix

The *concrètistes* distanced themselves from standard musical traditions in using sound from non-traditional sources. Though requiring no performers, such works draw upon significant organizational and engineering skills. Forsaking all organizational composition skills, some experimentalists use existing music to make novel works thus applying readymaking to composition. For instance, Christopher Hobbs cuts up and then randomly re-assembles conventional pieces, and thus designedly 're-articulates' the classics. Bach, Bull, Tchaikovsky, Czerny, Scriabin and others have been fed through his 'dislocating procedures'. In *The Remorseless Lamb* (1970), he cut up a two-piano version of Bach's *Sheep May Safely Graze*. After separating the right and left hand parts of each bar, the scraps were randomly re-organized and then played. A performance, nearly fifty minutes long, was described as 'comfortingly disorienting'.[4] I call these works 'snip-n-mix'.

Compositionally, the snip-n-mix conforms nicely to certain readymade themes.[5] Though they involve some intervening agency, anyone can learn to make such pieces just by exposure to one instance, particularly if random selection determines the result. The chance selection process in composition is designed to deflate any compositional vanity.

All considered, such pieces may be even more demanding for the player than the source repertoire. Besides frustrating the player's aural expectations, the technical-mechanical flow of otherwise standard repertoire becomes utterly disjointed and consequently may render such works devilishly difficult to play. On the performance side, then, they easily call upon all the primary skills demanded by any of their source works.

Responding to this very bias, Hobbs composed *Czerny's 100 Royal Bouquet Valses for Piano by Lanner and Strauss arranged for such as cannot reach an Octave* (1970), drawing one hundred fragments of one to six bars from the mentioned music sampler. These can be played in any order by players of dubious accomplishment. But, if one can still make mistakes, if there is a right way and a wrong way, this will not make for a skill-free performance. Duchamp can be neither praised nor faulted for the aesthetic qualities of the curves on *Fountain*. Once one can be described as departing from a standard, one's activity can be judged against it. Accuracy is an achievable snip-n-mix performance virtue. Evaluatively, snip-n-mix players fall in with the rest.[6]

Found sound

However compositionally like readymades, snip-n-mix pieces still require primary skill in performance. Closer to readymaking, works of the genus 'found sound' display freely occurring, unaltered sounds which arise without the express intention or intervention of some music-maker. There are two kinds which I dub 'ambient' and 'prepared'.

In ambient found sound, the work's sound constituents are neither directly nor indirectly produced by the player, but arise whether or not the work is staged. The player's role approximates that of a presenter-auditor and thus shares much with the displayer-spectator counterpart in the visual arts. Sometimes neither composer nor player knows in advance of the performance occasion which sounds will constitute that occasion.

Prepared found sound is modified by a participant player, but the modifications demand no more skill and expertise than any non-musician has. One instance, the 'event' piece *Drip Music* by George Brecht, requires no more than 'a source of dripping water and an empty vessel [which] are arranged so that the water falls into the vessel'. Another event piece, *Micro I* by Takehisa Kosugi, calls for a live microphone to be wrapped in a large sheet of paper. As the paper unfolds, the microphone amplifies its crackling. One enthusiast describes such works as seeking 'the mono-structural and non-theatrical qualities of the simple natural event, a game, or a gag. It is the fusion of Spike Jones, vaudeville, gag, children's games and Duchamp.'[7]

Ambient found sound considered

Ambient found sound pieces putatively illustrate readymade themes concerning primary skill. Consider Max Neuhaus' ode to industrial sound in *Listen: Field Trips Thru Found Sound Environments*. Described by the composer as one of six 'sound oriented pieces for situations other than that of the concert hall', Neuhaus performed *Listen* by working 'in and on the public, man-made sector of environmental sound'.[8] In a performance, 'an audience expecting a conventional concert or lecture is put on a bus, their palms are stamped with the word *listen* and they are taken to and thru an existing sound environment'. Among the venues visited were the Consolidated Edison Power Station in New York City (1966), the Hudson Tubes subway (1967), and New Jersey Power and Light Power Plant (1968).

One central readymade theme predominates; namely, the independence of the objects taken as art. Though the sound is 'framed' by singling out some determinate acoustic phenomenon for attention, the framing itself does not cause those sounds. Ambient found sound pieces are declared works. In contrast with musical sound, the sounds emanate from characteristically non-musical sources in contexts unconventional for ordinary music-making. Why we should regard such displays as works or pieces, let alone associate them with music proper, are doubts Neuhaus invites us to entertain.

Ambient found sound pieces work well as compositional readymades but say nothing about performance other than that it is dispensable. Those who stage ambient found sound works no more perform them than the disc jockey performs the songs being played. The DJ may call attention to a certain sound, frame it, occasion it, exhibit it, display it, show it off, but, the DJ does not make it – with or without skill. In ambient found sound, the displayer has no hand whatever in either the sounding episode or even the reason for the sounding.

What would a performance quasi-readymade minimally require? Though the sound must be autonomous, it cannot be causally detached as a concrete readymade is from its readymaker. Quasi-readymade music must somehow be performer-made. One way of approximating quasi-autonomous player-caused sound is by detaching, not the player, but the player's intentions from the sounds made; that is, they become unintended agent-made sounds. Some experimenters reckon that to detach intention from the sounds players make, one must introduce indeterminacy into performance. We will see that that does less than is supposed.

Prepared found sound considered

Prepared found sound requires active intervention in sound production. Typically, some sound-making device is set up to ensure a specific quality of sound. Although the sound does not derive spontaneously from the ambient environment, the immediate cause of and precise progress of the sound is significantly removed from human agency. Instead, the natural forces of the world generate what we hear. Though both *Drip Music* and *Micro I* employ non-musical sound sources, this feature is incidental. The Aeolian harp, a wind-driven six-string resonator popular around 1800, exemplifies an instrumental prepared found sound device.[9] Though no such sound-making episodes were then declared instances of specific works, they could have so served.[10]

Explaining sound: are sounders performers?

Prepared found sound pieces work well as compositional readymades. For prepared found sound to work as an interesting performance quasi-readymade, it must somehow count as being performed. For terminological convenience, I use the term 'sounder' to refer to the causal agent participating in pieces like *Drip Music* or *Micro I*. Are sounders performers? Though event pieces consist of relatively autonomous and spontaneous sound, the sound is, nevertheless, causally linked to the sounder. Is this causal linkage sufficient for performance? I think not. The remoteness of the sound from the sounder is of a different order from that between sound and conventional performer. This relative remoteness becomes clear in the way we would explain the sound occurrences. To explain non-musical sound sources like dripping water and paper crackling we do not generally appeal to human agency. An appeal to physics would best suit an explanation of the immediate sound determinants because no explanatorily pertinent human activity intervenes in the sound-generating process. Event pieces are short on a central species of agency. (Convention, though, counts. The recognized instruments of music could include such water-drop and paper-crackling instruments.)

To explain why a listener heard a middle-C in a conventional performance, one would ordinarily offer that the performer played it or that the performer fingered a certain fret stop. To explain why the player sounded that very pitch, one would refer to the particular work in progress and the player's intentions regarding its proper execution. In such circumstances, any reference to the physics of sound would be inappropriate unless one had independent reason to believe the sound occurred inadvertently. The 'intentional stance' fails to apply to the ongoing sounds of *Drip Music* and *Micro I*.[11]

Though one may properly explain the dripping sound by appealing to the sounder's setting up the apparatus in a certain way, the causal details get very loose. Though roughly true, this account cannot be extended to further details; for example, why some particular dripping sound occurred. Although many qualities of conventionally produced sound are equally outside the player's agency and control, the found sound cases attach agency only minimally and incidentally to the sound emitted. What sounders do relative to the acoustic content of the drip sounds seems as remote from them as I am to the electro-magnetic content of my study when I turn on the light.

Sounder agency ranks very low in the larger causal nexus. Doesn't the stage-hand who wheels the piano onto the stage also 'set it up'? Is the stagehand thereby part of the performance? Consider the massive list of credits attached to most feature films and ask: just how many of these are genuinely *sine qua non*?

True, they all played their small causal part, but it is also reasonable to reflect on the fact of overdetermination or causal fat. Sounders play a bit part. Dripping water survives as well in a universe without us. Sounders are just triggers – or facilitators, to be polite. They turn on certain independent causal mechanisms. Differences in the distance in agency create an explanatory asymmetry between the sounder/found-sound and performer/made-sound relationships. Sounders cannot be performers if the explanation of performed sound can never be so causally thin as to make human agency largely incidental.

What sounders do: performing and playacting

Might sounders be mere sound-jockeys? This raises issues about skill. Can any sounding sequence lack skill and count as a performance? Consider the relative importance of musicianly activities in performance; for example, skilled actions like drawing a bow, strumming a rasgueado, or fingering an arpeggio. Normally, performing activities are distinct from anything audiences do while listening. Conventional performance requires performers to learn new bodily man-oeuvres. Must such musicianly actions be present in any performance?[12]

Compare acting cases where seemingly skilled actorly actions are indistinguishable from ordinary ones. Actors frequently act out many sequences we can all do without acting. For instance, actors on stage may have to 'read the newspaper' or 'settle down comfortably in a sofa', and usually do so without reading anything or feeling comfortable. That any of us may be as convincing in these action patterns just by doing them ordinarily does not detract from the professional performance status such activities have on stage. Just because I can read a newspaper gives me no cause to think myself as good at acting at reading a newspaper as any actor, even if I appear to others just as the actor appears. Why? Because there is a difference between convincingly giving others the impression that one is reading a newspaper and merely reading a newspaper.

Conventional music performance is considerably less related to ordinary life enterprises. Practically no musicianly activities have ordinary life models, except perhaps some in singing. Are distinctive musicianly activities integral to musical performance? Certainly, such trained movements are currently necessary for traditional musical goals and must be mastered to achieve those goals. What goes on in *Drip Music* fails to distinguish the sounder's capacities from the listener's. Prepared found sound cases provide the impression of identifiable musical activity, though nothing in the activity distinguishes it as musical except the setting. We all can serve as unrehearsed understudies for any sounder. Such pieces, then, call for no musicianly cause; but, if so, the musical status of the event is forfeit. At least, so the conservative story goes.

Are sounders musicians?

In prepared found sound, the sounder focuses attention upon some selected

115

sound. Sounding is event framing. Even if sounders prepare the causal back-drop, they witness the sounds as if members of the audience. If sounders thus dissolve functionally into the audience, prepared found sound pieces involve no music-making role.

What makes for musicianhood? I brush past a chandelier and set it tinkling. This makes no musician out of me. Suppose I brush past it deliberately and set it tinkling. Does my deliberation make any difference? Mere deliberation can sometimes make a difference. Compare my unwittingly brushing past someone who falls off a cliff and dies with my deliberately doing this. My deliberation makes all the difference between accidental death and murder. My status as a murderer hangs on my deliberation. It is a fact I may have led to someone's death; it is not similarly a fact that I am a murderer. Only law can confer that status. Musicians are not born quite so officially. The chandelier case no more makes me a musician than my deliberately hitting the keys on a typewriter makes me a poet. Compared with musicians, sounders are much more like anyone gratuitously making sound. Though musicianhood is a status rank, it is earned and not conferred. Sounders in event pieces are not musicians because their actions do not earn them that status.

Fortuity and performance

Instead of this appeal to ornate qualities of agency and musicianship, why not simply call upon the place of intention in performance? The argument runs thus: Found sounds are fortuitous occurrences. As such they cannot have been intended. Any sounds in performance must be intended. So, found sounds cannot be considered performed. Though interesting, the argument is inadequate.

In Chapter 1, the agent's intentions are necessary for performance. One writer concurs when he dismisses the suggestion that 'the wind blowing through the rocks' counts as a performance even though it may be 'an occurrence having all the acoustic properties' specified by some work. He ranks such cases alongside 'someone's doodling on a piano, or an electronic organ's going berserk'.[13] These examples are of fortuitous, unplanned, even random events. What makes the difference to performance is the context of sound production. Without the purpose and the intention one has caused but unperformed sound.

Every performance contains accidental, incidental, unintended, involuntarily made sounds. The cellist's bow squeaks, the horn bobbles, the violinist's peg creaks, the flautist breathes in with a gasp. All are constituents of the performance. Deliberate but distracting sounds also occur; for example, the renowned thump of Lully's mace used to keep the beat. Only the recording engineer's power can banish these sounds effectively. If performances have unintended sounds, why not allow found sounds their rightful place? If *4'33"* was about performance silence, perhaps *Drip Music* is about background noise.

The matter is perhaps one of degree. Could all or most of the sounds of a performance be fortuitous? Some scores contain sections directing the player to lose direction and to fill in the sound by any means, even 'doodling on a piano'. But one doesn't abandon intention thereby. One is following instructions.

Every prepared found sound case can be transformed into an intentional exercise with score directives: 'Bring your boss to hear the wind blowing through the rocks'; 'Get uncontrollably drugged and then doodle at the piano'; 'Send a high voltage surge through your Roland Jupiter-8'. Directives may make the difference, even if the results cannot be anticipated, controlled, or repeated. Though performance requires intention, who can say just what strictures on intention apply? Since found sound pieces are scripted, their sounders act intentionally. Any fortuitous sounds can be easily made into the object of some intention, so more is needed to distinguish found sound and performance.

Manner and fact in performance

Perhaps the causal story makes all the difference. In the visual arts, our appreciation of how an effect is achieved (a matter of manner) does not necessarily influence our valuing that it was achieved (a matter of fact). Artists themselves may admire or condemn certain techniques in each other's work, but these need not influence a spectator's aesthetic appreciation. If an artist employs a trick, a shortcut, a gimmick, that need not bias the viewer's attitude toward the work. Such subterfuge concerns the viewer only if appreciation hangs on full information about the work's origin. Ordinarily, this has not been called for even if the appearance of specified origin counts.[14]

This manner/fact distinction has enjoyed a long life partly because the primary craft tradition has been taken for granted between artist and art consumer. The readymade broadcasts the manner/fact separation by denouncing the pact, or at least treating it as nothing more than a hollow gentlemen's agreement. That readymades have been adopted into the family of fine art underlines the literal reading of the manner/fact distinction.

Musical performance is not so indulged. Conventional performance primitively requires that performing activities and the production of musical sound be causally co-extensive. The worth of a performance typically depends upon both the actual manner and fact of achievement. If tricks are used, the performance will be condemned by listeners and fellow performers alike no matter how closely it ranks in appearance with the best. Our appreciation of performance, then, is strongly connected with our awareness of and regard for its manner. Where manner simply doesn't count in an activity, we are uninclined to recognize it as a performance. In prepared found sound pieces, the sounders do not even intervene musically. Without musical intervention, there is no discernible intervention manner *a fortiori*.

Event pieces like *Listen* and *Micro I* are ideologically kin to electronic and computer-based pieces in that they both dispense with musicians. In so doing, electronic music returns musical control to the composer. For some composers, musicians introduce an uncontrollable indeterminacy in the form of third-party interpretation. Electronic music is not executed, and so is uninterpretable by an executant. Like bronze, it is cast, and persists historically independent of and uninfluenced by any performance traditions. By fixing the last detail of each sound, nothing remains for any performer to do. Thus, Stockhausen, discussing the differences between electronic and instrumental composition, speaks of discovering how the composer may compositionally control all the qualities of sound:

> I found [in working on *Kontakte*] for the first time ways to bring all properties under a single control. I deduced that all differences of acoustic perception can be traced to differences in the temporal structure of sound waves. . . . If nowadays, it has become necessary to find one general set of laws to govern every sphere of musical time itself, that is simply the result of a condition imposed by electronic music that each sound in a given work must be individually composed.[15]

Control is not the goal of found sound composers even though the sounds called for in *Listen* and *Drip Music* leave as little for any performer to do as the pre-cast finality of computer music. Their goal concerns hearing. In that respect, musicians (and even composers) are redundant because this is listener-centred music. As such, found sound falls entirely outside the performing arts and resembles more a form of sensory therapy which uses the institutional setting of the scheduled concert to lend it greater influence in capturing the listener's full attention.

Fancy-free: indeterminacy and freeflow

I name the last group 'fancy-free' after its spiritual ancestor, the free fantasy or 'fancy'. Fancy-free pieces enjoin players to cause sound directly as if traditionally engaged, but discourage conventional preparedness. Such works, often shaped by fortuity, are systematically open-textured.

In indeterminate or chance works the sounds constituting the piece are revealed by means of some randomizing process chosen by the composer.[16] Although direct and full causation of sound takes place, the player (and composer), lacking any foreknowledge of the sound sequence for any occasion, forfeits preparation. In Christopher Hobbs' *Voicepiece* (1967), for example, the details of individual executions are determined by sets of numbers chosen at random from the telephone directory. Participants take any final four digit sequence and to each digit an 'interpretation' is attached. Digit 1 relates to types of sound production (for example, humming, screaming, throat noises, etc.), digit 2 to duration from very short to very long, digit 3 to pitch and amplitude, and digit 4 to the duration of silence after each event. The score indicates that each performer makes his own part.

Freeflow or impulse pieces allow one to play on impulse, no conditions having to be met. These range from the mystic search for the purest non-thinking spontaneity of Stockhausen's *Es* to the chummy anarchy allowed non-musicians in Frederic Rzewski's *Les Moutons de Panurge* (1969). Consider Stockhausen's instructions for his meditatively impulsive piece *Es*, an instance of *musique intuitive*, and one seeking uncontaminated spontaneity:

> Within the cycle, the text '*Es*' reaches an extreme of intuitive playing in the instruction to play only when one has achieved the state of non-thinking, and to stop whenever one begins to think. By this means a state of playing should be achieved in which one acts and reacts purely intuitively. As soon as a player thinks of something (e.g., that he is playing; what he is playing; what someone else is playing or has played; how he should react; that a car is driving past outside, etc.) he should stop, and only start again when he is just listening, and at one with what is heard.[17]

Frederic Rzewski, searching for musical community, instructs that participating non-musicians are:

> to make sound, any sound, preferably very loud, and if possible are provided with percussive or other instruments. The non-musicians have a leader whom they may follow or not . . . [Musicians are advised to] stay together as long as you can, but if you get lost, stay lost. Do not try to find your way back into the fold.[18]

While found sound pieces provide no opportunity for musicians, fancy-free works are roughly unified by the illusion of conventional performance roles. Many such pieces have scores calling for active performers. Room exists for interpretive discretion within the confines of a pre-ordained structure. Fancy-free works often call for improvisation, though they usually shun the competitive and demonstrative mannerisms connected with virtuosic ingenuity and musical brinkmanship.

From these descriptions, these works seem scarcely different from the usual. Fancy-free works are intended, however, to reshape the tasks, expectations, and credentials of the traditional musician. Because they apparently respect conventional institutions, fancy-free pieces provide the most interesting source of challenge to tradition from the inside. Fancy-free music putatively responds to tensions between the alleged universality of musical expression and the barriers to music-making imposed by the Guilds. These challenges involve:

Musicianship Why must music call upon conventionally trained musicians? Why not call upon players unconstrained by formal musical training?

Notation   What purpose is served by formal notation? Why not replace it with a more intuitive, universal, less expert and clubbish language?

Scores   Shouldn't the score interfere minimally with the decisions of the performers and not impose external standards of correctness? Shouldn't composers through their scores be non-judgemental?

Spontaneity   Mightn't we achieve true musical spontaneity by relinquishing the fixity and forethought typical of conventional music-making and instead turning to mechanisms of chance to create the work/performance in progress?

Because fancy-free participants make their own sounds, often on conventional instruments, the immediacy of agency is not at issue. Tradition is purportedly challenged by: rejecting primary skill; using non-traditional means; avoiding evaluative scales, and the relative autonomy of the resulting sound. This final item is most intriguing, for how can something directly caused by an agent also be independent of that agent? Here is where chance plays a part, and where the sounds made need detaching from the performer's intentions.

Abandoning skill, notation, evaluation

To create a universally accessible music, fancy-free pieces forsake the specialized demands of traditional musicianship. In forsaking traditional musicianship, fancy-free pieces call for participants uninformed about traditional sources of musical information. To engage these people, new, more immediately accessible musical behaviour and ways of conveying musical information are required. This inspires the adoption of new notation (for example, graphic notation) and novel, 'non-professional' capacities in musical contexts (for example, humming, whistling, uncorking bottles). As notation, instrumentation and participation are democratized, musical expectations slacken. As more people, manners, and means are musically sanctioned, admission and rejection standards weaken. An open-door admissions policy with no threat of rejection spells the end of all comparative evaluation of one party against another or of any party against some external objective standard.

We are left with sound-making unfettered by skill, preparation, or standards which anyone can do just by wanting to. What makes this a musical exercise is the institutional skeleton of the musical establishment; for example, schools of composition, the concert format, organized gatherings of participants for rehearsal-like preparation, the sense of occasion, the will and intention to present certain designated works, use of scores, and so on. That the result may sound like a racket just betrays the tunnel-hearing of taste. So thought Beethoven's first audience about the last movement of his *Second Symphony*, and so think prissy critics of contemporary grunge. What greater challenge to tradition than 'music-making for everyone'?

Musical training divides people. Where native impulse alone suffices, no one is excluded from active participation. Some composers deliberately sought out 'musical innocents' as best suited for interpreting their works. Notation, too, has been a secret code dividing the *cognoscenti* from the rest. One way to remove the barrier between official musicians and the laity was to swap pitch for graphics notation. The latter demands visual but not necessarily musical sophistication. One such work, Cornelius Cardew's *Treatise* (1963–7), was notated graphically using circles, lines, triangles, squares, and ellipses. The performer, provided with no instructions for the score, forms various ideas about acoustic correspondences and acts on them. In principle, no performance can be inconsistent with the score. *Treatise*, unfortunately, failed to isolate musical innocents because of its reliance upon visual acuity, a virtue Cardew thought largely absent in the acoustically oriented. His remedy, *The Tiger's Mind* (1967), 'demands no musical education and no visual education; all it requires is a willingness to understand English and a desire to play in the widest sense of the word'.[19]

Music like this removes all but the willingness to participate as essential to performance. Performance is thereby transformed into an amorphous phenomenon of willing engagement which requires no orthodox credentials. Skilled execution is not banished from the new music, but it is demoted to being a needlessly formal way of approaching what others engage in with equal thoroughness, less formally. This closely allies music-making to other social co-operative ventures. In the spirit of the concrete readymade, fancy-free pieces provoke tradition by displaying hitherto unacceptable objects as artworks the making of which summons no technical or professional distinction.

Fancy-freedom and chance

Why bother to develop new notations? Wouldn't the infusion of extreme randomness alone guarantee a music which is both made and come upon? Wouldn't chance unhinge and frustrate both novice and professional alike, thus levelling all grades of pedigree?

Despite the disarming effect of chance, not all pieces driven by randomizers are egalitarian. Skill and training sometimes count. Some forms of chance music require enormous musical concentration. The demands placed upon players by the complex and exacting notation of Christian Wolff in such works as *Duo for Pianists II* (1958) and *For Pianist* (1959) prompted the remark that 'the technical equipment needed to play . . . are extreme presence of mind, a mental as well as physical agility, and an acute grasp of the capabilities of your instrument'.[20] How else could one hope to summon and control the twenty-two different types of sound production called for in *For 1, 2 and 3 People*?

How then does chance contribute to the fancy-free philosophy? Chance mechanisms assist rather than create the participatory spontaneity sought by fancy-free proponents. These mechanisms are meant to furnish the musical counterpart to the fortuitousness of the features in concrete readymades, no feature of the found object having been planned and realized by the ready-maker. Each is as if an article of fortune. With sounds created on the cue of signals unknown both to composer and performer, the emerging execution is as if a discovery. The piece is found while being made.

Where 'chance' means 'unpredictability', it is a platitude that every composer injects chance into works which are interpreted by autonomous third parties. This unpredictability, though, affects the composer, not the performer. The performer has a twofold predictive advantage over the composer: the composer yields everything and hides nothing from the player; and the players fully know their own interpretation.

Indeterminacy confounds the player's discretion itself in the interests of spontaneity. One may know roughly in advance the available options but never how they will emerge. The role of the work is to frustrate preparation. In such settings, no one can be guilty of music aforethought. Indeed, one invites freedom verging on anarchy.

Autonomy, agency, impulse, and chance

Apart from their broadmindedness, do fancy-free works succeed at shaking down the performance establishment? Among prominent readymade themes are the detachment of the result from any formal skill and from the 'artist'. Fancy-free works don't quite deliver on either.

Fancy-freedom as fraud Some complain that unskilled 'performers' acting purely on impulse or madly complying with random directives to squeal or snort just make haphazard noise comparable at best to hopelessly bad conventional performance. Nothing new arises here; just another misguided attempt at originality. The scorn dumped on such music draws its thunder from the conviction that its practitioners are either crazy, frauds, or crazy frauds. Here's Pierre Boulez:

> The most elementary form of the transmutation of chance would lie in the adoption of a philosophy tinged with Orientalism that masks a basic weakness in compositional technique; it would be a protection against the asphyxia of invention, the resort to a more subtle poison that destroys every last embryo of craftsmanship; I would willingly call this experiment . . . since the individual does not feel responsible for the work, but merely throws himself by unadmitted weakness, by confusion, and for temporary assuagement into puerile magic – I would call this experiment *chance through inadvertence*. . . . This kind of narcotic indeed constitutes protection against the goad inflicted upon you by all inventiveness; it is to be observed that its action is exaggeratedly soothing, sometimes mirth-provoking, like what hashish fanciers

describe. Peace to these angelic creatures; we can be sure they run absolutely no risk of stealing any thunder, since they wouldn't know what to do with it.[21]

Though these words might inspire the experimentalist who tastes legitimacy by having triggered the fury of the establishment, it is difficult not to sympathize with Boulez's version of the *Emperor's New Clothes*.

Autonomy, indeterminacy and impulse The independence of the musical result from the artist faces a familiar problem: to the extent that sounds are directly made by human agents, they are agent-dependent. The closer an agent gets to the sound the less autonomous it is; the more autonomous the sound, the less performed it is. With agent-dependency, skill assessment threatens to return. The elements of indeterminacy and impulse are meant to make such autonomy possible by changing the quality of agent-causation enough to liberate the sound from the sound-maker. Neither does the job.

Indeterminacy Consider first indeterminacy in performance which can be either immediate or assigned. With assigned indeterminacy, the composer offers a set of raw materials and a random choice procedure. The final selection and assembly takes place before presentation and requires practice and other conventional features of rehearsal. These cases clearly fall under the thumb of the Guild.

Immediate indeterminacy pre-empts practice and rehearsal. The materials, randomly selected and ordered, must be presented on the spot. Though one can get a feel for responding spontaneously to randomly generated directives, one remains systematically unprepared for what happens on stage. In responding to the pressures of the moment, one must react purposively without reflection. This resembles automatic response to emergencies. One doesn't 'think'; one registers a signal and acts. This 'thought-free' exercise putatively yields soundings which are from the player but not of the player, so to speak; hence their quasi-independence.

But this won't work. Though unreflective, such acts are voluntary and intentional. The agent owns and takes responsibility for the actions, and conceives them as part of a larger plan. Further, just as one can prepare for emergencies by practising drill, so one might prepare for random music. Whatever one's aptitudes, there is a point to practising drill for contingencies. Can't one get better at this sort of music? But surely this smacks of skill. Indeterminacy fails to free such performances from the performer's background. They run on directives. It's just that the performer has to follow orders in a terrible rush.

Spontaneity and impulse Does spontaneously or impulsively made music challenge the Guild? Spontaneous occurrences seem just to occur. They are unplanned, unexpected, and unconnected with whatever is going on. The ultimate spontaneous event requires true randomness; for example, particular radioactive emissions. Spontaneous human actions cannot be truly random. Spontaneity is occasionally contrasted with restraint and inhibition. Negatively, spontaneous acts may seem impetuous and reckless. Positively, they may seem refreshing, spirited, or dynamic. Spontaneous acts cannot be pre-meditated, planned, rehearsed, prepared, reflective, designed, practised, or routine; nor for which the agent can have any immediate conscious reason. They are actions their agents will but cannot adequately explain or justify. In that, they seem random.

Musical spontaneity is valued where it contrasts with plodding, academic playing. 'Spontaneity' may refer either to how something sounds or how the sounds are caused. Some highly planned events seem utterly spontaneous. Inner free spirit does not guarantee free-spirited sounds. Stockhausen's call in *Es* for 'an extreme of intuitive playing' demands both the inner free spirit and musical free-spiritedness.

Such spontaneity would hardly liberate the sound from the player. The sound is intended, even if not planned and even if the player cannot say what will happen next. As intended, it expresses its maker, however temporarily unencumbered by self-conscious musical obligation. What of Stockhausen's anti-directive which directs one to do as one will for as long as one wishes? Supposing the context is musical, we are no better off. Here is where skill would tell. That the player enjoys some musical grounding, to that extent, the player would treat this as 'free' improvisation. Thus 'spontaneity' issues in something fiercely deliberate. To the extent that no background whatever is present besides a willingness to participate, one gets not freedom but arbitrariness.

Impulsive playing fares no better. Impulsive action is capricious, done without concern for consequences. Typically non-rational, it usually is viewed negatively. (While criticized for acting on impulse, people are seldom chastised for their spontaneity.) Far from freeing the maker from the sound, impulsive playing, like many thoughtless enterprises, is often that about which one has later regrets.

Autonomous musical results require automatism – actions performed while sleep-walking or under various drug-induced or pathological states. With respect to Boulez, no one would suppose such performance to demand systematic mindlessness. One would expect a player in a state of automatism to perform much worse than a normal one. The only reliable automata, of course, are machines like computers, but that's another game altogether.

In the end, appeals to chance and spontaneity merely mask the tight bond between agents and the sounds they make. While certain readymade themes like the use of unconventional processes are represented, the principal requirements of autonomy and absence of skill are not met. Far from departing radically from performance traditions, fancy-freedom easily falls under traditional criteria of appraisal.

6

ARTISTS, PROGRAMS, AND PERFORMANCE

Introduction

Years pass. An unassuming research team, decades on from the designers of the ultimate synthesizer, describes a trial of a new prototype in the Notes & News section of a modest engineering quarterly.

The setting: a prestigious international piano competition presided over by a panel of judges drawn from the most accomplished, respected, and astute virtuosi, pedagogues, and critics currently active. The session rules have been altered. Under the pretext of minimizing predictable nationalistic and doctrinal prejudice, not only the players' identities but the players themselves have been concealed from the judges. The judges are blindfolded before entering the hall. Each player is labelled by number. The judges are also unaware that not a single person will participate in the competition. The prize will go to a program which drives a conventional piano. No human player participates.

The contest proceeds. Although the level of talent is impressive, the accolades converge in the end on one player whose future developments will be anticipated eagerly, so the judges inform the musical world. The call goes out for the winner to appear. Player #8 appears in a clear acrylic jacket and is respectfully laid on a disk stand specially fashioned for the occasion. As from one voice, a great gasp echoes through the hall.

Something seems to have gone wrong. One impulse is to deny that there ever was a music competition. There cannot have been a 'winner' in any respectable sense. The whole peculiar episode is surely a mis-trial. Are we witness to a musical performance here? Have such eventualities hope of full standing in our musical culture or are they artistically aberrant?

In Chapter 2 we examined challenges to the conservative model of performance involving instrumental resources and the degree of skill in making music. Throughout, we assumed an environment of intentional human agents. Here, in focusing on the performing artist, we seek grounds for the human agency assumption. The conservative basis for refusing Guild membership to computer programs presupposes a concept of the artist as a person in the 'thick' sense.[1] This takes us beyond the bare requirement of a causal source delivering appropriately expressive musical sound and also past the formal professionalism of the Guild.

The six sections below attempt to defuse or discredit the program performance. Section 1 examines the example as a 'mere' simulation. Section 2 develops a sketch of the type of machine needed for such performance. In section 3, various contextualist and institutionalist avenues designed to make peace with the program performance are explored, while section 4 questions the implications of blindfold tests. Section 5 examines the authority of competition judgements. In section 6, a consideration of what we appreciate in performers as performers sets some boundaries for an analysis of performing artists. This last part faces squarely the inherent thickness of our notion of performing artists.

The simulation setting

Does the case fail as a competition because we cannot even begin to talk about performing artists at the outset? Since the competition is an artistic one, and since no artist participates, no competition has transpired. J.L. Austin pointed out that a phoney priest performs no marriage, however correct the service.[2] Here we have merely to imagine an ordained priest trying to marry two robots. The mis-trial is kindred. The priest's ignorance of the true nature of those before him does not affect the fact that he cannot have married two machines.

Unfortunately, this dissolution begs all the questions about what counts as a performer. Why can't non-organic mechanisms enter on equal terms? Because we have here a human–machine boundary, a distinction drawn from artificial intelligence is helpful; namely, between programs and devices designed to do what we do just as we do it, and those designed to achieve similar results without regard for matching inner causes.[3] I will call the first devices 'adulators' and the second 'simulators'.

We design adulators to enhance understanding of how we do what we do. Fodor characterizes this as a search for 'strong functional equivalence' between certain devices and us, the ultimate prize being a theory of psychology deeper than that provided by behaviourism.[4] Since successful comprehensive adulators would be very like us in all functionally relevant respects, we would reasonably (and even spontaneously) be inclined to treat them just like us; for example, to take an interest in how they were feeling. Such is the android approach. Simulators, by contrast, are just machines. They interest us only because they perform certain useful tasks better than we can. In seeking faster, cheaper, safer, more accurate and efficient production means, we need not bother closely matching these means to our own inner and outer states unless, for purely practical purposes, selective matching is maximally effective. What use could there be in designing simulators that get tired, bored, or sore when sorting mail? Such is the robotics approach.

Given this distinction, wherein lies the misfire? One may argue that if a felicitous contest requires artists, then the imagined one counts only if the devices employed are at least artist-adulators.

But this is terribly presumptuous. We certainly have no working theory of the inner mental side of artistic performance any more than we have of the creative process. And even if such theories eventually emerge, they will not likely be presupposed in any artistic setting; not, at least, if we are satisfied with the traditional style of adjudication. Besides, how could one require that the contestants enjoy appropriate states of mind during competition the absence of which would disqualify them? Thus, 'Zoltan played the piece with feeling and a true sensitivity to the style period' entails nothing particular about Zoltan's mental states, though it might say something about his hands. Nor have we any cause to feel cheated if we learn that Zoltan really despises both the piece and the period, however disappointed we may be. Perfectly effective playing need not be sincere. One cannot mislead by playing feelingly that for which one has no feeling any more than an actor's playacting a furious outburst warrants any beliefs about the actor's anger. (Indeed, a player's having to be mournful when playing mournfully could be a professional liability. How could one concentrate properly on the job at hand?) Performers at work may have their minds on any manner of things. In the spirit of professional entertainment, someone performing sensitively might simultaneously be bored to distraction and hankering after a restful career in real estate. Because we can have no reasonable expectations of specific inner attitudes, we cannot reasonably require artist-adulators for the competition.

An artist-simulator, a weak functional equivalent, should suffice so long as it doesn't do its job so well as to rouse suspicion. If we concede this, we legitimize the competition case. Even if human performers must have certain human performance-specific inner states, it doesn't follow that artistic performances must be caused by humans. Granted that we know (and, perhaps, care) so little about how performers perform, we would be arrogant indeed to cut off artistic membership on the basis of circuitry. However, as we will see, the inner story is relevant, though not necessarily as a causal account of performance.

Such liberality has been assaulted by John Searle.[5] Briefly, he contends that any theory of human cognitive processes like understanding will fail unless the brain (or something just like it) figures centrally in their explanation because 'intentionality . . . is a biological phenomenon'. Mental functions cannot be logically independent of physical functions because the mind is 'both conceptually and empirically' inseparable from the brain. Since programs are just formalized routines for the manipulation of binary digits, they cannot explain cognitive processes because they do not exemplify the way brains work. So 'no program, by itself, is sufficient for intentionality'.

Presumably, artistic performance falls under the same argument. The imaginary competition could not obtain because there are no genuine performances; merely simulations and not duplications. No one gets burned in a fire drill.

Dismissing simulations, however, is not very effective here. The competition seemingly supplies everything the judges need to base their decision. We may customarily presuppose the biological pedigree of performers, but we don't build that in as a condition of success. The judges may be surprised when they learn the truth, but surprise alone does not warrant a retraction of the judgement. The case is analogous to the surprise a biologist might experience upon discovering that an amoeba can master a maze as adeptly as a mouse. Does the amoeba 'learn' as does the mouse? The innards are dramatically different, to be sure, but we cannot dictate before the fact that amoeba-learning must differ from mouse-learning. Pianos are played, music fills the hall, audiences are thrilled. Some simulation! Have we all been taken in?

How the simulators work

Are the hypothesized simulators plausible? What do they do? What is the relationship between them and the sounds we hear? Are they glorified stereos, like player pianos and other mechanized instruments? What can they do with the music they're meant to perform? The competition requires performing machines which count as creatively expressive. Is this excessive?

Music machines like music boxes or player pianos have been around for centuries. A player piano roll instantiates a program which causes sound as output given the appropriate hardware. The relationship between CDs (records or tapes), their source, and their output devices is different. The CD's sound through the speakers is not strictly the sound of the hardware; that is, it is not the acoustic output of the amplifier, the reading device, or the speakers themselves. One should ideally hear only the sound of that which has been recorded, a piano, say; and not the amplifier's 60 Hz 'background' hum. The piano along with its 'driver', the pianist, are not physically present in the playback setting.

With recordings, we could talk about 'traces' or 'images', the effects of past causes, which are restored in the form of the playback or acoustic output. The playback is no more a performance than the photograph is the thing photographed, or the footprint is the prime suspect. In a recording, I hear an acoustic image of a performance given necessarily at some past time. Recordings, like photographs, capture and fix past events. With recordings, one is ideally meant to hear not the playback system but the piano itself through the playback system, its immediate medium of re-delivery. But the most highly prized recorded sound is meticulously scrubbed. Recordings are seldom true and faithful records of performances. What one really hears is a decryption of a piano-sound simulation, which is as if a trace of a single prior episode. Charitably put, one hears an idealized performance; less charitably, recordings typically tidy up (if not fake) the past.[6]

Player pianos are not devices for reproducing the sound of a piano, but pianos activated by means other than human hands. Player pianos cannot, however, match the expressive potential in typical performance because they cannot change anything. They cannot vary their roll any more than a stereo can alter its recordings. The pianola roll does not stand to the performance as the score (or the piece in case there is no score) stands to the human executant. Instead of an interpretation, there is just a hard mechanical link between physical perforations and the release of the keys. Nothing mediates between the roll and the execution.

However much we may admire the sensitivity of a player piano rendition, the epithet 'expressive' does not attach to the machine. If anything, we esteem the driver roll's proximate source, presumably some human executant. The roll's immediate source is the manufacturing process. In this respect, both player piano and CD player are kindred playback devices driven by traces of some past performance which alone merits praise for its artistic qualities.

My imaginary player-programs are much more sophisticated. Each must be individual, must operate autonomously, must be capable of nuances that make for interpretive diversity, and each must be able to cope with a range of repertoire. None merely mimics human performances. I imagine each program to have been devised by engineers who, appropriately consulting with the performing community, have analysed the stock repertoire into a sequence of abstract structures and have derived a workable formalization of music or music theory. The player-programs, fitted with music theories and relevant historical data, are also equipped with heuristic strategies on how to proceed with new input, typically a score. They derive 'interpretations' consonant with the input which are then mapped onto a preliminary ordered set of instrument activation commands. These, in turn, determine the physical effects upon the instrument's sounding mechanism. On this model the same piece may be performed differently on different occasions depending on changes to the data banks (for example, 'experience' with more pieces by the same composer or new information on performance practice) or to the heuristics (for example, changes to 'fingerings' by way of facilitating the smoothness of a passage). Further, in any given performance, changes may be effected on the go in the original command set as a result of ongoing feedback which files reports on output effectiveness; for example, adjustments to instrumental idiosyncrasies by matching more closely the 'interpretation' to the physical qualities of the instrument, or to the hall's acoustic ambience, and the like. Once activated, such player-programs develop on their own. They are not mere tools or mere extensions of their makers, any more than one would think thus of one's children or students. They are no more 'used' by their engineers than imaginative disciples can be said to be 'used' to express the doctrines of their masters.

I tacitly assume that what the metronome did for the quantization of tempo could be matched for other dynamic interpretive aspects. Unless one can defend an anti-reductionistic theory regarding certain qualitative features of performance, one cannot block the claim that any relevant aspect of performance can be reduced to a form compatible with program content.

Performance and the artworld

Whatever the outcome of debates about the formalization of musical intention, these may be incidental to the matter at hand; namely, trying to characterize criteria for inclusion into and exclusion from the performance context. Consider two well-known views; namely, the 'open texture' and 'institutional' theories of art.[7] On either view, the program-driven performance can be accommodated within or excluded from the artworld depending upon certain prevailing conditions; namely, either by a decision to expand or restrict the concept of performance (the open texture approach), or by appeal to the appropriate institutional setting (the institutional approach). Neither position, however, seems equipped to deal with special performance features, nor does the issue seem terribly dependent upon the kinds of artworld conventions to which both theories commonly appeal. It is fitting to review each, indicating where inadequacies crop up.

The open texture theory

The open texture theory applies a Wittgensteinian family resemblance analysis to: 'Is this work an F?', where F picks out some sub-category of art; for example, 'novel', 'poem', 'sonata', etc.:

> what is at stake is no factual analysis concerning necessary and sufficient properties, but a decision as to whether the work under examination is similar in certain respects to other works, already called 'novels', and consequently warrants the extension of the concept to cover the new case . . . [N]ew art forms, new movements will emerge, which will demand decisions on the part of those interested, usually professional critics, as to whether the concept should be accepted or not.[8]

Relevant similarities are made and not born. The open texture adherent would charge that the competition problem is overplayed since it presupposes some underlying essence, dependence upon which violates the true nature of the concept 'performance'. Why can't the judges just decide the competition to be close enough to the conventional standard and consent to the revision of the concept 'performance'?

The open texture theory assumes a smooth transition from talk about artworks to performances. In the competition case, no one denies that Mozart's *D Minor Fantasy* is being heard. The artworld's inventory remains intact. But can the open texture theory deal comfortably with the question: is this rendering of the Mozart an artistic performance? I do not think so. The worry arises over the cause and not the effect. Since no predicate is logically necessary for the correct use of the concept 'art', the open texture theory cannot require that human activity be involved in art-making. The issue of agency in art, therefore, plays no logically central role:

One would scarcely describe X as a work of art if X were not an artefact, or a collection of elements sensuously presented in a medium, or a
product of human skill, and so on. . . . But, even so, no one of these or
any collection of them is either necessary or sufficient.[9]

From this it follows that a world may exist, otherwise just like this world,
which contains works of art none of which is a product of human skill; for
example, a world in which every piece of art is a natural readymade. Though
conceivable, it is nonetheless peculiar because we would have trouble understanding what the world's inhabitants appreciated in all such items as artworks.
No one has trouble understanding our appreciation of the aesthetically appealing
qualities of natural objects like pebbles or clouds, but such aesthetic appreciation
is quite independent of our thinking the pebbles or clouds to be works of art.

If human intentional agency in art were strictly contingent, one oddity would
be this: if the 'winning' sounds came from a machine, that should not deter us
from awarding the machine a prize after congratulating it for its efforts. Can any
judge 'decide' to do that? (The machine's designers may have been other
machines. How far back does one usually extend congratulations? To the artist's
teachers, perhaps? The parents? The human gene pool? Honours normally go to
the player.) Surely, the qualities of artistic agency do not even arise in aesthetic
deliberations, because they lie outside the range of features people normally find
interesting in the music. Indeed, because the open texture theory focuses single-
mindedly upon works, art scholars and critics – those exercising decisions about
inclusion in a category – have no more prerogative legislating over the program
competition than they do in deciding whether something is an orchestra properly
so-called if its entire wind section is replaced with one synthesizer.

The claim that one may identify a performing artist as nothing more than the
cause of some output independently accepted as an artwork would invalidate
the impulse to question (let alone decide) whether the computer program was a
performer. But the logical parasitism of the implication: 'If A is an artwork,
then, if A is caused by X, X is a performing artist' leads to weird results.
Consider: a harp is stirred by the wind which miraculously causes a poignant
rendition of the *Londonderry Air*. Could anyone freely decide by simple
consensus or legislation that a performance has taken place? The open texture
theory view cannot thus casually allow a spill-over from conceptions of artworks
to art-makers.

The institutional theory

The institutional view emphasizes 'the context within which the production of
the artefact takes place'.[10] Responding to concerns about whether chimpanzee
paintings are art, institutional theory advocates are openly relativistic: 'It all
depends on what is done with the paintings. . . . It all depends on the institutional setting.'[11] The essential art-making context is the artworld, 'the complex

131

of differentiated roles which must be fulfilled by persons in order for art to be created . . . a broad, informal cultural practice'.[12] Our opening case simply falls into (or out of) the conventional practices of music competitions.

But the institutional theory too has limitations. Artworks and artefactuality are strongly linked. If one denies the link to program output, it should be denied to readymades as well. Readymades are accommodated by referring to the use to which such objects are put within the artworld. The program competition, however, does not challenge the standing inventory. Mozart's *D Minor Fantasy* remains just that whether it is rendered in formal recital or on an otherwise uninhabited planet. It can't really be anything else; not, at least, in the way that Harding's driftwood and Duchamp's urinal are obviously and primarily something else. One need not use the Mozart in some deliberate way to make it into an artwork (though it can be used for other purposes; for example, as a device in hypnosis). There can't be any worry about its failing to secure that status unless extraordinary steps are undertaken.

Consider the setting in the competition case. It employs textbook conventionality. Established competition protocol is observed, standard repertoire is offered, a typical recital venue is used, and so on. These 'central conventions' are commonly specified rituals designed to unify procedure. Were this all that were necessary, because no central conventions are violated, our competition case falls right in with the rest.

I have supposed that some unease or even shock would result when the winner is called to appear. Because this is a first experience for the listeners, the unease indicates the violation of certain further expectations. Call whatever is sensed as missing 'shadow conventions'; that is, those factors, present alongside the central conventions, which also mould our expectations.[13] Some instances are: the ability of a player to appear for an award, the willingness to take the applause, the eagerness to follow up with recordings, and so on. In the program competition, these are snipped out. We are deprived of one high moment of spectatorship; having watched and heard someone win what they set out to win. Watching a computer chess program which plays both white and black is not as engaging as watching two people play. Why? Because, apart from the formalities, no sense of winning occurs in the solo-machine competition. Nothing whatever hangs on the outcome. Where two programs battle each other, the interest in the competition derives from its really being between human programmers who use their programs as the tools of the competition.

Are these 'conventions'? Should we talk in the same terms about institutional-procedural protocol, say, and tacit expectations? Calling these 'conventions' seems untoward given the institutional theory requirement that conventions be rule-governed.[14] Shadow conventions are clearly not formally rule-governed; however they are kindred to the abilities, sensitivities, and background knowledge audiences must cultivate for proper appreciation. As such, they are neither incidental to the object of appreciation, nor irrelevant to matters requiring formal procedure.

132

The institutional theory holder may accept that shadow conventions embody perfectly legitimate expectations, and still declare these ones as immaterial. Because performances are relativized to social circumstance, the only problem in our case stems from the judges having mistaken one self-contained context (human-performance) for another (program-performance). Since each form of performance is set in its own context, expectations attached to the one cannot willy-nilly be grafted onto the other.

This response is too convenient. It is not obvious how many contexts are in place at any time, how one counts them, how they come into being and pass away. Genuine first cases obviously belong to no pre-established context nor have we a pre-packaged supply of appropriate responses to them. But if contexts are inventions and arise as a result of mere decisions designed to fit each case, that would deflate the currency of 'context' considerably.

Program-driven concerts may well become institutionalized events, ones we even call 'performances'. The fuss here concerns general categories. Are these artistic or engineering events? Are they more like the sort of thing ambitious violinists endure in their search for stardom, or like a high budget science fair? If our attachment to the shadow conventions persists, the institutional theory holder cannot arbitrarily appeal to some artistic context in which such conventions can never be satisfied.

To distinguish his theory from others proposing essential art-making properties, Dickie talks of the 'thickness' of the context, one which grows into a complex 'web of cultural relations'.[15] The context, it transpires, is thicker still than the institutional theory allows; indeed, as we will see, it is so thick as to draw in a range of features about human life, personality, experience, and fortune which overflow the restraints of rule-governed institutional activity. This embarrassment of riches makes unlikely the discovery of any interesting universal truths about art-making. More modestly, to welcome the program episode as a recital proper is to tolerate a fundamental change in our conception of artists. Though the open texture and institutional theories may provide insight about works of art, they are unhelpful when it comes to the players.[16]

Blindfold tests

Like Turing's blindfold test for intelligence,[17] the performance case requires certain information to be concealed. What do such tests prove? Supposedly, if a person cannot tell the difference between two items under fair conditions, then no rational grounds exist for preferring one over the other. So: If X and Y cannot be distinguished in a standard blindfold test, then whatever value attaches to X must also attach to Y. X and Y may be distinct in many ways. The principle is neutral on that score. Still, you cannot trumpet the virtues of X over Y if you cannot tell them apart in all the ways that count.

Is this so? What, besides predictable embarrassment, do blindfold tests establish? Someone claims to be an undying champion of X over anything else.

This entitles us to assume that the person can distinguish X from any Y which is other than X; but in a blindfold trial the person proves incapable of making the distinction. Suppose the person has never experienced Y before. If so, the claim 'I like X the best of all' is merely rash. After all, some Y may be so like X that no one would normally be able to distinguish them. This shows that blindfold tests may require us to revise our conceptions of what we like exactly by forcing a focus upon particular qualities rather than blanket types. If the judges had never before heard simulator-performances, and cannot distinguish them from human performances, that may suggest that what they have really valued all along about performances are certain sound properties pure and simple.

Suppose both X and Y have been experienced previously and that a preference has been stated. What follows if the same blindfold failure results? The blindfold test rests on the assumption that rational preferences can be traced back to distinguishing marks of the items under scrutiny. To state 'I prefer X to Y' entails 'I can tell X from Y', which further implies: 'X and Y are manifestly distinct with respect to some discernible feature F'. A test failure allegedly shows either that the judge lacks the competence to detect the presence of some such feature even though it is present; or that the judge is mistaken about which distinguishing feature is significant; or that there is no significant distinguishing feature at all.

But we have omitted a telling possibility; namely, that the relevant distinguishing marks of X are concealed by the test itself. Test failures might merely signal that the conditions related to rational preference are more complex; for example, that preferences combine complex, even shifting, clusters of distinguishing features and variable states of mind. The experimentally controlled conditions under which blindfold tests are conducted are, by that very token, artificial and unnatural. By limiting certain perceptions one might well forbid access to those factors which, in combination, really count. To determine precisely in advance 'all the ways that really count' involves specifications which take one considerably beyond the standard institutional conventions, if such precision is achievable at all. The person may not be able to articulate these preference factors or even be able to isolate them in experience. The test designer is in an even weaker position. So, the sceptic concludes, one never can tell whether or not failure of the blindfold test marks a weakness in the basis for rational preference or a defect in the experimental conditions. So, just because the competition judges and audience suspect nothing and just because they treat the episode exactly as they would treat any human event does not imply that there is nothing untoward about the artistic qualities of engineered concerts.

Still, this is too optimistic. The embarrassments remain, and a retreat to the mysteries of preference looks increasingly like a defeat the more the judges rely upon the imputation that they cannot really say why they prefer what they do.

The paradigm test failure involves the wine taster. Experimentally, all that really counts are the nose and palate. The tasters bring to the challenge their senses, experience, and conviction that certain qualities of sense reveal certain details about the wine. One sniffs, sips, spits, and renders judgement: 'A Rhine wine, from such-and-such a region, such-and-such a vintage, possibly from such-and-such vineyards'. The bottle is undraped. Oh my! It's from Bright's bottling plant in Oliver, British Columbia.

Suppose our taster has tried them all. Sampling a wine with a Bright's label, they anticipate the worst. Even if mildly surprised under those conditions, one is unlikely to exclaim then and there: 'Zounds! A match for any of the Niersteiners.' Indeed, one will not necessarily make this judgement even if it is true – even if someone has filled the Bright's bottle with the best of the Niersteiners. The flipside case of filling the German bottle with the pride of the Okanagan might conceivably yield greater praise than ever for Oliver's product. That these are instances of deceit and trickery doesn't lessen their import. It's just possible that the label makes or breaks the wine. People do judge books by their covers, and each other by their grooming. Sometimes, good inductive background works well in judgement; at other times, the same background fouls judgement with pre-packaged anticipations. Many times, we cannot know in advance whether our background is working fair or foul. If it weren't so very difficult to see things as they are, the truth would be ever so much easier to grasp. In matters of value, we may be entitled to set whatever standards we like. But we may also fool ourselves into believing that certain qualities are the ones that really count. That foible may not be confirmed absolutely by the blindfold test, but it is a charge that must be met.

If a program cannot be a performing artist, the onus is on the judge and anyone else who objects to say why not. That forces consideration of what really counts – even after we've realized that it can't all be told by the ear. If what we hear is insufficient to distinguish the machine from the artist, we have to reconsider not only how one identifies artists but also what expression and expressiveness are about.

How competitions are judged

What is the status of competitions? What content in a competition of this sort falls under the judges' jurisdiction? Shades of the 'other minds' problem lurk here. Supposing that no human judge could distinguish by ear alone between a human and a simulator, on what rational basis could judges withdraw judgement after learning that they had been witness to a 'mechanical' episode? Would one be entitled to call a mis-trial or have to liberalize their talk about expressive execution, interpretative innovation, and the like?

In a contest between a chess-playing program and a chess-player, it is fitting to talk about winners and losers and also about strategies and blunders.[18] It seems equally reasonable to talk in these terms even if a competition featured nothing but chess-playing programs. Why not treat the music competition thus?

To judge music and chess competitions similarly, we have to ignore certain prominent differences. These competitions are of different sorts.

The winner of a chess match can be determined independently of any judges.

Victory in chess is as explicitly determinable through the rules of the game as is any other rule-sanctioned move. It is not 'subject to interpretation', requiring the judicious scrutiny of expert third parties, except in cases involving misdemeanour.

Unlike chess players, music competitors do not achieve victory by defeating their opponents face-to-face in the exercise of their skills. Music competition runners-up have not been vanquished by the winner. A sole competition chessplayer awaiting an absentee opponent wins a game never played 'by default'. Winning by defeating and winning by default are clearly distinct. The former is definable exclusively in terms of the rules of play; the latter makes sense only in terms of the protocol of competition. In music competitions, no one can win by default. Even if only one performer turns up, there is no guarantee of a prizewinner. All the playing might be substandard.

Whereas in chess matches, any two judges must reach the same decision about a given match, no such requirement or expectation attaches to judgement about music performance. Judgements of victory in music competitions are reached by a consensus-like procedure. For Isabella to win, not every judge need concur that Isabella was the best. Isabella need not have scored highest on a majority of judges' reports. Such could never arise in a chess match or baseball game; though it does occur in boxing matches and is typical in gymnastics and synchronized swimming. Sometimes, no one wins, not because there is a draw but in the more complex sense that no one deserved to win for want of relevant merit.

Victory in artistic competition is a function of the token context of victory. The selfsame performances will not necessarily be equally ranked by different panels of judges. Such different verdicts are not due to differences in expertise in the judges. Imagine a dozen independently acknowledged competent judges to comprise a pool from which six different juries of six members are selected at random. By convention, we accept the possibility of a lack of agreement as between juries about the rankings. Even if more are likely to agree about the very worst performance than about the very best, no truly objective standards exist, so no one expects hard consistency in ranking. This reflects major differences between the types of adjudicative judgement in different undertakings.

But why shouldn't the determination of the best performance also be amenable to unambiguous characterization? Suppose that performance could be gauged against an external set of criteria so that anyone could identify correctly when such criteria had in fact been met. If music can be determinately decomposable, why not critical judgement? Some might argue that such standards exist. Disagreements would subsequently indicate failures in some judges to apprehend them correctly. Intriguingly, the manifest failure to apply rigid standards in music competitions does not lead people to think victory is settled by subjective appeal only, nor is it thought the best of an unfortunate circumstance as if we await the discovery of such unequivocal standards. I will deal with this later.

To anticipate, the story lies in the shadow conventions raised above. Chess matches, unlike music performances, are exhaustively governed by a finite set of

ARTISTS, PROGRAMS, AND PERFORMANCE

explicit rules. Indeed, the rules of chess alone properly explain why any match has been won, lost, or drawn. Though chess strategy may be 'fuzzy', the rules and boundary conditions are not. The manner of winning at chess does not determine the fact of victory, and the fact of victory is never a matter of degree. Music performance differs, in part because what we value and appreciate in it hasn't everything to do with adherence to any determinable rules we may set in advance. Those rules may, for example, set boundaries for allowable repertoire, age of contestants, qualifications of juries, venues, times, etc.; but, we wilfully allow that what really counts in performance may sometimes be created on the go in performance and subsequently discovered to count by the jury. That kind of allowance which currently makes music performance of interest to us demands a format in which, of necessity, there cannot be decision procedures governed utterly by the kind of blind formal rules typical of chess. This requires that the judges bring to bear in their judgements their personally varying backgrounds, a condition which leaves any putative set of criteria open-ended.

Comparing the judgement of machine-chess and machine-performance is, perhaps, uninteresting. Imagine a competition where human- and machine-made handicrafts are presented for blind refereeing. The merits of the items are subject to the same vagaries in judgement attaching to the music competition. Would the judges here be quite as aghast in this case? Probably not. Why should they be? After all, we have long become used to acknowledging the contest and, indeed, conflict between hand- and machine-crafted items. Can custom be the only barrier to accepting machine-performance?

One reason to resist the propriety of the program contest is because we take aesthetic interest to depend upon qualities in the performance which derive from qualities in the performer. The link between the states a performer goes through and the features of the performance is causal and involves intention. The simulator calls into question the significance of the causal link. But that causal link must implicitly be regarded as a non-contingent feature of artistic output, one which traces back to a special kind of source which we are accustomed to calling 'the artist'. If simulators do not rob humans of their expressive thunder, they must be missing something.

The challenge flows from two directions. Simulator supporters who accept weak functionalism believe the artistry in robot or Martian art is indeed a function of certain inner mechanisms of the Martian or the robot; however, the significance of any specific causal link between the expressive output – the artistic behaviour – and the inner motive force (however characterized psychologically) is minimized. The simulator story takes the precise content of the inner mechanism which originates the causal process to be a black box, and thus immaterial to the judgement of artistry under 'relevant' test conditions. All that matters is that whatever is 'inside' does nothing disappointing.

For 'adulator' supporters who support strong functionalism not any old inner constitution will do. Some strong functional equivalence between adulator and human inner structure and content is necessary. But if this requirement were

137

dogmatically applied, we would have to refuse any extension of the predicate 'artistically expressive' to any robot or Martian just because the innards of robots and Martians differ radically from ours.

We can't quite brush off the simulators. The dilemma is this: if the simulator model is sufficient for attributions of artistry, nothing artistically interesting distinguishes program and human performances. If the adulator model is necessary for such a distinction, we just don't have an adequate account of the requisite inner mechanism behind human artistic performance to specify what is lacking in the program competition. Further, we would have to restrict artistry proper to beings just like us. Since the adulator view is deeply deficient, we seem forced to accept the artist-simulator on full and equal terms.

Ought we, then, to tolerate the simulator? Should we allow our player-program the same credit we attribute to human performers? Are there any special features humans have which would make it impossible for anything else to be artistic, especially machines? Do we, wittingly or not, build seemingly peripheral psychological and culture-relative notions into the concept of artistry and thus bar it from liberal transfer to bloodless machines?

Performers as persons

To give the vagaries their vague say, one must travel the Romantic Express. Just one year after Jack Kilby produced the world's first Integrated Circuit chip at Texas Instruments, Paul Ziff had these thoughts:

> [N]o robot could sensibly be said to feel anything. Why not? . . . Because there are no psychological truths about robots. . . . Because we can program a robot to act in any way we want it to act. . . . Because we could make a robot say anything we want it to say. . . . Because robots are replaceable. Because robots have no individuality. . . . Because no robot would act tired.[19]

Though assailed by his critics for parochialism,[20] Ziff's unease echoes our doubts about program-artists.

The resolution of such doubts must partly lie in our conception of the artist. Program-driven performance can be perfectly individual. Such is trivially true of any spatio-temporal object or event. The telling question remains: Is it individualistic? Our interest in the arts occupies a sphere broader than that of the objectified public result – the sound, the composition, the painting. After all, if such program-driven artistry were to proliferate, would that not tend to eliminate any special interest attaching to human artists?

Can we comfortably countenance such an eventuality? Supposing we can, we might have to accept that our programmers had, strictly as programmers, solved the question of creativity by having produced an explanatory theory capable of dealing with individuality of expression while dispensing with persons and, in a word, culture. But that seems extravagantly optimistic – at least to those travellers on the Romantic Express convinced of the interconnectedness of things. If we reject this type of account, what stands in its stead? Herewith a hesitant and decidedly unscientific postscript.

One standing assumption has been that the artistry in the performance is exhausted by the immediate performance context, that the only artistically interesting objects emerge in an auditor's immediate perception in the appropriate institutional context of display. It is as if we place a frame of protocol around the delivery of sound such that, once we learn to attend strictly to perceptibles bounded by the frame, we are thereby party to all the content pertinent to appropriate aesthetic judgement and experience.

This frustrates any impulse to value features outside the frame. We tend to shield ourselves thereby from various matters doctrinally excluded as lacking special artistic relevance. Such 'externalist' views tend to locate all aesthetic content in publicly accessible forms, whether by reference to some inherent qualities in works indifferently apprehendable by any suitably positioned or qualified spectator, or by reference to complex relational properties linking works, institutions, art-makers, and art consumers. Externalist views differ about what should be excluded. Whereas all of them would rule out the artist's subjective states (except within causal accounts about the origin of a work), some are less stringent than others about the extent of the public domain. Some, for example, tolerate certain public but non-institutional features like the artist's personality as pertinent to interpretive and evaluative judgement. The institutional theory is clearly externalist, as are any other views (such as those antagonistic to intention) which regard any reference to the inner life of the artist as aesthetically incidental.

Though no unified anti-externalist theory of art exists, there are certain irrepressible attachments ignored by externalist views. Risking the poverty of labels, I will call the cluster of anti-externalist sympathies 'personalism'. Various personalist focal points capture our interest and imagination, and often sculpt what we hear and want to hear. We are drawn to personal details, and these seamlessly intertwine with our aesthetic expectations; for example, the riotous life of the performer, his cranky, immature conduct at august gatherings, his wayward attitude to his listeners, his crippling depressions, his bitter envy of his colleagues, his rapt intensity on stage, his savage career ambitions, and the like. We may even want our artists to be personally 'different'. There is no formulaic continuation for 'and the like'; just a familiar gist. That possible limitation is overcome by the fact we can't often go wrong, that just about any constituent of human personality, history, and fortune may occupy a privileged, however temporary, place in our aesthetic apprehension. Contrary to externalism, such constituents may be blatantly inner (for example, pent up fury), or openly unconventional and asocial (for example, open disdain for the rules of play); nor does any special authoritative monopoly regarding their choice fall to the critics and other artworld bosses, contrary to open texture views.

This diffuse domain incorporates entrenched habits which guide our identification of artists. We hear a performance not only as a sequence of perceptibles but also as the effect of real effort expended, as the product of a complex of inner affective and cognitive states, as a stage in a developmental continuum – in a word, as deriving from a story which drags in with it all the peculiarities of any human life. In many ways, there are just human beings involved – mortal, self-absorbed, dependent upon others, giving and taking, fallible, under the skin much the same. Outside that familiar unlovely foundation, we could never enjoy and appreciate what it is like for one of our very own limited kind to display occasional magnificence. Once we forget this, the performance becomes merely so much institutional ritual, and might as well be machine-driven, if all we want are perfect results. The spontaneous appeal of personalism has no serious tendency to mislead. Within such rich variegation, we map out what counts as artistic success and failure, interest and dullness. Stripped of this dimension, the question of merit in the full artistic sense cannot be raised. Our program-players have been endowed with an eerie otherworldly essence precisely because nothing whatever 'inside' them counts.[21]

The personalist starts by assuming that an aesthetic difference exists between listening to a recording of a performance and listening to a performance, even if the sound quality were indistinguishable. If one went to a concert and shut one's eyes throughout, one would miss something important about music.

What would be missed? There are, of course, the overt institutional aspects; for example, the type of seating, the physical distance and isolation of the performer from the audience, the dress and manner of the audience, and so on. These features any sociologist or cultural historian would describe. The recital is, after all, a highly structured, ritualized, and brazenly public event. But there is more afoot. The performing artist, after all, occupies centre stage. One hears, of course, but one also sees the hands or voice causing musical sound, the players' shifting facial attitudes, their bodies moving, their occasional recognition of the audience, their sweat. Some of it distracts, some of it flatters. No two players have it quite the same way. All this and more feeds what one hears and affects how one values what one hears.

Some performers take advantage of this and play for rapport by staging a choreographed show. This is performance theatre. Some conductors are so prone theatrically. Rock groups are professionally committed to performance theatre. Other players are less actorly. All the same, the performer exhibits a range of behaviour coincident with the sounds made which influence what we hear and how we judge what we hear. The personalist anticipates the individualistic in performance, the person-centred particularities of performance and manner. Much value in performance is pegged to this quality which is richer than uniqueness (which connotes simple difference from all other things), individuality (which connotes a degree of independence from other things and persons) and idiosyncrasy (which connotes mere quirkiness). An individualistic performance is not just unique, individual or idiosyncratic; it displays the signature of a person.

140

As such, it is not the mere signature of a functional operator, of that which merely occupies a role within a context of production and delivery. (Though ensemble playing displays its own signature, it is an interesting question whether ensemble playing can display as broad a range of signatures as solo playing given the need in ensemble to compromise and reach musical consensus.)

Public behaviour is just the natural cue for beliefs about the performer's circumstances and inner states which both cause and are occasioned by the music created in performance. Our unhesitant positing of these inner states affects our views of the expressive richness of the performance or the structural clarity of the technique. A few examples give the gist. Many of those who have seen Glenn Gould play Bach (usually on film or television) are invariably drawn to his mannerism of 'conducting' the active voice with his spare hand. Watching this allows some listeners to separate voices much more effectively. The uncanny clarity in Gould's voice separation is further heightened by this quirk. Further, one becomes more intricately involved in Gould's own way of making his music. Who ever remained impervious to Louis Armstrong's beaming grin, his exuberance, his rivers of sweat? And David Helfgott – well, there's another story![22] On a good night, Julian Bream gets lost in his own playing. He will stare at the ceiling during certain passages, biting his lip near to the point of drawing blood, and drift to the verge of tears. For those familiar with Bream on stage, this has a deep impact upon his listeners to many of whom his intensely visceral emotions are imparted. This, no doubt, makes his audience experience more, and also gives insight into his recorded sounds which occasionally strike those who know Bream only through ghostly recordings as gratuitously moody. In concert it all works together as one musical occasion.

There are also very rare occasions where formal performance barriers simply evaporate. In one Oxford concert, Bream served us Paganini's murderously flashy *Sonata in A* for guitar. By the time he reached the slow movement, he obviously realized this was an extremely silly piece, and so, forsaking tiresome recital solemnity, he hammed it up. In playing, he invited us all to play. Healthily, and much to his delight, many in the audience burst out laughing while he was at work. Though much of the virtuosic display was drowned out by our own laughter, it was perfect Paganini and unforgettable Bream. On the recording he made, the Paganini is, by comparison, a phantom, flawlessly musical though it is. All one can rely on here is anecdote, personal stories. But that's what it's all about, so the personalist insists. What anecdotes could draw life from our program-players?

Even the Guild has its hand in this. Stage presence and inner affect have ever been thought crucial if one is to play expressively and to 'master the feelings of [the] audience':

Those who maintain that all this can be accomplished without gesture will retract their words when, owing to their own insensibility they find themselves obliged to sit like a statue before their instrument. Ugly grimaces are, of course, inappropriate and harmful: but fitting expressions help the listener to understand the music.[23]

To the personalist, all this counts because it controls and intensifies the aesthetic climate. Performance becomes the fullest display of skill and affect, not to speak of the sound everyone hears, and even the biography everyone may follow. To exclude all this from the intrinsic aesthetic experience of performance seems an unintelligible deprivation. After all, the more we rule out of the world immediately available to us, the more we have to substitute in imagination. Why fantasize when the world is to hand? To argue further that the worth of that experience is not diminished by such exclusion seems counter to the very forces that draw performers and listeners together in the first place.

Many personalist qualities are, of course, evanescent, likely to affect some more than others, often inarticulable and outside the scope of rules and social conventions. As such, most are not amenable to systematic treatment, though they do carry the warning that any theory of performance, if possible, cannot just comprise a compartment of the externalist theory of art.

For the personalist, the program concert goes wrong because, though 'live', it is even more remote than a recording of a human performance. From the vantage point of the listener prone to enrich the live source of musical display with a fuller sense of the person making it, the program performance is altogether mysterious out-of-body sound.

Every performance manifests the dimensions of musicality and musicianship in the form of expression and technical skill. The former displays affect, mood, personality, and, for the personalist, draws its power from some inner source on which it is modelled. Technique, skill, and control are at their apex in virtuosity. Virtuosity matters because of an obvious banality of life; namely, most things that most humans do competently most of the time are simple to do. Most people can do them. We are, for most things, functionally intersubstitutable. As complexity and difficulty are imposed upon us, our native proneness to error shows itself more and more prominently. Virtuosity displays the near miracle of a mere human being doing something savagely difficult perfectly – on call; hence, the Guild's dogged determination to preserve it by reserving for it a special place. True virtuosity is a temporary suspension of predictable human fallibility. Recognizing this, one draws once more upon an inner story without which the victory over human limitation loses all substance.

The program show offers us nothing of comparable significance 'behind' the display, no opportunity at all to fill in, even speculate upon, details of the affective and cognitive backdrop. There is an engineering victory, to be sure, but that shifts the focus utterly. The simulator ranks, on the personalist view, as a 'hi-tech' music box, nothing more. Mirroring Ziff's complaints, the personalist continues the litany of denunciation:

No program could sensibly be said to perform artistically. Why not? Because the program did not, in any convoluted sense, learn what it performs. Because

142

programs do not overcome difficulties. Because programs do not choose the repertoire they perform for any personal reasons. Because programs never decide to scuttle a performance in defiance of the rules of the contest, or make people laugh. Because programs neither envy their fellow programs, nor alter their performance in an attempt to emulate what they regard as better, more sensitive, more insightful artistic reflections than their own. Because programs do not get nervous before they generate their output, nor do they worry about what their teachers, friends, and lovers will think of them if they fail. Because programs have no life plans, no personal histories. 'Because no [program] would act tired.'

And so on. Nothing mentioned above hinges centrally on the displayed acoustic output. Most of it is backstage, most of it inescapably internal and ineluctably familiar. Artist and artwork, performance and performer are quite as inseparable as people are from their histories, external and internal.

The imagined competition with which we began fails as an artistic episode because the elemental background is stripped from us once it is revealed that we have witnessed nothing but technological wizardry. I say 'nothing but' with respect. My imaginary engineers have performed engineering wonders, to be sure. Still, they have not, in the end, offered us a musical performance. Nor could they have done; not, at least, until Player #8 thanks its lucky stars. Should that happen, our quandary is over. Player #8 will have become just another one of us.

Epilogue

In Chapter 1, I drafted a model designed to be sensitive to the complex of parties and events directly involved in performance. Performances were conceived as rather large and messy events which pay due respect to players, listeners, and works. Chapter 2 added details about the supporting cast which further crammed the stage with the ghosts of tradition and its very live professional communities which guard the good name of the craft. Performing was there portrayed as essentially a highly regulated undertaking, a primary action craft.

Here we press matters further afield. Personalism reminds us of aspects within the performance environment which colour our experience of performance and which, if purged altogether, would impoverish it utterly. Why do we attend performances? Not just for the sound, obviously, and not just for the sights. We go to be moved, to be delighted, to learn, to be charmed, entertained, and transported. We go for the uneasy void of silence, the gush of sound for its own sake, the surprises of the not-yet-transpired and the comforts of the familiar. All these our engineers may conceivably offer us. But we also go to be engaged by someone we count on recognizing, to be addressed by someone, to work vicariously with them, to admire a fallible, vulnerable being able to remind us briefly of infallibility. In every human performance, something is at stake, something matters for all involved. The machine recital, like the solo computer chess tournament, is, in all these respects, indifferent, without risk, failure, success, or creation.

Personalism reminds us that performance is a way of communicating, not especially a work or a composer's notions, but a person, the performer, through music. This has repercussions. The original model, though weighed down heavily, kept performance within the art-aesthetic household. We respected the need to conceive it on its own music-specific terms and in terms of the artworld generally. Personalism intimates that a proper understanding of performance must move beyond these confines by coming to appreciate ritual, forms of communication, action and its significance, human benefit and reciprocity, and a good many other concerns belonging naturally to social conduct. This implies that performance is probably most fully understood in a domain of study much broader than aesthetics can ever encompass.

Surely, one might protest, there is always room for trim and manageable models which afford modest but secure insights. Abstractions, after all, free us from the confusion of gratuitous detail. But, theoretical abstractions often behave like more than mere abstractions. They have ambitions. They often want to smooth over all the lumps and creases which make life interesting in our creased and lumpy world.[24] So, maybe we'd best take things as we find them. Maybe the crazy brother of a famous one-armed piano player got it largely right when he said: 'What's ragged should be left ragged'.[25]

NOTES

INTRODUCTION

1 To name a few, the following concentrate on works and notation: Goehr, *The Imaginary Museum of Musical Works*, New York, Oxford University Press, 1992; Goodman, *Languages of Art*, Indianapolis, Hackett, 1968; Kivy, 'Platonism in Music', *Grazer Philosophische Studien*, 1983, vol. 19, pp. 109–29; Levinson, 'What a Musical Work Is', *Journal of Philosophy*, 1980, vol. 77, pp. 5–28; Levinson, *Music, Art, and Metaphysics*, Ithaca, Cornell University Press, 1990; Price, 'What is a Piece of Music?', *British Journal of Aesthetics*, 1982, vol. 22, pp. 322–36; Walton, 'The Presentation and Portrayal of Sound Patterns', in Dancy *et al.*, pp. 237–57; Webster, 'Music is Not a Notational System', *Journal of Aesthetics and Art Criticism*, 1971, vol. 29, pp. 489–97; Webster, 'A Theory of the Compositional Work of Music', *Journal of Aesthetics and Art Criticism*, 1974, vol. 33, pp. 59–66; Wollheim, *Art and its Objects* 2nd edn, New York, Harper & Row, 1980; Wolterstorff, 'Toward an Ontology of Artworks', *Nous*, 1975, vol. 9, pp. 115–42 (Reprinted in Margolis, *Philosophy Looks at the Arts*, pp. 229–52); and Wolterstorff, *Works and Worlds of Art*, Oxford, Oxford University Press, 1980.

   Musical theory and analysis also assume this perspective.

2 Performance is the theme in Alperson, 'On Musical Improvisation', *Journal of Aesthetics and Art Criticism*, 1984, vol. 43, pp. 17–30; Cone, *Musical Form and Musical Performance*, New York, W.W. Norton, 1968; Davies, 'Authenticity in Musical Performance', *British Journal of Aesthetics*, 1987, vol. 27, pp. 39–50; Kivy, 'On the Concept of the "Historically Authentic" Performance', *Monist*, 1988, vol. 71, pp. 278–91; Kivy, *Authenticities: Philosophical Reflections on Musical Performance*, Ithaca, Cornell University Press, 1995; Levinson, 'Authentic Performance and Performance Means', in Levinson, *Music, Art, and Metaphysics*, pp. 393–408; Mark, 'The Work of Virtuosity', *Journal of Philosophy*, 1980, vol. 77, pp. 28–45; Mark, 'Philosophy of Piano Playing: Reflections on the Concept of Performance', *Philosophy and Phenomenological Research*, 1981, vol. 41, pp. 299–324; Thom, *For an Audience*, Philadelphia, Temple University Press, 1994; and Walton, 'Style and the Products and Processes of Art', in Lang, *The Concept of Style*, pp. 45–66. Also see the great tutors: Couperin, *L'Art de Toucher le Clavecin*, Paris, 1716; Quantz, trans. Reilly, *On Playing the Flute*, London, Faber & Faber, 1966; and Bach, trans. Mitchell, *Essay on the True Art of Playing Keyboard Instruments*, London, Eulenberg Books, 1974; as well as modern classics such as Dart, *The Interpretation of Music*, London, Hutchinson, 1954; and Donington, *The Interpretation of Early Music*, London, Faber & Faber, 1963.

3 Some notable works emphasizing the qualities of musical sound and our experience of music are Beardsley, 'Understanding Music', in Price, *On Criticizing Music: Five Philosophical Perspectives*, pp. 55–73; Budd, *Music and the Emotions*, London, Routledge & Kegan Paul, 1985; Budd, 'Music and the Communication of Emotion', *Journal of Aesthetics and Art Criticism*, 1989, vol. 47, pp. 129–38; Davies, 'The Expression of Emotion in Music', *Mind*, 1980, vol. 89, pp. 67–86; Davies, *Musical Meaning & Expression*, Ithaca, Cornell University Press, 1994; Higgins, *The Music of our Lives*, Philadelphia, Temple University Press, 1991; Karl and Robinson, 'Shostakovich's Tenth Symphony and the Musical Expression of Cognitively Complex Emotions', *Journal of Aesthetics and Art Criticism*, 1995, vol. 53, pp. 401–15; Kivy, *The Corded Shell: Reflections on Musical Expression*, Princeton, Princeton University Press, 1980; Kivy, *Sound and Semblance*, Princeton, Princeton University Press, 1984; Kivy, *Sound Sentiment*, Philadelphia, Temple University Press, 1989; Kivy, *Music Alone*, Ithaca, Cornell University Press, 1990; Levinson, 'Music and Negative Emotions', *Pacific Philosophical Quarterly*, 1982, vol. 63, pp. 327–46; Levinson, *Music, Art, and Metaphysics*, Ithaca, Cornell University Press, 1990; Meyer, *Emotion and Meaning in Music*, Chicago, University of Chicago Press, 1956; Ridley, *Music, Value and the Passions*, Ithaca, Cornell University Press, 1995; and Scruton, *The Aesthetic Understanding*, London, Methuen, 1983.

1 A MODEL OF MUSICAL PERFORMANCE

1 The intended context is the familiar Western 'classical' music tradition of the formal performance in which independently identifiable notated works are performed. In so far as an improvisation constitutes the making of a work, improvisational performances also involve works, though ones which completely emerge in performance.
2 For a sympathetic defence of the resistance put up by common sense, see Tilghman, *But Is It Art?*, New York, Blackwell, 1986.
3 See Mark, 'Philosophy of Piano Playing: Reflections on the Concept of Performance', *Philosophy and Phenomenological Research*, 1981, vol. 41, pp. 299–324. Intention is also a key ingredient for Wolterstorff, *Works and Worlds of Art*, Oxford, Oxford University Press, 1980.
4 See Alperson, 'On Musical Improvisation', *Journal of Aesthetics and Art Criticism*, 1984, vol. 43, pp. 17–30.
5 Though one need not necessarily labour to acquire skill, the relative value attached to certain skills is often partially a function of the toil they typically exact in their acquisition.
6 My position is a footnote to Plato's insight about the bond between *aretē* and *technē*. I also draw upon Alasdair Macintyre's treatment of virtues and their relation to 'goods internal to practices' and traditions. See Macintyre, *After Virtue* 2nd edn, Notre Dame, University of Notre Dame Press, 1984; especially Chapter 15.
7 For further information see Bateman, *Introduction to Computer Music*, New York, John Wiley, 1980, pp. 179–80. Note that 'frequency shifting is radically different than simple transposition' (p. 180) because of effects upon the overtone series. See also Manning, *Electronic and Computer Music*, Oxford, Oxford University Press, 1987, pp. 61–3. Basic ring modulators are easy to build. Although now old-fashioned, Anderton, *Electronic Projects for Musicians*, New York, Amsco Publications, 1972, pp. 99–104 remains instructive. Newer designs are found in Anderton, Moses, and Bartlett, *Digital Projects for Musicians*, New York, Amsco Publications, 1994.
8 Thanks to Allen Strange for information on these devices.
9 Roads (ed.), *Composers and the Computer*, Los Altos, William Kaufmann, 1985, p. xvii.

10 Max Mathews, in his 'Foreword' to Roads and Strawn (eds), *Foundations of Computer Music*, Cambridge, MIT Press, 1985. Mathews' confidence concerning the relaxation of technical demands is compromised in his brief comment on intelligent instruments played as 'super organs':

> The performer controls every aspect of the sound by means of the instrument's sensors, and must make a separate gesture for each note played. Intimate control over the sound is available, but to master it requires a virtuoso. Because of the richness of its timbres, the instrument needs many controls. In this mode it is more demanding than any normal instrument.

11 Suppose, in reverse, one sounds something simple like *Twinkle, Twinkle* by playing something difficult like the *Chaconne*? Here, though one might spontaneously attribute to the player the ability to play the easier piece, one would not be justified in saying that the musician has played it. Thanks to Catherine Wilson for the example.

12 The analogy is limited. Motives are internal states; here we deal with external episodes. Motives are taken to be analogous to movement sequences. In moral efforts, we accept reluctantly that our motives usually underdetermine the intended results so that we can never guarantee success. By contrast, in music, we normally expect a performer's chosen movements to result in a certain audible result. A performance, the product of a musician's efforts, is supposed to be completely under control. We aren't nearly as charitable regarding performance mishaps because performance contexts are causally much simpler than those involving moral effort and are prey to far fewer unforeseeable upsets, and performances are typically rehearsed, practised, prepared in advance. Whatever moral training comes to, it does not involve dry-runs with the right motives.

13 Quoted in Machlis, *Introduction to Contemporary Music*, New York, W.W. Norton, 1961, p. 352.

14 On the public function of artistic activity, see Wolterstorff, *Works and Worlds of Art*, Oxford, Oxford University Press, 1980, Part I; especially, pp. 29–32. See also Thom, *For an Audience*, Philadelphia, Temple University Press, 1994.

15 Bach, trans. Mitchell, *Essay on the True Art of Playing Keyboard Instruments*, London, Eulenberg Books, 1974, Chapter III, 1, section 14. Quantz, ever more pragmatic, chastises self-indulgent players:

> If we were to demand that all our listeners be connoisseurs and musical scholars, their number would not be very great; we would have to seek them out, one at a time, among the professional musicians. And from the latter it would be most unwise to hope for many benefits. . . . Thus it is most important that the professional musician seek to play each piece distinctly and with such expression that it becomes intelligible to both the learned and the unlearned, and hence may please them both.
>
> Quantz, trans. Reilly, On Playing the Flute, London,
Faber & Faber, 1966, Chapter IX, 7.

16 See Chapter 3, 'Performances and musical works'.

17 This case involves a single work with two attributions. Interesting discussions treat the case of two identically sounding but distinct 'works' by two composers. See the Beethoven/Marthoven example in Walton, 'The Presentation and Portrayal of Sound Patterns', in Dancy *et al.*, pp. 237–57, and the Sterngrab/Grotesteen case in Levinson, 'What a Musical Work Is', *Journal of Philosophy*, 1980, vol. 77, pp. 5–28.

18 On the nature and influence of some such constraints in and on performance see, for example, Davies, 'Authenticity in Musical Performance', *British Journal of Aesthetics*, 1987, vol. 27, pp. 39–50, and Davies, 'Transcription, Authenticity, and Performance', *British Journal of Aesthetics*, 1988, vol. 28, pp. 216–27.

19 See Godlovitch, 'Aesthetic Judgement and Hindsight', *Journal of Aesthetics and Art Criticism*, 1987, vol. 46, pp. 75–83, and Goehr, 'Being True to the Work', *Journal of Aesthetics and Art Criticism*, 1989, vol. 47, pp. 55–67. Also, relatedly, discussions on authentic performance in Davies, 'Transcription, Authenticity, and Performance', *British Journal of Aesthetics*, 1988, vol. 28, pp. 216–27; Young, 'The Concept of Authentic Performance', *British Journal of Aesthetics*, 1988, vol. 28, pp. 228–38; Kivy, 'On the Concept of the 'Historically Authentic' Performance', *Monist*, 1988, vol. 71, pp. 278–91; Godlovitch, 'Authentic Performance', *Monist*, 1988, vol. 71, pp. 258–77, and Levinson, 'Authentic Performance and Performance Means', in Levinson, *Music, Art, and Metaphysics*, pp. 393–408.

20 See Sharpe, 'Type, Token, Interpretation, and Performance', *Mind*, 1979, vol. 88, pp. 437–40, and Sharpe, *Contemporary Aesthetics*, New York, St Martin's Press, 1983 on interpretation classes. Also Zemach, 'Nesting: The Ontology of Interpretation', *Monist*, 1990, vol. 73, pp. 296–311.

21 Success may, to a degree, be relativized to the gifts and expectations of the players and listeners. Ultimately, however, it is the performance community which maintains the standard. See Chapter 2.

22 The break can occasionally be deliberate. In a scene in the pulp fiction film biography *Rhapsody in Blue*, Gershwin's *Concerto in F* is being performed. A page rushes on stage and hands the conductor a note with the news that Gershwin had just died. The conductor stops the orchestra, reads the note to the audience, and then asks the players to resume where they left off. This performance has been interrupted and then continued. One need not judge it as flawed because the break was intentional and had a musical point, however eccentric. Such suspensions, however, require special justification precisely because they violate a standing norm. See *Rhapsody in Blue* (Director: Irving Rapper, Hollywood: Warner Brothers, 1945) (Oscar Levant played piano). In a rougher, more charming sequence in *The Oklahoma Kid* (Director: Lloyd Bacon, Hollywood: Warner Brothers, 1939), the Kid (James Cagney) interrupts his rendition of *I Don't Want to Play in Your Yard* by flattening a rudely interfering heavy, and then carries on, without losing the spirit.

23 Nyman, *Experimental Music*, New York, Schirmer's Sons, 1981, pp. 140–2.

24 Suppose a work requires an ensemble of twelve players. Suppose the staffing is continually rotated in performance by one player at a time. Would this be less disconcerting than rotation in the solo case?

25 Kivy, *Music Alone*, Ithaca, Cornell University Press, 1990, p. 11.

26 Sharpe, 'Type, Token, Interpretation, and Performance', *Mind*, 1979, vol. 88, pp. 437–40, and Sharpe, *Contemporary Aesthetics*, New York, St Martin's Press, 1983.

27 The proponents of historically authentic performance might, of course, disagree. Enormous effort has been expended on articulating some of these very norms. See, for instance, these classics of re-construction: Dolmetsch, *The Interpretation of the Music of the XVIIth and XVIIIth Centuries Revealed by Contemporary Evidence*, London, Novello & Co., 1946; Dart, *The Interpretation of Music*, London, Hutchinson, 1954, and Donington, *The Interpretation of Early Music*, London, Faber & Faber, 1963.

28 Related criticisms are developed by Dipert, 'Types and Tokens: A Reply to Sharpe', *Mind*, 1980, vol. 89, pp. 587–8, and Davies, 'The Ontology of Musical Works and the Authenticity of Their Performances', *Nous*, 1991, vol. 25, pp. 21–41.

29 On related themes, see Levinson and Alperson, 'What is a Temporal Art?', in French (ed.), *Midwest Studies in Philosophy: Philosophy and the Arts*, University of Notre Dame Press, 1991, pp. 439–50. Note, even a work which calls for seeming disruption obeys ritual norms which can be violated if one interrupts the performance by ignoring the call to disrupt.

30 The connection has long-standing roots. Thus Thomas Mace is 'ready to Prove by Demonstration (to any Person intelligible) That Musick is a Language, and has its Significations, as Words have . . . ' (Mace, *Musick's Monument or a remembrancer of the best practical musick both divine and civil, that has ever been known to have been in the world*, London, 1676, p. 11). Edward Cone adopts a 'picture of music as a form of utterance to be compared and contrasted with the verbal utterances of ordinary speech' (Cone, *The Composer's Voice*, Berkeley, University of California Press, 1974, p. 160). Finally, Thomas Carson Mark develops an elaborate speech-act model of performance involving both assertion and quotation of musical works in Mark, 'Philosophy of Piano Playing: Reflections on the Concept of Performance', *Philosophy and Phenomenological Research*, 1981, vol. 41, pp. 299–324. For a powerful critique of the linguistic model of musical meaning see Davies, *Musical Meaning & Expression*, Ithaca, Cornell University Press, 1994; especially Chapter 1.

31 One could, of course, multiply examples. Consider poetry readings and drama performances. These seem far less serializable than lectures though one can envisage acceptable delivery discontinuities between various formal sections. Presumably no one delivered the entire *Iliad* at a sitting, and very long dramatizations are commonly broken into discrete bits, particularly on television.

32 See Mace, *Musick's Monument...*, London, 1676; Cone, *The Composer's Voice*, Berkeley, University of California Press, 1974, or Mark, 'Philosophy of Piano Playing: Reflections on the Concept of Performance', *Philosophy and Phenomenological Research*, 1981, vol. 41, pp. 299–324.

33 For an interesting and characteristically intricate listener's side to the story about why anyone tolerates this, see Levinson, 'Music and Negative Emotions', *Pacific Philosophical Quarterly*, 1982, vol. 63, pp. 327–46.

34 Thanks to John H. Brown for this example.

35 Such accounts range from stringent expectations of listening expertise, through basic technical awareness, to much less demanding, more qualitative and 'metaphorical' apprehension. Rosen provides an instance of the first in discussing the true composer's listener. Brahms' *Piano Concerto no. 2* alludes to Beethoven's *Emperor Concerto* by mirroring the scheme of the latter. 'This sort of allusion is like the modernized quotation from Horace practised by poets of the time of Pope. It creates an intimate link between poet and educated reader, composer and professional musician – and excludes the ordinary reader and listener' (Rosen, 'Influence: Plagiarism and Inspiration', in Price, *On Criticizing Music: Five Philosophical Perspectives*, pp. 16–37). Less demanding, but still no dilettante's game, is the call to understand music in a full music-specific sense through attention to structural and dynamic factors, detailed knowledge of which cannot be gained without formal musical study. See Scruton, *The Aesthetic Understanding*, London, Methuen, 1983, pp. 34–101, and Scruton, 'Analytical Philosophy and the Meaning of Music', *Journal of Aesthetics and Art Criticism*, 1987, vol. 46, pp. 169–176. In discussing the last form of attentive listening, Beardsley shelters various qualitative, affect-laden, and metaphorical accounts of music against the positivistic reductions of the Schenkerians and other formalists, and makes room for listeners attending to just those properties of aesthetic noteworthiness music exemplifies; for example, affective ones (sadness, bitterness) all the way to 'modes of continuation' (Beardsley, 'Understanding Music', in Price, *On Criticizing Music: Five Philosophical Perspectives*, p. 70). My account is

neutral regarding these variants, though, clearly, Rosen's 'connoisseur' can scarcely claim title to being a typical listener.

36 Cone, *Musical Form and Musical Performance*, New York, W.W. Norton, 1968, p. 12.

37 Though building into his player the intention 'that his listeners will take the sounds produced to have [an] authority' as a condition of performance, Mark places no correlative requirement on the listener (Mark, 'Philosophy of Piano Playing: Reflections on the Concept of Performance', *Philosophy and Phenomenological Research*, 1981, vol. 41, p. 312). This undervalues the intrinsically social quality of performance. The best-intentioned player can still fail to give a performance. It takes two to communicate.

38 See Aristotle on mutilations. Mutilations are superficial imperfections in things which do not violate their essence; for example, 'a cup is not mutilated if a hole is made in it, but only if the handle or some projection is broken'. Such is a failure in a cup, but not, like the cup with the hole in the bottom, a failure as a cup. Aristotle (trans. Tredennick), *Metaphysics*, London, Heinemann, 1933, Book V, xxvii, 1024a12ff.

39 'Instance' here is meant in a bland sense to avoid reference to any complex relations between universals and particulars, or types and tokens.

2 SKILLS AND GUILDS

1 Interpretive directives did not become prominent until the nineteenth century. See Dorian, *The History of Music in Performance*, New York, W.W. Norton, 1942.

2 Dennett, *Elbow Room,* Cambridge, MIT Press, 1984, p. 56.

3 See Walton, 'Style and the Products and Processes of Art', in Lang, *The Concept of Style*, pp. 45–66.

4 Examples abound in Plato's Socratic dialogues; for example, in Plato (trans. Grube), *Republic*, Indianapolis, Hackett, 1974, Book I.

5 For a refurbishing of the notions of *technē* and virtue under the concept of 'practice' see Macintyre, *After Virtue* (2nd edn), Notre Dame, University of Notre Dame Press, 1984, especially Chapter XIV; also, Carroll, 'Art, Practice, and Narrative', *Monist*, 1988, vol. 71, pp. 140–56.

6 For a parallel conception of the scientific or research community identified in terms of its dedication to a particular paradigm, see Kuhn, *The Structure of Scientific Revolutions* (2nd edn), Chicago, Chicago University Press, 1970, pp. 176–81. Strongly realist variants are found in Hacking, *Representing and Intervening*, Cambridge, Cambridge University Press, 1983, and Kitcher, *The Advancement of Science*, New York, Oxford University Press, 1993.

7 Consider, for example, Thomas Zach's highly asymmetrical 'Violino-Harpa' (1873), designed to improve the violin. See Young, *The Look of Music*, Vancouver, Vancouver Museums and Planetarium Association, 1980, p. 230.

8 These and related issues are considered in: Davies, 'Authenticity in Musical Performance', *British Journal of Aesthetics*, 1987, vol. 27, pp. 39–50; Young, 'The Concept of Authentic Performance', *British Journal of Aesthetics*, 1988, vol. 28, pp. 228–38; Kivy, 'On the Concept of the 'Historically Authentic' Performance', *Monist*, 1988, vol. 71, pp. 278–91; Godlovitch, 'Authentic Performance', *Monist*, 1988, vol. 71, pp. 258–77; and Levinson, 'Authentic Performance and Performance Means', in Levinson, *Music, Art, and Metaphysics*, pp. 393–408.

9 Massey *et al.*, *A Synthesist's Guide to Acoustic Instruments*, New York, Amsco Publications, 1987, p. 5. Also, Dodge and Jerse, *Computer Music*, New York, Schirmer, 1985.

10 Munrow, *Instruments of the Middle Ages and Renaissance*, London, Oxford University Press, 1976.

11 I exaggerate for effect. The guitars and lutes developed independently and co-existed for a long while because they served different musical functions. And so with the viols and violins, the latter being for 'rude' types, the former for the gentility. Still, the guitar ultimately assumed all the roles of the lute thus leaving no one to mourn the latter's disappearance.

12 Dodge and Jerse, *Computer Music*, New York, Schirmer, 1985, p. 79.

13 Championing the obvious advantage microscopes provide over naked vision, Ian Hacking remarks that 'it is doubtless of some small interest to know the limits of the naked eye, just as it is a challenge to climb a rock face without pitons or Everest without oxygen. But if you care chiefly to get to the top you will use all the tools that are handy. . . . Any skilled artisan cares for new tools' (Hacking, 'Do We See Through a Microscope?', in Brody and Grandy (eds), *Readings in the Philosophy of Science*, p. 31). Clearly, mountaineers don't 'care chiefly to get to the top' in Hacking's sense. They care to climb to the top. This puts them in with the naked eye school of visual prowess.

14 Stephen Davies brought this example to my attention.

3 PERFORMANCES AND MUSICAL WORKS

1 Apel, *Harvard Dictionary of Music* (2nd edn), Cambridge, Harvard University Press, 1972, p. 418.

2 Regarding the import of 'musical work', I rely on common paradigms; for example, that Beethoven's *Pastoral Symphony* and Dowland's *Forlorne Hope Fancy* are musical works, and that such works are typically represented in score. Important analyses of the concept of a musical work are found in Wolterstorff, 'Toward an Ontology of Artworks', *Nous*, 1975, vol. 9, pp. 115–42, in Margolis, *Philosophy Looks at the Arts*, pp. 229–52; Wolterstorff, *Works and Worlds of Art*, Oxford, Oxford University Press, 1980; Levinson, 'What a Musical Work Is', *Journal of Philosophy*, 1980, vol. 77, pp. 5–28; and Walton, 'The Presentation and Portrayal of Sound Patterns', in Dancy *et al.*, pp. 237–57.

3 Functional subordination is suggested in Walton, 'The Presentation and Portrayal of Sound Patterns', in Dancy *et al.*, pp. 237–57; ontological subordination in Mark, 'Philosophy of Piano Playing: Reflections on the Concept of Performance', *Philosophy and Phenomenological Research*, 1981, vol. 41, pp. 299–324.

4 See Wolterstorff, *Works and Worlds of Art*, Oxford, Oxford University Press, 1980, and Alperson, 'On Musical Improvisation', *Journal of Aesthetics and Art Criticism*, 1984, vol. 43, pp. 17–30.

5 Bach (trans. Mitchell), *Essay on the True Art of Playing Keyboard Instruments*, London, Eulenberg Books, 1974, Chapter VII, 1, Section 5; Chapter III, 1, Section 15.

6 'Judging by composers' products, they have worked consistently toward increasing control of musical elements (that is, sound, harmony, melody, rhythm, and growth), extending this control also into steadily larger dimensions' (Larue, *Guidelines for Style Analysis*, New York, W.W. Norton, 1970, p. 202). Control for Larue represents a musical norm. Improvisation itself involves a composer's 'transferring partial responsibility to the performer' (p. 203), a perspective improvisers might reject.

7 See Pousseur, 'The Question of Order in New Music', in Boretz and Cone, *Perspectives on Contemporary Music Theory*, pp. 97–115; and Cone, 'Beyond Analysis', *ibid.*, pp. 72–90.

8 In Wollheim, *Art and its Objects* (2nd edn), New York, Harper & Row, 1980; Wolterstorff, *Works and Worlds of Art*, Oxford, Oxford University Press, 1980, and Levinson, 'What a Musical Work Is', *Journal of Philosophy*, 1980, vol. 77, pp. 5–28.

9 See Harrison, 'Types and Tokens and the Identity of the Musical Work', *British Journal of Aesthetics*, 1975, vol. 15, pp. 336–46; Sharpe, 'Type, Token, Interpretation, and Performance', *Mind*, 1979, vol. 88, pp. 437–40; and Sharpe, *Contemporary Aesthetics*, New York, St Martin's Press, 1983.

10 On case (1), consider the physically impossible chord in *Etude #6* (MM.5, 1st chord) in Villa-Lobos, *Douze Etudes pour Guitare*. This was not a type-setting error. On (2), Mario Castelnuovo-Tedesco's guitar pieces undergo revision by editors with guitar savvy who provide alternate versions of the genuine article and the playable article; for example, Tedesco's *Suite Escarraman Opus 177* (Gilardino (ed.), Edizioni Musicali Berben). The *ossia* convention is occasionally adopted to offer a technically easier alternative, though usually with musical improvement in mind.

11 Differing accounts as to the essential components of the work are developed in Wolterstorff, *Works and Worlds of Art*, Oxford, Oxford University Press, 1980; Levinson, 'What a Musical Work Is', *Journal of Philosophy*, 1980, vol. 77, pp. 5–28; Walton, 'The Presentation and Portrayal of Sound Patterns', in Dancy *et al.*, pp. 237–57, and Kivy, 'Platonism in Music', *Grazer Philosophische Studien*, 1983, vol. 19, pp. 109–29, among others.

12 See Levinson. 'What a Musical Work Is', *Journal of Philosophy*, 1980, vol. 77, pp. 5–28.

13 There is a Rylean temptation to scoff. Nonetheless, that paintings too are ultimately free of the toils of time is explored in Zemach, 'No Identification Without Evaluation', *British Journal of Aesthetics*, 1986, vol. 26, pp. 239–51. See also Levinson, 'Zemach on Paintings', *British Journal of Aesthetics*, 1987, vol. 27, pp. 278–83. Webster, 'A Theory of the Compositional Work of Music', *Journal of Aesthetics and Art Criticism*, 1974, vol. 33, pp. 59–66, develops the view that musical works exist only in their instantiations.

14 This is not to deny that such models exist. For a discussion about works and time, see Anderson, 'Musical Identity', *Journal of Aesthetics and Art Criticism*, 1982, vol. 40, pp. 285–91 and Anderson, 'Musical Kinds', *British Journal of Aesthetics*, 1985, vol. 25, pp. 43–9. On the formalist side, see Martin, 'On the Proto-Theory of Musical Structure', in Boretz and Cone, *Perspectives on Contemporary Music Theory*, pp. 91–6, who characterizes any musical work as 'a virtual class of virtual couples'.

15 One would scarcely say that any general principle of classical mechanics or any theorem of Euclidean geometry underdetermined its instances because, say, the former neglected to specify the purchase price of the projectile or the latter the colour of the quadrilateral.

16 Pitch fixity may just be a Terran fixation. See Walton, 'The Presentation and Portrayal of Sound Patterns', in Dancy *et al.*, pp. 237–57.

17 Scheibe, 'Der critische Musicus', in David and Mendel, *The Bach Reader*, p. 238.

18 Walton, 'The Presentation and Portrayal of Sound Patterns', in Dancy *et al.*, pp. 237–57.

19 If there is a problem about not being able to hear a set of execution directives, this cannot be more awkward than hearing a structure or pattern.

20 These represent the type well or poorly relative to the standards overseeing the instantiation. See Levinson, 'Evaluating Musical Performance', *Journal of Aesthetic Education*, 1987, vol. 21, pp. 75–88.

21 The idea that performances cannot stand to the work as copies of a book stand to the novel because the former unlike the latter involves interpretation has been carefully explored in Sharpe, 'Type, Token, Interpretation, and Performance', *Mind*, 1979,

vol. 88, pp. 437–40, and Walton, 'The Presentation and Portrayal of Sound Patterns', in Dancy *et al.*, pp. 237–57.

22 Dependent types are like abstract particulars as portrayed, for instance, by Webster, 'A Theory of the Compositional Work of Music', *Journal of Aesthetics and Art Criticism*, 1974, vol. 33, pp. 59–66, and Margolis, 'The Ontological Peculiarity of Works of Art', in Margolis, *Philosophy Looks at the Arts*, pp. 253–60. I resist, however, Webster's suggestion that a work is as amply instantiated in a score or magnetic trace on tape as it is in a performance.

23 Cone, *Musical Form and Musical Performance*, New York, W.W. Norton, 1968, p. 56.

24 Mark, 'Philosophy of Piano Playing: Reflections on the Concept of Performance', *Philosophy and Phenomenological Research*, 1981, vol. 41, pp. 302–4. I disagree with Mark's view that performances are only contingently related to musical works.

25 While works do not need scores, a full score is sufficient for the existence of a work. See Mark, 'Philosophy of Piano Playing: Reflections on the Concept of Performance', *Philosophy and Phenomenological Research*, 1981, vol. 41, pp. 300–1.

26 Twain, *The Adventures of Tom Sawyer*, 1876, Chapter 26.

27 See, for example, Christopher Plummer's Holmes in *Murder By Decree* (1979) (Director: Bob Clark) and its take on the Jack the Ripper legend. Nor should we forget Basil Rathbone's Holmes stalking Nazi spies in *Sherlock Holmes and the Voice of Terror* (1942) (Director: John Rawlins). Must Holmes at least be a sleuth? Not necessarily if one traces his teenage or retirement years. But what makes this Holmes? A few anchors here and there do the trick. What matters is that, if we want this very character to be Holmes, we can and will make the necessary adjustment.

28 Cone remarks: 'Even the performance that seems a revelation may become boring through repetition. This is why recorded performances inevitably lose their excitement and sometimes eventually become unbearable' (Cone, *Musical Form and Musical Performance*, New York, W.W. Norton, 1968, p. 35).

29 The work may benefit from this lenience. Let 'a person of delicate, sensitive insight who knows the meaning of a good performance [play certain works], and the composer will learn to his astonishment that there is more in his music than he had ever known or believed. Good performance can, in fact, improve and gain praise for even an average composition' (Bach (trans. Mitchell), *Essay on the True Art of Playing Keyboard Instruments*, London, Eulenberg Books, 1974, Chapter III, 13).

30 Analogies always invite further comparisons. We might have distinguished the story-teller (analogous to the improviser) from the story-reader (parallel with the score-player), the latter bound by more constraints and conventions. If performing is communicating, the score-player doesn't necessarily communicate a text with meaning.

31 Two translation moods are captured in the following remarks. Of Homer's *Odyssey*, translator Ennis Rees comments: 'For most people the more and better a myth is translated into their own language the more effective it is likely to be, and needless to say the translation of poetry is effective only insofar as it approaches re-creation . . . I have tried to be faithful to the sentiments, ideas, and images of the original. . . . But I have also done what I could to make a readable English poem' (Homer (trans. Rees), *The Odyssey of Homer*, New York, The Modern Library, 1960, p. xv). Rilke's translator Norton sees his job as follows: 'The translator's prime effort has gone into the translation itself, into the search for equivalents – not dictionary equivalents, but those that should take in the special flavour, the corresponding ambiguity, the poet's usage, the "secret name"'. I still believe that the closest adherence to the poetry itself is best achieved through the most literal possible rendering of word, phrase, image, far as the result may prove to remain from the final perfection, the 'indescribable

"being-there" of the original poem' (Rilke (trans. Norton), *Sonnets to Orpheus*, New York, W.W. Norton, 1942, p. 11).

4 COMPUTERS, READYMADES, AND ARTISTIC AGENCY

1 For a brisk antidotal reaction see Wolterstorff, 'The Philosophy of Art After Analysis and Romanticism', *Journal of Aesthetics and Art Criticism*, 1987, vol. 46, pp. 151–68.

2 There is a partner case in the philosophy of science involving observability. Bas van Fraassen argues for the significance of the fact that, whereas one can see Neptune's moons with the unaided eye (if brought closer to Neptune), one cannot analogously ever directly see a blood cell because we're just too big. See van Fraassen, *The Scientific Image*, Oxford, Oxford University Press, 1980.

3 A good survey is in Manning, *Electronic and Computer Music*, Oxford, Oxford University Press, 1987, Chapter 10.

4 Walton puts this down to what we can call the 'foreign agency' quality of the sound. The listener cannot get 'a sense of the physical activities by which they were made . . . scraping, banging, blowing, and so forth' (Walton, 'Style and the Products and Processes of Art', in Lang, *The Concept of Style*, pp. 53–4). But isn't this a matter of imagination? Electronic sounds are as physically evocative as any, even if they need not remind one of conventional instruments. My point is stronger. The music is remote aurally because it is literally remote physically. Whether it sounds 'ethereal, disembodied, unreal' is not very telling. The first time I ever heard the celesta was in Bartok's *Music for Strings, Percussion, and Celesta* (1937). It sounded ethereal, disembodied, and unreal to me. Was I mistaken thinking of it this way?

5 'Whatsoever . . . he removes out of the state that Nature hath provided and left it in, he hath mixed his labour with it, and joined to it something that is his own, and thereby makes it his property' (Locke, *Second Treatise of Civil Government 1690*, Chapter 5, in Locke (Laslett (ed.)), *Two Treatises of Government*, New York, The New American Library, 1965).

6 Manning, *Electronic and Computer Music*, Oxford, Oxford University Press, 1987, p. 14.

7 Manning, *Electronic and Computer Music*, Oxford, Oxford University Press, 1987, p. 11.

8 For an interesting discussion of control see Dennett, *Elbow Room*, Cambridge, MIT Press, 1984, Chapter 3.

9 See Danto, *The Transfiguration of the Commonplace*, Cambridge, Harvard University Press, 1981.

5 EXPERIMENTS WITH MUSICAL AGENCY

1 Most of the examples of experimental music are drawn from Nyman, *Experimental Music*, New York, Schirmer's Sons, 1981, a stimulating, sympathetic, and densely packed survey of 'Cage and Beyond'. The page references to works, often in score, are to Nyman, *Experimental Music*, New York, Schirmer's Sons, 1981: *Voicepiece* (p. 4), *Drip Music* (p. 60), *Micro I* (p. 67), *Listen* (pp. 88–9), *Les Moutons* (p. 136), and *Remorseless* (p. 140). Other fine surveys are Holmes, *Electronic and Experimental Music*, New York, Scribner's Sons, 1985, and Manning, *Electronic and Computer Music*, Oxford, Oxford University Press, 1987.

2 See Manning, *Electronic and Computer Music*, Oxford, Oxford University Press, 1987, Chapter 2.

3 On the moral message side, Arthur Honegger, relishing the retaliatory rise of 'mechanical music', reflects unkindly in a 1928 interview upon the parasitic player who doesn't compose:

Honegger: 'Mechanical music permits the establishment of the master-interpre-
             tation. The future is with the completely mechanical orchestra, which
             will offer first the advantage of being no longer limited by the human
             possibilities of extent and duration . . . I believe in the future of the
             mechanical in the domain of music . . . which alone [is] capable of
             solving the problems created by the growing demands of human
             interpreters'.
Interviewer: 'By suppressing them?'
Honegger: 'Yes.'

Quoted in Pincherle's charming book, Pincherle (trans. Brockway), *The World of the Virtuoso*, New York, W.W. Norton, 1963. Igor Stravinsky had equally caustic things to say about such 'growing demands'. See Stravinsky, *An Autobiography*, New York, W.W. Norton, 1962, pp. 34, 150–1.

4 Nyman, *Experimental Music*, New York, Schirmer's Sons, 1981, pp. 140–2. Nyman describes Hobbs' procedures merely as 'random controls of different kinds'. The randomizing devices of other composers include computer-generated number tables, the telephone directory, shuffled cards, etc. Not all random samplers are the product of great cleverness.

5 Hobbs offers a variant on the infamous 'dice music'; for example, the *Musikalisches Würfelspiel* (1806) consisted of sets of measures labelled 'First measure', 'Second measure', and so on. One's 'choice' of an item in each set was determined by a throw of the dice. One thereby built up a sequence of randomly selected measures from an ordered set of sets. This was intended as 'an easy system to compose an unlimited number of Waltzes, Rondos, Hornpipes and Reels'. See Apel, *Harvard Dictionary of Music* (2nd edn), Cambridge, Harvard University Press, 1972, p. 27.

6 Among the random regroupings is a version identical to the original. Though Hobbs may, in his shuffled Bach, have 'removed the harmonic glue from the harmonic texture', a number of random re-organizations are bound to furnish mildly convincing Baroque repertoire. How tempting it is to view that random but orthodox variant of *Remorseless* which is identical to *Lamb* as an acoustic cousin to *L.H.O.O.Q. Shaved*! See Binkley, 'Piece: Contra Aesthetics', in Margolis, *Philosophy Looks at the Arts*, pp. 80–99.

7 George Maciunas, an exponent of the 1960s Fluxus movement, as quoted in Nyman, *Experimental Music*, New York, Schirmer's Sons, 1981, p. 64.

8 Nyman, *Experimental Music*, New York, Schirmer's Sons, 1981, pp. 88–9. Nyman describes *Listen* as a cousin of *4'33"* meant to remedy the so-called hindrances of the Cage classic; namely, its occurrence in a concert hall, its lack of directives for the audience, and its not leaving the listening experience purely to chance.

9 Designs emerged for a wind-driven keyboard in J.-J. Schnell's *Aeroclavichord* (1789) and H. Herz's *Piano eolien* (1851), but these betrayed too much control to match the harp case. Air was to have been forced across the strings to achieve the Aeolian effect. See Apel, *Harvard Dictionary of Music* (2nd edn), Cambridge, Harvard University Press, 1972.

10 George Brecht himself wrote instrumental works rather more conventional than the gust blown harp. Consider his *Flute Solo, Solo for Violin, Piano Piece (1962)*, and *String Quartet*. No matter that the flute work requires just assembling and

disassembling a flute; the violin work, the polishing of the instrument; the piano piece, placing a vase of flowers upon the piano; and the quartet, just shaking hands. Peripheral to these works is any sound or, indeed, even silence.

11 See Dennett, 'Intentional Systems', in Dennett, *Brainstorms*, pp. 3–22.

12 Roger Scruton banks on a kindred feel for the perceivable qualities of sound *qua* musical in Scruton, *The Aesthetic Understanding*, London, Methuen, 1983, Chapter 8. One may conceivably argue that any notion of musical sound must itself be built atop a view of what it is to make music. That in turn will draw from craft-specific musicianly undertakings. The auditor's ear-view of musicianly ventures is nicely captured in Walton, 'Style and the Products and Processes of Art', in Lang, *The Concept of Style*, pp. 45–66.

13 Wolterstorff, *Works and Worlds of Art*, Oxford, Oxford University Press, 1980, p. 74.

14 Walton notes that an appreciation of style derives from a sense of causal origin. Appreciators must have a sense of 'how a work appears to have been made, what sort of action or actions it looks or sounds or seems as though the artist performed in creating it, . . . the apparent manners in which works were created' (Walton, 'Style and the Products and Processes of Art', in Lang, *The Concept of Style*, p. 52). However, Walton does not require successful appreciators to know exactly how a work was made. Indeed, 'sometimes it would be rash to suppose that a work was actually made in the manner it appears to have been; yet the appearance alone is important'.

15 Stockhausen, 'The Concept of Unity in Electronic Music', in Boretz and Cone, *Perspectives on Contemporary Music Theory*, pp. 215, 225.

16 Cage used as devices the *I Ching*, imperfections on paper, random overlaying of shapes on plexiglas, star maps, and computers to create indeterminacy at the time of performance. Apologists for such techniques argue that compositional skill is merely transplanted from work within an existing system already imposed upon the composer (for example, diatonic harmony, the tone row) to work upon a new system. This has the composer composing the rules (or system) of composition while leaving the composition to the vicissitudes of the system itself. See Nyman, *Experimental Music*, New York, Schirmer's Sons, 1981.

17 Holmes, *Electronic and Experimental Music*, New York, Scribner's Sons, 1985, p. 151.

18 Instructions in score facsimile reprinted in Nyman, *Experimental Music*, New York, Schirmer's Sons, 1981, p. 136.

19 Nyman, *Experimental Music*, New York, Schirmer's Sons, 1981, pp. 99–101. Also, see the discussion of the Scratch Orchestra, a democratic assemblage dedicated to fancy-free music-making, *ibid.*, pp. 112–18.

20 *Ibid.*, pp. 56–8

21 Boulez, 'Alea', in Boretz and Cone, *Perspectives on Contemporary Music Theory*, p. 44.

6 ARTISTS, PROGRAMS, AND PERFORMANCE

1 On 'thick' concepts in ethics, see Williams, *Ethics and the Limits of Philosophy*, Cambridge, Harvard University Press, 1985, pp. 129, 143–5; also Williams, 'Truth in Ethics', in Hooker, *Truth in Ethics*, pp. 19–34.

2 See Austin (Urmson (ed.)), *How To Do Things With Words*, Oxford, Oxford University Press, 1962.

3 For a clear account see Winston, *Artificial Intelligence*, Englewood Cliffs, Prentice-Hall, 1977.

4 Fodor, *Psychological Explanation*, New York, Random House, 1968.

5 Searle, 'Minds, Brains and Programs', *The Behavioral and Brain Sciences*, in Feinberg, *Reason and Responsibility*, pp. 286–97.

6 These are idealized simplifications. One is never completely free from the sounds of the playback machines. Further, many 'performances' heard are assembled from many takes. Given the sound itself, one cannot tell just how it was caused and how many takes were involved. Even with a 'direct-to-disc' recording, one always hears engineered sound; that is, the engineer's balanced mix of the original input.

7 A major proponent of the open texture theory is Morris Weitz. See Weitz, 'The Role of Theory in Aesthetics', *Journal of Aesthetics and Art Criticism*, 1956, vol. 15, reprinted in Werhane, *Philosophical Issues in Art*, Prentice Hall, 1984, pp. 447–54. George Dickie has advanced the institutional theory in many works including 'Defining Art', *American Philosophical Quarterly*, 1969, vol. 6; in Werhane, *Philosophical Issues in Art*, pp. 464–9; *Art and the Aesthetic*, Ithaca, Cornell University Press, 1974; 'The Return to Art Theory', *Modern Trends in Philosophy*, Vol. II, Tel-Aviv, Yachdav Publishers, 1983 reprinted in Werhane, *Philosophical Issues in Art*, pp. 469–77; and *The Art Circle*, New York, Haven, 1986. For further refinements of the institutional theory, see Davies, *Definitions of Art*, Ithaca, Cornell University Press, 1991.

8 Weitz, 'The Role of Theory in Aesthetics', in Werhane, *Philosophical Issues in Art*, pp. 450–1.

9 *Ibid.*, pp. 452.

10 Dickie, 'The Return to Art Theory', in Werhane, *Philosophical Issues in Art* p. 475.

11 Dickie, 'Defining Art', in Werhane, *Philosophical Issues in Art*, pp. 468–9.

12 Dickie, 'The Return to Art Theory', in Werhane, *Philosophical Issues in Art*, p. 473.

13 Regarding computer music concerts, Manning tellingly remarks: 'In the concert hall serious environmental problems are encountered. Tradition has cultivated an expectation of live action as an integral part of performance . . . [T]he vista of a platform empty except for an arrangement of loudspeakers does not encourage a heightened concentration on the aural dimension. On the contrary, it frequently leads to feelings of detachment or even alienation. The social aspects of concert-going are firmly rooted, and habits of a lifetime are hard to change' (Manning, *Electronic and Computer Music*, Oxford, Oxford University Press, 1987, p. 261). These may be species habits, and impossible to change.

14 Dickie, 'The Return to Art Theory', in Werhane, *Philosophical Issues in Art*, p. 476.

15 *Ibid.*, pp. 471, 476.

16 In fairness, Dickie gestures in this direction (Dickie, 'The Return to Art Theory', *Modern Trends in Philosophy*, Vol. II, Tel-Aviv, Yachdav Publishers, 1983 reprinted in Werhane, *Philosophical Issues in Art*, pp. 469–77) where he tries to relieve the restraints upon institutional contexts with phrases like 'cultural and historical background' (p. 471), 'broad, informal cultural practice' (p. 473), 'a kind of background against which individuals . . . create works of art' (p. 473), 'a cultural pattern . . . a practice of human beings' (p. 475), 'a web of cultural relations' (p. 476). Unfortunately, to read him literally takes the wind out of his tougher talk of institutions and rule-governed conventions. If his conventions turn out to be extremely loose, that removes the force of talking about rules, institutions, and conventions themselves.

17 Turing, 'Computing Machinery and Intelligence', *Mind*, 1950, vol. 59, pp. 433–60. Reprinted in Anderson, *Minds and Machines*, pp. 4–30.

18 Dennett, 'Intentional Systems', in Dennett, *Brainstorms*, pp. 3–22.

19 Ziff, 'The Feelings of Robots', Analysis, 1959, vol. 19, reprinted in Anderson, *Minds and Machines*, p. 102. See also the anti-mechanist Dreyfus, *What Computers Can't Do*, New York, Harper & Row, 1979; and the 'fragmentarians', advocates of 'micro-

worlds' and 'problem the contributions by J.J.C. Smart, 'Professor Ziff on Robots', *Analysis*, 1959, vol. 19, reprinted in Anderson, *Minds and Machines*, pp. 104–5; and N. Smart, 'Robots Incorporated', *Analysis*, 1959, vol. 19, also reprinted in Anderson, *Minds and Machines*, pp. 106–8.

21 Cone, *The Composer's* spaces', like Minsky, 'A Framework for Representing Knowledge', in Haugeland, *Mind Design*, pp. 95–128; also Haugeland, *Artificial Intelligence: The Very Idea*, Cambridge, MIT Press, 1986.

20 Consider, for example, *Voice*, Berkeley, University of California Press, 1974, expresses kindred sentiments in his non-formalist faith in the ineliminable yet often murky element of human expressive values in music; also Cone, 'Beyond Analysis', *Perspectives of New* Music, 1967, reprinted in Boretz and Cone, *Perspectives on Contemporary Music Theory*, pp. 72–90.

22 The Helfgott phenomenon represents a dramatic audience-centred personalist revolt against the externalism or formalism of the critics. So I have tried to argue in Godlovitch, 'Is There a Critic in the House?', Symposium on the David Helfgott Debate, *Philosophy and Literature*, 1997, vol. 21, pp. 368–75.

23 Bach (trans. Mitchell), *Essay on the True Art of Playing Keyboard Instruments*, London, Eulenberg Books, 1974, Chapter III, 1, 13 Marpurg (in footnote 9, p. 152) described (9 September 1749) K.P.E. thus: 'I know a great composer on whose face one can see depicted everything that his music expresses as he plays it at the keyboard'. The French preferred composure. The great harpsichordist François Couperin spends much time in his *L'Art de Toucher le Clavecin* advising his students not only to maintain a dignified posture, but to adopt an indifferent and blasé facial posture. In contrast, the Italians used to burst into flames as one gathers from stories about the violin duels between Corelli and Locatelli in Pincherle (trans. Russell), *Corelli, His Life, His Music*, New York, W.W. Norton, 1968.

24 ' "Where are my favourite passages?", Schoenberg is said to have exclaimed on seeing Schenker's diagram of the *Eroica*; "Ah, there they are in those tiny notes" ', quoted in Charles Rosen, *The Classical Style*, New York, W.W. Norton, 1972, p. 35.

25 Wittgenstein (trans. Winch), *Culture and Value*, Chicago, University of Chicago Press, 1981, p. 45e.

BIBLIOGRAPHY

Alperson, Philip, 'On Musical Improvisation', *Journal of Aesthetics and Art Criticism*, 1984, vol. 43, pp. 17–30.

Alperson, Philip (ed.), *What is Music?*, New York, Haven, 1987.

Anderson, Alan Ross (ed.), *Minds and Machines*, Englewood Cliffs, Prentice-Hall, 1964.

Anderson, James, 'Musical Identity', *Journal of Aesthetics and Art Criticism*, 1982, vol. 40, pp. 285–91.

Anderson, James, 'Musical Kinds', *British Journal of Aesthetics*, 1985, vol. 25, pp. 43–9.

Anderton, Craig, *Electronic Projects for Musicians*, New York, Amsco Publications, 1972.

Anderton, Craig, Moses, B. and Bartlett, G., *Digital Projects for Musicians*, New York, Amsco Publications, 1994.

Apel, Willi, *Harvard Dictionary of Music* (2nd edn), Cambridge, Harvard University Press, 1972.

Aristotle (trans. H. Tredennick), *Metaphysics*, London, Heinemann, 1933.

Austin, John Langshaw (J.O. Urmson (ed.)), *How To Do Things With Words*, Oxford, Oxford University Press, 1962.

Bach, Karl Philipp Emanuel (trans. W.J. Mitchell), *Essay on the True Art of Playing Keyboard Instruments*, London, Eulenberg Books, 1974.

Bateman, Wayne, *Introduction to Computer Music,* New York, John Wiley, 1980.

Beardsley, Monroe, 'Understanding Music', in Price, *On Criticizing Music: Five Philosophical Perspectives*, pp. 55–73.

Binkley, Timothy, 'Piece: Contra Aesthetics', *Journal of Aesthetics and Art Criticism*, 1977, vol. 35, pp. 265–77. Reprinted in Margolis, *Philosophy Looks at the Arts*, pp. 80–99.

Boretz, Benjamin and Cone, Edward (eds), *Perspectives on Contemporary Music Theory*, New York, W.W. Norton, 1972.

Boulez, Pierre, 'Alea', *Perspectives of New Music*, 1964. Reprinted in Boretz and Cone, *Perspectives on Contemporary Music Theory*, pp. 45–56.

Brody, Baruch and Grandy, Richard (eds), *Readings in the Philosophy of Science*, Englewood Cliffs, Prentice-Hall, 1989.

Budd, Malcolm, *Music and the Emotions*, London, Routledge & Kegan Paul, 1985.

Budd, Malcolm, 'Music and the Communication of Emotion', *Journal of Aesthetics and Art Criticism*, 1989, vol. 47, pp. 129–38.

Carroll, Noel, 'Art, Practice, and Narrative', *Monist*, 1988, vol. 71, pp. 140–56.

Cone, Edward, 'Beyond Analysis', *Perspectives of New Music*, 1967. Reprinted in Boretz and Cone, *Perspectives on Contemporary Music Theory*, pp. 72–90.

Cone, Edward, *Musical Form and Musical Performance*, New York, W.W. Norton, 1968.

Cone, Edward, *The Composer's Voice*, Berkeley, University of California Press, 1974.

Couperin, François, *L'Art de Toucher le Clavecin*, Paris, 1716.

Dancy, Jonathan, Moravcsik, J. and Taylor, C.C.W. (eds), *Human Agency: Language, Duty, and Value*, Stanford, Stanford University Press, 1988.

Danto, Arthur, *The Transfiguration of the Commonplace*, Cambridge, Harvard University Press, 1981.

Dart, Thurston, *The Interpretation of Music*, London, Hutchinson, 1954.

David, Hans and Mendel, Arthur (eds), *The Bach Reader*, New York, W.W. Norton, 1966.

Davies, Stephen, 'The Expression of Emotion in Music', *Mind*, 1980, vol. 89, pp. 67–86.

Davies, Stephen, 'Authenticity in Musical Performance', *British Journal of Aesthetics*, 1987, vol. 27, pp. 39–50.

Davies, Stephen, 'Transcription, Authenticity, and Performance', *British Journal of Aesthetics*, 1988, vol. 28, pp. 216–27.

Davies, Stephen, *Definitions of Art*, Ithaca, Cornell University Press, 1991.

Davies, Stephen, 'The Ontology of Musical Works and the Authenticity of Their Performances', *Nous*, 1991, vol. 25, pp. 21–41.

Davies, Stephen, *Musical Meaning & Expression*, Ithaca, Cornell University Press, 1994.

Dennett, Daniel, 'Intentional Systems', in Dennett, *Brainstorms*, pp. 3–22.

Dennett, Daniel, *Brainstorms*, Cambridge, MIT Press, 1979.

Dennett, Daniel, *Elbow Room*, Cambridge, MIT Press, 1984.

Dickie, George, 'Defining Art', *American Philosophical Quarterly*, 1969, vol. 6. Reprinted in Werhane, *Philosophical Issues in Art*, pp. 464–9.

Dickie, George, *Art and the Aesthetic*, Ithaca, Cornell University Press, 1974.

Dickie, George, 'The Return to Art Theory', *Modern Trends in Philosophy*, Vol. II, Tel-Aviv, Yachdav Publishers, 1983. Reprinted in Werhane, *Philosophical Issues in Art*, pp. 469–77.

Dickie, George, *The Art Circle*, New York, Haven, 1986.

Dickie, George, Sclafani, R. and Roblin, R. (eds), *Aesthetics: A Critical Anthology*, New York, St Martin's Press, 1989.

Dipert, Randall, 'Types and Tokens: A Reply to Sharpe', *Mind*, 1980, vol. 89, pp. 587–8.

Dodge, Charles and Jerse, Thomas, *Computer Music*, New York, Schirmer, 1985.

Dolmetsch, Arnold, *The Interpretation of the Music of the XVIIth and XVIIIth Centuries Revealed by Contemporary Evidence*, London, Novello & Co., 1946.

Donington, Robert, *The Interpretation of Early Music*, London, Faber & Faber, 1963.

Donnellan, Keith, 'Reference and Definite Descriptions', *Philosophical Review*, 1966, vol. 75, pp. 281–304.

Dorian, Frederick, *The History of Music in Performance*, New York, W.W. Norton, 1942.

Dowland, Robert (ed.), *A Varietie of Lute Lessons*, London, Thomas Adams, 1610.

Dreyfus, Hubert, *What Computers Can't Do*, New York, Harper & Row, 1979.

Etheridge, John, 'Jazz Guitar', in Stimpson, *The Guitar*, pp. 237–55.

Feinberg, Joel (ed.), *Reason and Responsibility* (6th edn), Belmont, Wadsworth, 1985.

Fodor, Jerry, *Psychological Explanation*, New York, Random House, 1968.

French, Peter (ed.), *Midwest Studies in Philosophy: Philosophy and the Arts*, Notre Dame, University of Notre Dame Press, vol. 16, 1991.

Glickman, Jack, 'Creativity in the Arts', in Lars Aagaard-Mogensen (ed.), *Culture and Art*, Eclipse Books, 1976. Reprinted in Margolis, *Philosophy Looks at the Arts*, pp. 169–186.

Godlovitch, Stan, 'Aesthetic Judgment and Hindsight', *Journal of Aesthetics and Art Criticism*, 1987, vol. 46, pp. 75–83.

Godlovitch, Stan, 'Authentic Performance', *Monist*, 1988, vol. 71, pp. 258–77.

Godlovitch, Stan, 'Artists, Programs and Performance', *Australasian Journal of Philosophy*, 1990, vol. 68, pp. 301–12.

Godlovitch, Stan, 'Music Performance and the Tools of the Trade', *Iyyun*, 1990, vol. 39, pp. 321–38.

Godlovitch, Stan, 'Music – What to Do About It', *Journal of Aesthetic Education*, 1992, vol. 26, pp. 1–15.

Godlovitch, Stan, 'The Integrity of Musical Performance', *Journal of Aesthetics and Art Criticism*, 1993, vol. 54, pp. 573–87.

Godlovitch, Stan, 'Innovation and Conservatism in Performance Practice', *Journal of Aesthetics and Art Criticism*, 1997, vol. 55, pp. 151–68.

Godlovitch, Stan, 'Is There a Critic in the House?', Symposium on the David Helfgott Debate, *Philosophy and Literature*, 1997, vol. 21, pp. 368–75.

Goehr, Lydia, 'Being True to the Work', *Journal of Aesthetics and Art Criticism*, 1989, vol. 47, pp. 55–67.

Goehr, Lydia, *The Imaginary Museum of Musical Works*, New York, Oxford University Press, 1992.

Goodman, Nelson, *Languages of Art*, Indianapolis, Hackett, 1968.

Gracyk, Theodore, *Rhythm and Noise: An Aesthetics of Rock*, Durham, Duke University Press, 1996.

Gunderson, Keith, 'The Imitation Game', *Mind*, 1964, vol. 73, pp. 234–45. Reprinted in Anderson, *Minds and Machines*, pp. 60–71.

Hacking, Ian, 'Do We See Through a Microscope?', *Pacific Philosophical Quarterly*, 1981, vol. 62. Reprinted in Brody and Grandy (eds), *Readings in the Philosophy of Science*, pp. 29–43.

Hacking, Ian, *Representing and Intervening*, Cambridge, Cambridge University Press, 1983.

Harrison, Nigel, 'Types and Tokens and the Identity of the Musical Work', *British Journal of Aesthetics*, 1975, vol. 15, pp. 336–46.

Haugeland, John (ed.), *Mind Design*, Cambridge, MIT Press. 1981.

Haugeland, John, *Artificial Intelligence: The Very Idea*, Cambridge, MIT Press, 1986.

Higgins, Kathleen, *The Music of our Lives*, Philadelphia, Temple University Press, 1991.

Holmes, Thomas B., *Electronic and Experimental Music*, New York, Scribner's Sons, 1985.

Homer (trans. Ennis Rees), *The Odyssey of Homer*, New York, The Modern Library, 1960.

Hook, Sidney (ed.), *Dimensions of Mind*, New York, New York University Press, 1960.

Hooker, Brad (ed.), *Truth in Ethics*, Oxford, Blackwell, 1996.

Karl, Gregory and Robinson, Jenefer, 'Shostakovich's Tenth Symphony and the Musical Expression of Cognitively Complex Emotions', *Journal of Aesthetics and Art Criticism*, 1995, vol. 53, pp. 401–15.

161

Kerman, Joseph, 'The State of Academic Music Criticism', in Price, *On Criticizing Music: Five Philosophical Perspectives.*

Keshen, Shmuel, *Reasonable Self-Esteem*, Montreal, McGill-Queen's University Press, 1996.

Kitcher, Philip, *The Advancement of Science*, New York, Oxford University Press, 1993.

Kivy, Peter, *The Corded Shell: Reflections on Musical Expression*, Princeton, Princeton University Press, 1980.

Kivy, Peter, 'Platonism in Music', *Grazer Philosophische Studien*, 1983, vol. 19, pp.109–29.

Kivy, Peter, *Sound and Semblance*, Princeton, Princeton University Press, 1984.

Kivy, Peter, 'On the Concept of the "Historically Authentic" Performance', *Monist*, 1988, vol. 71, pp. 278–91.

Kivy, Peter, *Sound Sentiment*, Philadelphia, Temple University Press, 1989.

Kivy, Peter, *Music Alone*, Ithaca, Cornell University Press, 1990.

Kivy, Peter, *Authenticities: Philosophical Reflections on Musical Performance*, Ithaca, Cornell University Press, 1995.

Kuhn, Thomas, *The Structure of Scientific Revolutions* (2nd edn), Chicago, Chicago University Press, 1970.

Lang, Berel (ed.), *The Concept of Style*, Philadelphia, University of Pennsylvania Press, 1979.

Larue, Jan, *Guidelines for Style Analysis*, New York, W.W. Norton, 1970.

Levinson, Jerrold, 'What a Musical Work Is', *Journal of Philosophy*, 1980, vol. 77, pp. 5–28.

Levinson, Jerrold, 'Music and Negative Emotions', *Pacific Philosophical Quarterly*, 1982, vol. 63, pp. 327–46.

Levinson, Jerrold, 'Hybrid Artforms', *Journal of Aesthetic Education*, 1984, vol. 18, pp. 5–13.

Levinson, Jerrold, 'Evaluating Musical Performance', *Journal of Aesthetic Education*, 1987, vol. 21, pp. 75–88.

Levinson, Jerrold, 'Zemach on Paintings', *British Journal of Aesthetics*, 1987, vol. 27, pp. 278–83.

Levinson, Jerrold, *Music, Art, and Metaphysics*, Ithaca, Cornell University Press, 1990.

Levinson, Jerrold, 'Authentic Performance and Performance Means', in Levinson, *Music, Art, and Metaphysics*, 1990, pp. 393–408.

Levinson, Jerrold and Alperson, Philip, 'What is a Temporal Art?', in French, *Midwest Studies in Philosophy: Philosophy and the Arts*, pp. 439–50.

Locke, John (Peter Laslett (ed.)), *Two Treatises of Government*, New York, The New American Library, 1965.

Mace, Thomas, *Musick's Monument or a remembrancer of the best practical musick both divine and civil, that has ever been known to have been in the world*, London, 1676.

Machlis, Joseph, *Introduction to Contemporary Music*, New York, W.W. Norton, 1961.

Macintyre, Alasdair, *After Virtue* (2nd edn), Notre Dame, University of Notre Dame Press, 1984.

Macintyre, Alasdair, 'Relativism Power and Philosophy', *Proceedings and Addresses of the American Philosophical Association*, 1985, pp. 5–22

Manning, Peter, *Electronic and Computer Music*, Oxford, Oxford University Press, 1987.

Margolis, Joseph, 'The Ontological Peculiarity of Works of Art', *Journal of Aesthetics and Art Criticism*, 1977, vol. 36, pp. 45–50. Reprinted in Margolis, *Philosophy Looks at the Arts*, pp. 253–60.

Margolis, Joseph (ed.), *Philosophy Looks at the Arts* (3rd edn), Philadelphia, Temple University Press, 1987.

Mark, Thomas Carson, 'The Work of Virtuosity', *Journal of Philosophy*, 1980, vol. 77, pp. 28–45.

Mark, Thomas Carson, 'Philosophy of Piano Playing: Reflections on the Concept of Performance', *Philosophy and Phenomenological Research*, 1981, vol. 41, pp. 299–324.

Martin, Richard M., 'On the Proto-Theory of Musical Structure', *Perspectives of New Music*, 1970. Reprinted in Boretz and Cone, *Perspectives on Contemporary Music Theory*, pp. 91–6.

Massey, Howard, Noyes, Alex and Shklair, Daniel, *A Synthesist's Guide to Acoustic Instruments*, New York, Amsco Publications, 1987.

Meyer, Leonard, *Emotion and Meaning in Music*, Chicago, University of Chicago Press, 1956.

Minsky, Marvin, 'A Framework for Representing Knowledge', *Memo 306*, Artificial Intelligence Laboratory at MIT, 1975. Reprinted in Haugeland, *Mind Design*, pp. 95–128.

Munrow, David, *Instruments of the Middle Ages and Renaissance*, London, Oxford University Press, 1976.

NGLA Standard Grading Rules for Canadian Lumber, Vancouver, National Lumber Grades Authority, 1977.

Nyman, Michael, *Experimental Music*, New York, Schirmer's Sons, 1981.

Pincherle, Marc (trans. L. Brockway), *The World of the Virtuoso*, New York, W.W. Norton, 1963.

Pincherle, Marc (trans. H.E.M. Russell), *Corelli, His Life, His Music*, New York, W.W. Norton, 1968.

Plato (trans.G.M.A. Grube), *Republic*, Indianapolis, Hackett, 1974.

Pousseur, Henri, 'The Question of Order in New Music', *Perspectives of New Music*, 1966. Reprinted in Boretz and Cone, *Perspectives on Contemporary Music Theory*, pp. 97–115.

Price, Kingsley (ed.), *On Criticizing Music: Five Philosophical Perspectives*, Baltimore, Johns Hopkins University Press, 1981.

Price, Kingsley, 'What is a Piece of Music?', *British Journal of Aesthetics*, 1982, vol. 22, pp. 322–36.

Quantz, Johann Joachim (trans. E. Reilly), *On Playing the Flute*, London, Faber & Faber, 1966.

Read, H.H., *Rutley's Elements of Mineralogy*, London, Thomas Murby, 1970.

Ridley, Aaron, *Music, Value and the Passions*, Ithaca, Cornell University Press, 1995.

Rilke, Rainer Maria (trans. M.D. Herter Norton), *Sonnets to Orpheus*, New York, W.W. Norton, 1942.

Roads, Curtis (ed.), *Composers and the Computer*, Los Altos, William Kaufmann, 1985.

Roads, Curtis and Strawn, John (eds), *Foundations of Computer Music*, Cambridge, MIT Press, 1985.

Rosen, Charles, *The Classical Style*, New York, W.W. Norton, 1972.

Rosen, Charles, 'Influence: Plagiarism and Inspiration', in Price, *On Criticizing Music: Five Philosophical Perspectives*, pp. 16–37.

163

Scheibe, Johann Adolph, 'Der critische Musicus', in David and Mendel, *The Bach Reader*.

Scriven, Michael, 'The Compleat Robot', in Hook, *Dimensions of Mind*, pp. 118–42.

Scruton, Roger, *The Aesthetic Understanding*, London, Methuen, 1983.

Scruton, Roger, 'Analytical Philosophy and the Meaning of Music', *Journal of Aesthetics and Art Criticism*, 1987, vol. 46, pp. 169–176.

Searle, John, 'Minds, Brains and Programs', *The Behavioral and Brain Sciences*, 1980, vol. 3, pp. 417–24. Reprinted in Feinberg, *Reason and Responsibility*, pp. 286–97.

Sharpe, R.A., 'Type, Token, Interpretation, and Performance', *Mind*, 1979, vol. 88, pp. 437–40.

Sharpe, R.A., *Contemporary Aesthetics*, New York, St Martin's Press, 1983.

Smart, J.J.C., 'Professor Ziff on Robots', *Analysis*, 1959, vol. 19. Reprinted in Anderson, *Minds and Machines*, pp. 104–5.

Smart, Ninian, 'Robots Incorporated', *Analysis*, 1959, vol. 19. Reprinted in Anderson, *Minds and Machines*, pp. 106–8.

Stimpson, Michael (ed.), *The Guitar*, New York, Oxford University Press, 1988.

Stockhausen, Karlheinz, 'The Concept of Unity in Electronic Music', *Perspectives of New Music*, 1962. Reprinted in Boretz and Cone, *Perspectives on Contemporary Music Theory*, pp. 214–25.

Stravinsky, Igor, *An Autobiography*, New York, W.W. Norton, 1962.

Thom, Paul, *For an Audience*, Philadelphia, Temple University Press, 1994.

Tilghman, Benjamin, *But Is It Art?*, New York: Blackwell, 1986.

Turing, Alan, 'Computing Machinery and Intelligence', *Mind*, 1950, vol. 59, pp. 433–60. Reprinted in Anderson, *Minds and Machines*, pp. 4–30.

Twain, Mark, *The Adventures of Tom Sawyer*, 1876.

Van Fraassen, Bas, *The Scientific Image*, Oxford, Oxford University Press, 1980.

Villa-Lobos, Heitor, *Douze Etudes pour Guitare*, Paris, Editions Max Eschig, 1929.

Walton, Kendall, 'Style and the Products and Processes of Art', in Lang, *The Concept of Style*, pp.45–66.

Walton, Kendall, 'The Presentation and Portrayal of Sound Patterns', in Dancy *et al.*, pp. 237–57.

Webster, William, 'Music is Not a Notational System', *Journal of Aesthetics and Art Criticism*, 1971, vol. 29, pp. 489–97.

Webster, William, 'A Theory of the Compositional Work of Music', *Journal of Aesthetics and Art Criticism*, 1974, vol. 33, pp. 59–66.

Weiss, Leopoldo Silvio (trascrizione di Miguel Abloniz), *Suite in La Maggiore*, Ancona, Edizioni Berben, 1964.

Weitz, Morris, 'The Role of Theory in Aesthetics', *Journal of Aesthetics and Art Criticism*, 1956, vol. 15. Reprinted in Werhane, *Philosophical Issues in Art*, pp. 447–54.

Werhane, Patricia (ed.), *Philosophical Issues in Art*, Englewood Cliffs, Prentice-Hall, 1984.

Williams, Bernard, *Ethics and the Limits of Philosophy*, Cambridge, Harvard University Press, 1985.

Williams, Bernard, 'Truth in Ethics', in Hooker, *Truth in Ethics*, pp. 19–34.

Winston, Patrick Henry, *Artificial Intelligence*, Englewood Cliffs, Prentice-Hall, 1977.

Wittgenstein, Ludwig (trans. P. Winch), *Culture and Value*, Chicago, University of Chicago Press, 1981.

Wollheim, Richard, 'Minimal Art', in Wollheim, *On Art and the Mind*, pp. 101–111.

Wollheim, Richard, *On Art and the Mind*, Cambridge, Harvard University Press, 1974.

Wollheim, Richard, *Art and its Objects* (2nd edn), New York, Harper & Row, 1980.

Wolterstorff, Nicholas, 'Toward an Ontology of Artworks', *Nous*, 1975, vol. 9, pp. 115–42. Reprinted in Margolis, *Philosophy Looks at the Arts*, pp. 229–52.

Wolterstorff, Nicholas, *Works and Worlds of Art*, Oxford, Oxford University Press, 1980.

Wolterstorff, Nicholas, 'The Philosophy of Art After Analysis and Romanticism', *Journal of Aesthetics and Art Criticism*, 1987, vol. 46, pp. 151–68.

Young, James O., 'The Concept of Authentic Performance', *British Journal of Aesthetics*, 1988, vol. 28, pp. 228–38.

Young, Philip, *The Look of Music*, Vancouver, Vancouver Museums and Planetarium Association, 1980.

Zemach, Eddy M., 'No Identification Without Evaluation', *British Journal of Aesthetics*, 1986, vol. 26, pp. 239–51.

Zemach, Eddy M., 'Nesting: The Ontology of Interpretation', *Monist*, 1990, vol. 73, pp. 296–311.

Ziff, Paul, 'The Feelings of Robots', Analysis, 1959, vol. 19. Reprinted in Anderson, *Minds and Machines*, pp. 98–103.

INDEX